Two Poets
of the Oxford Movement

Two Poets
of the Oxford Movement

John Keble
and John Henry Newman

Rodney Stenning Edgecombe

Madison • Teaneck
Fairleigh Dickinson University Press
London: Associated University Presses

Associated University Presses
440 Forsgate Drive
Cranbury, N.J. 08512

Associated University Presses
25 Sicilian Avenue
London WC1A 2QH, England

Associated University Presses
P.O. Box 338, Port Credit
Mississauga, Ontario
Canada L5G 4L8

Library of Congress Cataloging-in-Publication Data

Edgecombe, Rodney Stenning.
    Two poets of the Oxford Movement : John Keble and John Henry
Newman / Rodney Stenning Edgecombe.
        p.   cm.
    Includes bibliographical references and index.
    ISBN 0-8386-3669-1 (alk. paper)
    1. Christian poetry, English—History and criticism. 2. English
poetry—19th century—History and criticism. 3. English poetry—
England—Oxford—History and criticism. 4. Newman, John Henry,
1801–1890—Poetic works. 5. Keble, John, 1792–1866—Poetic works.
6. Anglo-Catholicism in literature. 7. Church of England in
literature. 8. Oxford movement. I. Title.
PR595.R4E34   1996
821'.809382—dc20   95-21769
                                                        CIP

PRINTED IN THE UNITED STATES OF AMERICA

This book
is dedicated
to Ronald Hall

Contents

Preface and Acknowledgments

The Oxford Movement had so wide an impact upon the literature of the nineteenth century that any commentator approaching the field must decide between general coverage and a focused selection of one or two aspects. The aftershocks of the movement that Newman dated from 1833 were still registering on the Richter scale decades later when he himself received Gerard Manley Hopkins into the church of his secession, or when Mrs. Humphry Ward, linked to Newman through her father's Catholicism, explored the domestic repercussions of religious allegiance in *Helbeck of Bannisdale*. Raymond Chapman has provided a general survey of the Oxford Movement's legacy in *Faith and Revolt*,[1] throwing the net as far forward as Reade and Kingsley, but focusing also on such prime movers as Keble and Newman. G. B. Tennyson, on the other hand, has opted to narrow the compass of *his* book[2] to the three chief poets (Keble, Newman, and Williams). My study is narrower still, since I have chosen to analyze only two items—*The Christian Year* and Newman's contributions (by far the most substantial) to *Lyra Apostolica*. This limitation is to some extent a function of my desire to look at the poetry qua poetry rather than as an index to the theology and poetics of the movement. Since these topics have been definitively handled by, amongst others, G. B. Tennyson, Gregory Goodwin,[3] and Stephen Prickett,[4] I have (I hope safely) taken this material for granted and stressed instead the structural, thematic, and textural aspects of the verse that their relatively broad projects have prevented them from pursuing in detail.

My decision to examine *The Christian Year* in preference to Keble's later volumes (*Lyra Innocentium* and *Miscellaneous Poems*) scarcely needs defending, since in this instance the first wine is by far the

9

best. The narrowed topical scope of the *Lyra Innocentium* is set forth in its subtitle—*Thoughts in Verse on Christian Children, Their Ways, and Their Privileges*—and it brings with it a corresponding curtailment in range and variety; while the *Miscellaneous Poems* is simply a posthumous catchall for various scraps and leavings, none of them, if we except the contributions to *Lyra Apostolica*, especially remarkable. In much the same way, nothing that Newman wrote after his conversion to the Roman Catholic Church can, with the exception of *The Dream of Gerontius*, be said to have bettered the achievement of *Lyra Apostolica*, and indeed some of the Catholic verse represents a distinct falling-off, as witness this thumping Sapphic salute to "Mary and Philip":

> This is the Saint of sweetness and compassion,
> Cheerful in penance, and in precept winning,
> Beckoning and luring in a holy fashion
> > Souls that are sinning.

> This is the Saint, who, when the bad world vaunteth
> Her many coloured wares and magic treasures,
> Outbids her, and her victim disenchanteth
> > With heavenly pleasures.[5]

In this sample, we have a distressing sense of movement without progression, of a gesturing and pointing more excitable than dignified. Newman's dactyllic clatter fails to mask the attenuation of his subject matter, and his choice of a "quantitative" meter seems doubly mistaken when we remember that Cowper had chosen the Sapphic measure for "Lines Written During a Period of Insanity":

> Hatred and vengeance, my eternal portion,
> Scarce can endure delay of execution,
> Wait, with impatient readiness, to seize my
> > Soul in a moment.[6]

Cowper has here managed to achieve a pathos entirely absent from "Mary and Philip"—and yet this note of stoic austerity lay well within Newman's grasp. It is a note that sounds again and again in his contributions to the Anglican *Lyra Apostolica*, where he was able to articulate the loneliness and isolation he dared not utter (however much he might have felt them) after his conversion to Rome.

The nineteenth century shied away from the analysis of devotional poetry for fear of trenching upon the spiritual experience of the reader and fenced it about with critical *noli me tangeres*. Newman, for example, flinched from having to dissect *The Christian Year*, claiming that the "volume which has made him [Keble] so specially famous, is of that rare kind, which scarcely comes under the idea of literature."[7] And Keble himself, having to review Conder's *Star in the East*, prefaced his assessment with many throat-clearings and demurrals:

> There are many circumstances about this little volume, which tend to disarm criticism. In the first place, it is, for the most part, of a *sacred* character: taken up with those subjects, which least of all admit, with propriety, either in the author or critic, the exercise of intellectual subtlety.

> But if they [religious poems] appear to have been written with any degree of sincerity or earnestness, we naturally shrink from treating them merely as literary efforts. To interrupt the current of a reader's sympathy in such a case, by critical objections, is not merely to deprive him of a little harmless pleasure, it is to disturb him almost in a devotional exercise.[8]

Such sentiments imply that a book like mine, which sets out to analyze the formal properties of *The Christian Year* and *Lyra Apostolica*, is nothing more than a foolish rushing in where angels have feared to tread. Yet is not Keble's claim that "intellectual subtlety" cannot be exercised on religious topics at least as old as the "Jordan" poems of Herbert, and quite as paradoxical? The poet who on one occasion reduces his whole utterance to an unrhymed, verbless acclamation ("*My God, My King*")[9] offers a contradictory declaration on another: "Wherefore with my utmost art / I will sing thee."[10] Keble's poetry, his impatience with formal criticism notwithstanding, reveals the same internal contradiction and opens itself to the same sort of inspection. A poet trying to serve God by means of his or her poetic gift cannot without irreverence write deliberately slipshod verse. Dean Church has noted that Isaac Williams recoiled from any form of self-glorification:

> This fear of display in a man of singularly delicate and fastidious taste came to have something forced and morbid in it. It seemed sometimes as if in preaching or talking he aimed at being dull and clumsy. But in all he did and wrote he aimed at being true at all costs and in

the very depths of his heart; and though, in his words, we may wish sometimes for what we should feel to be more natural and healthy in tone, we never can doubt that we are in the presence of one who shrank from all conscious unreality like poison.[11]

But even if we allow that Williams tried to suppress his individuality and selfhood, I find it hard to believe that he "wrote in" the defects and limitations of *The Cathedral* in a kind of aesthetic self-mortification. If, on the contrary, he did—in his verse at least—resort to "utmost art," that art would have necessarily entailed a degree of self-consciousness. The more polished the utterance, the more the reader will attend to its *curiosa felicitas* and de facto to the writers, however self-effacing they may pretend to be, in whom it originates. And so, in defiance of such misplaced Tractarian scruples, I have undertaken in this study to investigate the formal properties of the verse in hand. These were not properties by which Tractarians set much store. As Geoffrey Tillotson has pointed out, Newman sees "composition as the mere consequence of the poet's decision to communicate his poetry, and he sees that decision almost as a thing of accident."[12] Such theoretical perceptions of form as something secondary and incidental to the essence of poetry—a stance shared by Keble—did not, could not, issue in its practical abandonment.

—⁂—

I wish to thank the following people, who have helped me in many ways: Professors John Atkinson, Richard Whitaker, John Suggit, Drs. Ulrich Klingmann and Ronald Hall, the Rev. James Patrick, Tanya Barben of Special Collections, Celia Walters and Shanaz Morris of Reference, Pene Beamish, Vernon Bryant, Diana Dickinson, Ros Maree and Evelyn Rossmeisl of Inter-Library Loans and Pat Golding of Acquisitions, all in the Jagger Library at the University of Cape Town. My thanks also go to Wyatt Benner, who edited this book.

Two Poets
of the Oxford Movement

1

The Nature of
Tractarian Poetry

ALMOST all the books and articles that have hitherto addressed the poetry of the Oxford Movement have tended to follow a theological line. This bias—a perfectly proper one—has been conditioned by the writers' sense of the interest and importance of Tractarianism as a historical force and by misgivings about the poetic ability of its protagonists. When Charlotte Yonge wrote her *Musings Over "The Christian Year" and "Lyra Innocentium,"* Keble's verse commanded a respect far exceeding that accorded to his religious leadership, whereas in our century these priorities have been reversed. Here, for example, is how Geoffrey Faber beats the unfashionable mellifluities of *The Christian Year* with a modernist stick: "As a poet, Keble was the Ella Wheeler Wilcox of his time. There is no observation behind the images he employs; no thought behind his emotion; no emotion behind his thought, since there is no thought there, nothing but simple assertion; in Mr. T. S. Eliot's phrase, no 'mechanism of sensibility'."[1] "Nothing but simple assertion" is a judgment better passed upon this judgment in turn—a string of negations pretending to the irresistible force of a sorites.

Georgina Battiscombe attempts a more generous appraisal of *The Christian Year* in her study of Keble, but even she can muster only faint praise: "Keble was no seer in either sense of the word, nor did he perhaps regret this deficiency; 'Sight tempts the heart From sober walking in the Gospel way.' He did not see, he only observed. To see is an act of passion and immediacy, to observe is merely to notice facts or objects."[2] This ad hoc differentiation between seeing and observing is precisely that: ad hoc and insufficient. That seeing does not of itself carry an emotional correlative can be gathered from a line in Coleridge's "Dejection: An Ode"—"I see, not feel, how beautiful they are."[3] Indeed, observation, requiring an altogether more protracted encounter of percipient with percept, is much more likely to issue in an emotional bond. The very basis of Battiscombe's assessment therefore needs to be revised, and her appraisal to be qualified.

G. B. Tennyson's important work on Tractarian poetry goes a long way toward redressing the too-ready dismissiveness of critics like Faber, but the terms of his apologia remain—for good tactical reasons, no doubt—extremely guarded.

> Once we recognize that the form of *The Christian Year* is both its most distinctive feature and an exemplification of the Tractarian poetic, which construed literature as a mode of "seeking the Deity in prayer"—once, that is, we recognize the work as a devotional manual—we are able to take an equally Tractarian approach to the poetry in the volume. Such an approach reminds us that, however necessary it is for critical purposes to isolate a given poem or portion of it for examination, the poem still functions as part of the larger construct of a sequence of poetic devotions keyed to the Church year.[4]

These are wise words, but in my view they tend to weaken the claims of the poetry to withstand a more dispassionate examination. While no one would deny that the first task of critics is to ascertain the genre of the material at hand and to regulate their formal and thematic expectations, that generic adjustment ought to center on mode and not on quality. I cannot help feeling Tennyson concedes too much to Keble's detractors when he comes to assess the verbal performance of *The Christian Year*:

> The Tractarian ethos shapes also those aspects of the poetry of *The Christian Year* that come under the general heading of style, by which I mean such technical matters as language, diction, imagery, and metrics, as well as such elusive qualities as verbal complexity, ingenuity, ambiguity, irony, and the like. Most modern critics place a higher value on these aspects of poetry than on any others, certainly a higher value than did Tractarian poetic theory, which is notably silent on technical questions. Accordingly, Keble does not fare well when attention is directed exclusively to stylistic issues. Using these criteria alone we cannot but find Keble's poetic achievement is a rather modest one, and I have no intention of making extravagant claims for him on purely verbal grounds. But I do believe that even on purely verbal grounds much of what Keble does can better be understood if it is related to Tractarian poetic theory and to the personal ethos that in Keble so thoroughly complements it.[5]

Here, as in Battiscombe's appraisal, we detect a reluctance to inspect the poetry from close-up, as though the author, knowing the skeptical (and possibly hostile) outlook of his twentieth-century audience, feared being branded with poor taste in poetry. Patrick Scott's airy summation suggests that such misgivings would not have been unfounded:

> To link, even in passing, Tennyson's *In Memoriam* with Keble's *Christian Year* nowadays seems a striking comparison, for it goes so much against the critical categories within which we normally read Victorian poetry—Tennyson is canonical, Keble is not; Tennyson is linguistically interesting, Keble is not; Tennyson was intellectually progressive, Keble was not; Tennyson is read, Keble is not. The twentieth-century consensus, G. B. Tennyson's brave apology notwithstanding, has pretty much followed Geoffrey Faber's judgment that "as a poet, Keble was the Ella Wheeler Wilcox of his time. . . ."[6]

Like Faber, Scott seems too ready to damn by assertion, repeatedly tossing Keble off an antithetic seesaw of unequal weight and balance. While no one would claim that he bears comparison with Tennyson, the received wisdom of humankind has shown us that the excellent will always impoverish the value we would otherwise set upon the good and that odium almost always attaches itself to comparisons. Critics who are too cautious about defying the current shape of the canon (protean and evanescent though its outlines tend to be) and who fail to address the poetry qua poetry, have given carte blanche to sweeping denunciations of the kind sampled above.

There is another problem that surfaces in G. B. Tennyson's defense of *The Christian Year*—a problem of chronology. Raymond Chapman provides a useful check in this regard:

> Keble's poems, published as *The Christian Year*, do and yet do not stand as a manifesto of the Oxford Movement. They are Tractarian in their attachment to the Book of Common Prayer: each was written for a Sunday or Holy Day. They are Tractarian in their direction towards the disciplined personal life which was aided by following the ecclesiastical year, and in their emphasis on sacramental services.[7]

Given the fact that the Tractarianism of *The Christian Year* is at best partial and proleptic, one ought not perhaps to read back Keble's later aesthetic pronouncements too systematically. The *Praelectiones*, from which Tennyson has extracted the greater part of the Tractarian poetic, was decades away, and was written laboriously and duti-fully. Far from presenting a manifesto *ex animo* of ardent pronounce-ments, Keble struggled to get his ideas together and solicited friends and relations for help.

At the same time as we try to revise the harsh verdicts that the twentieth century has passed upon *The Christian Year*, we need also to reappraise the uncritical acclaim that its Victorian readership lav-ished upon it. Newman's tribute to the collection—to take a ran-dom instance—will not stand up to inspection:

> the two main intellectual truths which it brought home to me, were the same two which I had learned from Butler, though recast in the creative mind of my new master. The first of these is what may be called, in a large sense of the word, the Sacramental system; . . .
>
> I considered that Mr. Keble met this difficulty [probability as a cause of doubt] by ascribing the firmness of assent which we give to religious doctrine, not to the probabilities which introduced it, but to the living power of faith and love which accepted it.[8]

Since Newman's literary criticism reveals a disappointing indiffer-ence to formal issues—as witness his essay entitled "Poetry, with Reference to Aristotle's Poetics" (1829)—the textural and structural aspects of *The Christian Year* remain incidental to the doctrinal con-tent of the poetry, upon which he expatiates with much greater ea-gerness. Yet even here, if we bear in mind the swiftness and summari-ness with which Newman had to produce the installments of the *Apologia*, he uses the poems as a compressed metonym for those theological elements that Keble contributed to his education. It would take no great effort to refute the claim that *The Christian Year* reintro-duced the "sacramental" system into English poetry; what Newman ultimately means is that Keble introduced the "sacramental" sys-tem into *his* intellectual universe. Almost every instance of his sacramentalism or typology—to use a term less redolently Catholic—can paralleled in earlier poets, not least the Puritans of the seventeenth century. Marvell's "Bermudas" yields nothing to "Septuagesima Sunday" in the assiduity with which it reads the "book" of nature.

And as to Newman's belief that *The Christian Year* provided a unique endorsement to the idea that religious assent finds valida-tion in the feelings of the believer—how can it possibly be supported? The idea might have been unusual in high-and-dry Oxford in the 1820s, but its genealogy is coextensive with religion itself. Moreover, no one poem or subset of poems in *The Christian Year* takes this doctrine as a special thematic center—the entire collection, being an assembly of lyrics, adopts it as the basic premise of the genre. For Newman, as for many who follow him, poetry must function first and foremost as a theological platform; any formal or structural or textural felicities remain tangential.

So much for the theological line of approach. The results of such investigation can be cogent and satisfying, but in the case of *The Christian Year*, at least, it can occasionally fall wide of the mark. How, if we view Keble's verse as the ancillary of his Tractarian outlook, can we account for its catholic—rather than Catholic—appeal? Georgina Battiscombe's demurral needs to be considered. *The Christian Year*

> is less concerned with the doctrine of the holy Catholic Church which was to be in the very fore-front of Tractarian teaching than with the relationship of the individual soul to God, which was, and is, almost the only pre-occupation of Evangelical piety. Scattered over *The Christian Year* there are, of course, more references to the Church than one would expect to find in a book written by an extreme Evangelical, but the large majority of the poems are concerned with the purely personal aspect of religion.[9]

This concern with "the purely personal aspect of religion" is to some extent a corollary of Keble's chosen genre. Lyric poetry seldom admits of dogma: everything in the utterance must be personalized and mediated through the individual who utters it. This not to deny the existence of distinct traditions of Catholic and Protestant lyric—traditions attested by the difference between "I sing of a maiden" and John Newton's "Amazing Grace"—but it is to suggest that the distinction is less marked and less unbridgeable than in discursive genres like the sermon and the tract. The personalism of lyric rests on that set of common denominators—human feelings—and this engenders a sense of shared experience rather than sectarian division. Hurrell Froude clearly felt this when he observed—in his harsh, uncharitable way—that there was a "Sternhold-and-Hopkinsy [something] about the diction" of *The Christian Year*.[10] Metrified psalms were of course a liturgical meeting ground for all the major divisions of the Anglican church in 1827, but anything so temperate and conciliatory as a meeting-ground held little appeal for the likes of Froude. Not, of course, that *The Christian Year* was as consciously "syncretic" and "ecumenical" as Faber makes it sound when he claims that "Keble . . . made his high-church poetry a vehicle for the emotions of Evangelicalism."[11] Even the "primitive" proto-Tractarianism of *The Christian Year* had something of the bipolar tension that Anglicanism would develop in the wake of the Oxford Movement. Once more we can invoke Faber to clarify the issue: "The Tractarians possessed all the moral earnestness and religious emotion of the Evangelicals; but combined them with an intellectual power of analysis and exposition, to a degree long unknown in England."[12] And again:

> It should be needless to add that in the teaching of Keble, Pusey, Newman and the Tractarians generally the relationship of the individual soul to God was just as important as in the teaching of John Wesley. But the importance of that relationship was not to be thought of as transcending the importance of the Church. The Church was the divinely established means of grace. She was the continuing dwelling-place of God's spirit upon earth, and as such she was owed all the honour and glory within the power of men to pay her.[13]

This necessity for synthesis and integration was actually perceived by people much closer to the thick of things than Faber, writing in 1933. Cardinal Manning also noted the complementarity of the divergent traditions of Low and High Church, though by that time he had rejected the Oxford solution as a specious one: "I have always believed that Anglicanism and Puritanism are the ruins of the outer and the inner life of the Catholic Church, from which they separated at the Reformation and then split asunder. This accounts for the dryness of Anglicanism, and the disembodied vagueness of evangelical pietism."[14]

James Campbell Shairp, an Oxford undergraduate of the 1830s who had been born and bred in the Kirk, could nonetheless sympathize with many central tenets of Tractarianism, and observed that the "leading men of the movement," amongst whom he would naturally have included Keble, left pomp and ritualism to "the weaker brethren."[15] Not so a rather more intemperate Presbyterian commentator, Alexander Whyte. Writing at the start of the twentieth century, he remarked that he never found himself "chanting a Lyra to myself in the early morning. An Olney hymn or a Wesley hymn often— . . . but never once a *Lyra Apostolica*, nor any of its school, unless it is 'New every morning is the love,' or 'Help us this and every day to live more nearly as we pray.'"[16] The fact that Dr. Whyte found himself chanting Cowper and Wesley is explained by their having written congregational hymns, items altogether more hummable than lyrics that have internalized their music. While it is true that some sections of *The Christian Year* found their way into hymnals, the process forced severe excisions and curtailments upon the original drafts. "Morning" is a case in point, for *Hymns Ancient and Modern* has shorn its first five stanzas. While this might account for its inclusion in Whyte's morning repertoire (he quotes the beginning of the sixth verse), I am at a loss to explain why its final distich should be presented as a hymn in itself—unless, of course, his knowledge of this and other texts was as superficial as I suspect it was. The truth of the matter is that the Tractarians had no intention of writing congregational hymns, chiefly because of a perceived Nonconformist "taint." Newman's hymns date from after his secession to the Catholic Church, a church more genuinely popular than the elitist High Church party—in its early days, at least—could ever have hoped to be.

If we take Shairp as more reliable witness than Whyte, however, we can conclude that *The Christian Year* embodied a kind of ecclesiastical comprehension and exerted a pull across virtually the whole spectrum of beliefs and alignments. Something so accommodating will naturally be difficult to differentiate from the antecedent traditions it attempts to reconcile. I suspect that if the poetry is divorced from accompanying manifestos and Tractarian credos, and at the same time disengaged from the theorizing of the *Praelectiones* (which came a long time after), our sense of a distinctively Tractarian poetry will often blur and waver. Consider for example the following two stanzas:

> Can a woman's tender care
> Cease, towards the child she bare?
> Yes, she may forgetful be,
> Yet will I remember thee.[17]

and

> Fathers may hate us or forsake,
> God's foundlings then are we:
> Mother on child no pity take,
> But we shall still have Thee.[18]

Here are poets writing remarkably similar verse, but from entirely different theological positions—the first quatrain comes from one of Cowper's *Olney Hymns*, composed under the watchful Evangelical eye of John Newton, the second has been extracted from *The Christian Year*, that High Church document which, *secundum* Newman, prepared the ground for the Oxford Movement. Any reader approaching them in ignorance of the writers' avowed theology might be forgiven in finding the difference negligible, the consonance strong. Both, after all, are versifying Isa. 49:15.

As for the vaunted sacramentalism of *The Christian Year*, what qualitative difference does it reveal in relation to similar procedures followed by some Evangelical poets, not least by Cowper? Take this excerpt from *The Task*, book 5 *(The Winter Morning Walk)*:

> Acquaint thyself with God, if thou would'st taste
> His works. Admitted once to his embrace,
> Thou shalt perceive that thou wast blind before:
> Thine eye shall be instructed; and thine heart,
> Made pure, shall relish, with divine delight
> Till then unfelt, what hands divine have wrought.
> Brutes graze the mountain-top, with faces prone
> And eyes intent upon the scanty herb
> It yields them; or, recumbent on its brow,
> Ruminate heedless of the scene outspread
> Beneath, beyond, and stretching far away
> From inland regions to the distant main.
> Man views it, and admires; but rests content
> With what he views. The landscape has his praise,
> But not its author.[19]

Compare the more succinct (or summary) exposition of a similar idea in Keble's "Septuagesima Sunday":

> There is a book, who runs may read,
>   Which heavenly truth imparts,
> And all the lore its scholars need,
>   Pure eyes and Christian hearts.
>
> The works of God above, below,
>   Within us and around,
> Are pages in that book to show
>   How God Himself is found.[20]

Marked similarities of conception and phrasing link these two excerpts. Both poets stress the didactic value of the natural world and register that didacticism in images of books and instruction. Both, moreover, stress a well-disposed, receptive mind and spirit as preconditions for a proper reading, whether it be with a heart "made pure" or "Pure eyes and Christian hearts." Finally both Cowper and Keble convey the idea of being whelmed in God's providence, of lessons assailing us from every prepositional quarter—"Beneath, beyond, and stretching far away" and "above, below / Within us, and around." It is worth bearing in mind as we record Keble's debt to Cowper that the Evangelical poet himself was only Christianizing a topos closely associated with the loco-descriptive poem, many exemplars of which extract *moralitas* (rather than dogma) from the data of scene—as witness these lines from Dyer's *Grongar Hill*:

> 'Tis now the Raven's bleak Abode;
> 'Tis now th' Apartment of the Toad;
> And there the Fox securely feeds;
> And there the pois'nous Adder breeds,
> Conceal'd in Ruins, Moss and Weeds:
> While, ever and anon, there falls,
> Huge heaps of hoary moulder'd Walls.
> Yet Time has seen, that lifts the low,
> And level lays the lofty Brow,
> Has seen this broken Pile compleat,
> Big with the Vanity of State;
> But transient is the Smile of Fate!
> A little Rule, a little Sway,
> A Sun-beam in a Winter's Day
> Is all the Proud and Mighty have,
> Between the Cradle and the Grave.
> And see the Rivers how they run,
> Thro' Woods and Meads, in Shade and Sun,
> Sometimes swift, and sometimes slow,
> Wave succeeding Wave they go
> A various Journey to the Deep,
> Like human Life to endless Sleep!
> Thus is Nature's Vesture wrought,
> To instruct our wand'ring Thought;
> Thus she dresses green and gay,
> To disperse our Cares away.[21]

Even though the passive participial formation of "Thus is Nature's Vesture wrought" enables Dyer to suppress the agent noun, rather as Keble at first withholds the Author's name from the book of "Septuagesima Sunday," the assumptions informing both poems are identical. Moreover, almost all the details of Dyer's *sic transit* tableau can be paralleled in Keble's "Monday in Whitsun-week"—the difference lies in the acknowledgment of its biblical origin:

> Slumber is there, but not of rest;
> There her forlorn and weary nest
>   The famish'd hawk has found,
> The wild dog howls at fall of night,
> The serpent's rustling coils affright
>   The traveller on his round
>
> What shapeless form, half lost on high,
> Half seen against the evening sky,
>   Seems like a ghost to glide,
> And watch, from Babel's crumbling heap,
> Where in her shadow, fast asleep,
>   Lies fall'n imperial Pride?[22]

If we move from theory to practice, it is equally hard to claim a substantive difference between the nightingales of Keble's "First Sunday after Epiphany":

> Where the thickest boughs are twining
>   Of the greenest darkest tree,
> There they plunge, the light declining—
>   All may hear, but none may see.
> Fearless of the passing hoof,
> Hardly will they fleet aloof;
> So they live in modest ways,
> Trust entire, and ceaseless praise.[23]

and the nightingale in one of Cowper's *Olney Hymns*:

> The calm retreat, the silent shade,
>   With pray'r and praise agree;
> And seem by thy sweet bounty made,
>   For those who follow thee.

There if thy Spirit touch the soul,
   And grace her mean abode;
Oh with what peace, and joy, and love,
   She communes with her GOD!

There like a nightingale she pours
   Her solitary lays;
Nor asks a witness of her song,
   Nor thirsts for human praise.[24]

If anything differentiates the poems, it is the fact that Keble's night-ingales are slightly more realized than Cowper's. The latter's bird functions as fabular shorthand for Christian withdrawal (much as it does in Keble), but without the imaginative enlargement provided by its plunging through a green sea and singing in concert with the clip-clop of horses on the road. Cowper mastered the comparative nudity and clarity of fabular verse; Keble tended to broach his fabulism by way of nature poetry—nature poetry, however, not of a Wordsworthian but of preromantic cast, generalized and simplified to such a degree that the movement into the *epimythium* or conclud-ing moral follows quite naturally from the material that precedes it. The shift, in other words, is effected without any breach of deco-rum, that signal sin in the decalogue of Augustan "thou shalt nots."

Having stressed the continuity between *The Christian Year* and the traditions of eighteenth-century verse both religious and secu-lar, I should perhaps pause to comment on an area in which Tractarian poetry does reveal its own distinctive color and peculiar-ity. Here it might be well to move beyond *The Christian Year* to Car-dinal Newman's *Loss and Gain*, a novel published after his conver-sion to Rome:

Charles, to his surprise, saw distinctly a man kneeling on the little mound out of which the Cross grew; nay, heard him, for his shoul-ders were bare, and he was using the discipline upon them, while he repeated what appeared to be some form of devotion. Charles stopped, unwilling to interrupt, yet not knowing how to pass; but the stranger had caught the sound of feet, and in a few seconds vanished from his view. He was overcome with a sudden emotion, which he could not control. "O happy times," he cried, "when faith was one! O blessed penitent, whoever you are, who know what to believe, and how to gain pardon, and can begin where others end! Here am I in my twenty-third year, uncertain about everything, because I have nothing to trust."[25]

While Charles hails the continuity of Catholicism as a reason for converting, one cannot help thinking that a temperamental masochism has also played its part. In *St. Bartholomew's Eve*, a collaborative venture with John Bowden written in 1818, Newman had taken up the traditional Protestant position with regard to corporal penance:

> Mistaken worship! where the priestly plan
> In servile bondage rules degraded man,
> Proclaims on high in proud, imperious tone
> Devotion springs from ignorance alone;
> And dares prefer to sorrow for the past
> The scourge of penance or the groans of fast![26]

But even here—and it is worth recalling that Newman still had strong Evangelical tendencies in 1818—the poet does not decry self-mortification per se but rather its reduction to externals, proof that even at this point of his life, Newman saw nothing intrinsically wrong with the idea of self-inflicted suffering. As his alienation from establishment Anglicanism waxed, however, so his misgivings about the darker aspects of Catholicism waned. Or, put another way, his attraction to them strengthened. He had once thought it prudent to remove the corpus from a crucifix in his rooms at Oxford and so remove the torture of the Atonement. But Catholicism had all along, through such Franciscan devotions as the stations of the cross, invited the believer to a voluntary participation in the sufferings of Christ. When the Blesséd Julie Billiart avers that the "whole earth is one vast Calvary, where all good Christians carry their victim to be immolated,"[27] she is simply articulating a Catholic commonplace, attractive to someone who, like Newman, regretted the complacency and worldliness of the Anglican establishment. This denial of the flesh seems also to have issued in nausea at the idea of marriage, as witness another distressing episode from *Loss and Gain*: "Charles had a faintish feeling come over him; somewhat such as might beset a man on hearing a call for pork-chops when he was sea-sick."[28] Few readers would dissent from the judgment that Raymond Chapman has passed on this passage: "He [Reding] feels himself called to celibacy, a vocation emphasized to that pathological extreme which infuriated men like Kingsley. . . . The image succeeds only in inducing a Kingsleyan type of nausea in the reader; it does not rouse sympathy with the genuine celibate."[29]

If therefore we were to seek the thread that links such diverse writers as Keble, Newman and Williams, we would find it in a shared cult of mortification, engendered at first by their noble revulsion at worldliness but ultimately tainted by a masochism no less distressing. Persecution became in their eyes a state devoutly to be wish'd, as when Bishop Jebb (a forerunner of the Oxford Movement) claimed in 1814 that:

> Perhaps, too, a little persecution, or of somewhat resembling persecution, may be providentially permitted to train up men with an attachment to the Church as a hierarchy, as distinct from the State, and as dignified only by its intrinsic excellence, by its venerable antiquity, and by its apostolical institution.[30]

The note was sounded again in the first of the tracts (by Newman himself): "And, black event as it would be for the country, yet, (as far as they are concerned), we could not wish them a more blessed termination to their course, than the spoiling of their goods, and martyrdom."[31] Not surprisingly, the establishment bishops proved reluctant candidates for the martyr's crown and did everything they could to block the advance of the Movement. Failing to find the right predisposition for painful experience in Anglicanism, Newman accordingly began to seek it elsewhere. In *The Development of Christian Doctrine*, when he was on the brink of secession, he sought to establish persecution as the note of Christianity by examining its reception in the Roman Empire, a reception recapitulated, mutatis mutandis, in John Bull's attitude to Catholicism. While the analogy worked when it was applied to the Roman Church *in nineteenth-century England*, Newman did not seem to acknowledge its embarrassing breakdown with respect to the Continental founder and maintainer of the Inquisition.

If, therefore, we were to look for the romantic element in Tractarianism, we would find it not in the ecclesiastical medievalism in which it later issued (amongst the members of the Oxford Movement, only Hurrell Froude had any hankering for the Middle Ages), nor in the sacerdotalism that, in magnifying the office of the priesthood, seems at first sight to baptize the romantic conception of the poet-prophet—we would find it not in those things, but in the cultus of the "romantic agony." Flaubert was one of the first writers to explore the masochism associated with Catholic penance. This is how Mario Praz inventories the algolagnia of *La Tentation de Saint Antoine*:

> It would take too long to quote all the obvious passages of this kind—the Saint's vision when he pictures himself in the act of slaughtering the Arians at Alexandria, wading in the blood of slain women and children and shuddering with joy at the feel of it on his limbs; his religious flagellation which turns into algolagnia; the minute description (as of a sadistic *voyeur*) of the penitent woman baring her feet and whipping herself (in the 1849 version); the episode of Priscilla and Maximilla flogged by the eunuch Montanus . . .[32]

But we need to go further back still, for Tobin Siebers has suggested that the romantic cult of suffering has its origin in Rousseau and Goethe. Here, perhaps, are additional sources for Newman's delight in persecution, that social extension of private suffering:

> The Romantic tradition views the suffering self as a work of art, but if we wish to understand Romanticism, we need to acknowledge that it distinguishes some forms of suffering as possessing greater esthetic potential than others. Rousseau discovers the idea that the forms of suffering with the greatest esthetic value portray the self as victim of persecution.[33]

In *Lyra Innocentium*, ostensibly a collection designed for the benefit of Christian children, Keble went so far as to recommend the hair shirt as a means of grace:

> Thrice happy, in Repentance' school
> So early taught and tried!
> At JESUS' side
> And by his dread Fore-runner's rule,
> Trained from the womb!
> Who underneath the world's bright vest
> With sackcloth tame their aching breast,[34]

Well might a puzzled child ponder whether such a garment would not reduce a properly mental pain to a physical skin rash. The fact remains, however, that self-mortification played a large part in forming the Tractarian sensibility. Hurrell Froude's *Remains* recorded fasts and other self-inflicted discomforts, disengaged from any benefit to humankind. Here, for example, is his *Journal* entry for 10 November 1826:

> Fell quite short of my wishes with respect to the rigour of today's fast, though I am quite willing to believe not unpardonably: I tasted nothing till after half-past eight in the evening, and before that had undergone more uncomfortableness, both of body and mind than any fast has as yet occasioned me, having, I hope, laid a sort of foundation, on which I may gradually build up a fit spending of a fast calling my sins to remembrance.[35]

At least one contemporary critic of the *Remains* commented on the absence throughout this journal of any sense of a transcendent Redeemer, and passages like the one above certainly suggest a self-sufficiency in the one fasting, as though, like an Iron Man competitor, he were coldly pitting mind against body. The "calling my sins to remembrance" comes as a distinct afterthought to the measurement and appraisal of the subject's spiritual endurance. A Broad Church judgment on such otiose and self-centered mortification can be found in *Little Dorrit*, written decades later; it proves how similar in some respects the "Apostles" and the "Peculiars" could be. Mrs. Clennam would have denounced the Puseyites as popish conspirators, and yet she seems as ready as Froude was to confuse self-violation with selflessness: "'All seasons are alike to me,' she returned, with a grim kind of luxuriousness. 'I know nothing of summer and winter, shut up here. The Lord has been pleased to put me beyond all that.'"[36] Froude, however, unlike Newman in this regard, was honest enough to see the signs of masochism—"grim . . . luxuriousness"—in his conduct. The *Journal* entry for 18 November 1826 reads, "Bad as I am, it seems as if I might, not indeed be too penitent, but penitent in a wrong way; abstinences and self-mortifications may, themselves, be a sort of intemperance; a food to my craving after some sign that I am altering."[37]

It might be argued that, being the combative enfant terrible of the Movement, Froude ought not to be regarded as its exemplar. But if that is so, how are we to account for an establishment figure like Pusey who, in the same year that *Lyra Innocentium* hailed the sanctity of hair shirts, requested Keble's sanction for a private rule of discipline? "In the event he drew up his own set of rules; all that he needed from Keble was the semblance of an authoritative command to observe them. Keble uncomfortably complied. The rules were long and detailed. They prescribed the wearing of haircloth, the use of a hard chair and a hard bed, the disuse of gloves, abstinence from wine and beer and from food, except what was required for health."[38] One can be sure that Keble's reluctance to sanction these tortures had everything to do with his shrinking from positions of authority—never did a leader lead so passively—and nothing to do with doubts about their sanity.

Again and again in his poetry, he implies that it is wrong to seize the joy as it flies, and shuns the sunrise of eternity promised by Blake's epigram. Human delight ought always to be tempered by consciousness of its transience, not to intensify its fruition (as in the carpe diem topos) but rather to sober it with a memento mori:

> Grief will be joy, if on its edge
> Fall soft that holiest ray:
> Joy will be grief, if no faint pledge
> Be there of heavenly day.[39]

Which, being interpreted, means that one should practice emotional as well as doctrinal reserve—rein in and chasten all strong, spontaneous feeling. Even one of Keble's most sympathetic commentators has misgivings on this score: "When reading his sermons, one is struck by his austerity, so that one sometimes cannot help thinking that he was inclined to go too far in his demands. Indeed, he may easily make the impression of being almost anti-humanistic."[40] It is one thing to espouse Pelagianism, but surely it is another to wish for improvements in the physical lot of humankind. How distressing that both Adam Smith and Keble should agree in proclaiming, "Whatever is, is right," and how additionally distressing that the Oxford Movement should have sought not redress of suffering—whether social or individual—but should have tried to create it in the name of sanctity. An idée fixe of Newman's *University Sermons* was the exaltation of godliness above comfort, which, as so often, took a Kebelian idea to its logical extreme. (Keble had counseled sufferers thus: "Which do you really want of the Almighty? Comfort now, or pardon and acceptance hereafter?"[41] Comfort above godliness seems a sound enough priority until we consider the social record of the first Tractarians.)

Some comfort is indeed trivial, such as the luxuriousness that kept a daughter of Louis XVI from becoming a nun because (she claimed) she had been undone by armchairs. Other comfort is essential, such as the succor and physical well-being to which (as the third generation of human rights now recognizes) every human is entitled. There, perhaps, lies the root cause of Tractarian indifference to the terrible social conditions of Britain. It was the Latitudinarian Kingsley, so mocked and demeaned by Newman's *Apologia*, who realized the importance of fresh water and sewage disposal for the upliftment of the laboring poor; it was the Latitudinarian Dickens who saw no point in instructing foodless paupers about the Lamb of God—without first feeding them. It was the Evangelical Wilber-force who spearheaded the campaign against slavery and the Evan-gelical Shaftesbury who led the movement against child labor. We might therefore wish to differ from Chapman when he takes on trust the disavowal Newman makes towards the end of *Loss and Gain*: "Above all—and Newman was writing only some two years after the stormy night of his own submission—both author and character experience the final sacrifice of family and friends, not for love of sacrifice itself but because 'I have put the subject from me again and again, and it has returned'."[42] That Newman was not above loving "sacrifice" for its own pharisaical sake can be gleaned from the table talk at Littlemore some years before his secession to Rome: "In the uncritical society of Littlemore Newman's puerile love of supernatu-ral and miraculous stories revived unchecked. Mark Pattison ob-served this 'lurking fondness for the miraculous' during his stay. His diary recorded some specimens of the talk at dinner—how St. Macarius stood upright in his cell for a week without eating any-thing, but chewed a palm-leaf out of humility; how St. Goderick stood all night in the river up to his neck, and frozen."[43] While such topics certainly testify to Newman's "puerile love of supernatural . . . stories," they also furnish evidence as ample for the masochism that underlies his version of *contemptus mundi*.

Rejecting the rationalist temper of Liberalism opened the door to darker impulses that would otherwise have fled the light of rea-son. Here are some very sensible remarks of a Deist who nonetheless admired Newman for following his conscience and accepting the suffering that came with secession. They come from Leigh Hunt's review of *St. Simeon Stylites*, which he called "a powerfully graphic, and in some respects appalling satire on the pseudo-aspirations of egotistical asceticism and superstition"—"We say Christian, out of Christian charity; for though real Christianity is a quintessence of good sense, both in its human and angelical aspirations, as the flower of it in due time will make manifest, yet these and other dark absurdities, have, no doubt, lurked about its roots, and for a time, with equal absurdity, have been confounded with the flower."[44] For the Tractarians, the sticking point in this pronouncement—entirely wise and just—would have been the assimilation of Christianity to good sense, for it was good sense, after all, that had recommended the suppression of the Irish bishoprics in 1833 and good sense that lay at the heart of the theology propounded by Whately and Arnold. But an additional dark thought occurs—what if, consciously or unconsciously, Newman found pleasure in pain? Would not all the scourgings and fastings then have amounted to rank indulgence?

We have used Cowper to establish the continuity of Tractarian verse with other traditions of the religious lyric. Let us invoke him now as a foil. Turning from the Desert Father extremes of Newman and Keble to the Evangelical position Cowper typifies, we have to acknowledge his comparative mental healthfulness, his breakdowns notwithstanding. Indeed it is paradoxical that Charles Reding, Newman's fictional convert, should celebrate the poet who wrote "From Thee is all that soothes the life of man"[45] and at the same time feel a morbid frisson at the thought of a discipline. Cowper is quite as ready as any Tractarian to condemn mere materialism and self-interest, but he finds redress in the idea of temperance, not masochistic mortifications:

> Man in society is like a flow'r
> Blown in its native bed: 'tis there alone
> His faculties, expanded in full bloom,
> Shine out; there only reach their proper use.
> But man, associated and leagu'd with man
> By regal warrant, or self-join'd by bond
> For int'rest-sake, or swarming into clans
> Beneath one head for purposes of war,
> Like flow'rs selected from the rest, and bound
> And bundled close to fill some crowded vase,
> Fades rapidly, and, by compression marr'd,
> Contracts defilement not to be endur'd.[46]

This condemns the sinful aspects of urban life as fervently as any poem by Keble, but without any underpinning *Menschenhass*. Indeed, living as he did in the retirement of Olney, Cowper could still acknowledge the interinvolvement of society with the temporal improvement of humankind, a mark of dispassionate common sense that we rarely find in Keble. For all practical purposes, *The Christian*

Year implies that sanctity is the correlate of retirement—the Desert Father option—whereas Cowper's position would seem to accord much more with that avowed by Francis de Sales, a saint whom Hunt admired:

> Psychologist and humanist as he was, he [St. Francis de Sales] set himself to show how ordinary life "in the world" can be made holy, and that without singularity or exaggeration: "Religious devotion," he wrote, "does not destroy: it perfects"; "It is a mistake, a heresy, to want to exclude devoutness of life form among soldiers, from shops and offices, from royal courts, from the homes of the married."[47]

Since the Tractarian lyric—to a degree only matched by medieval exercises in *contemptus mundi*—is committed to undervaluing life as we know it, its sense of the real will accordingly seems a little attenuated.

Anyone approaching *The Christian Year* with the expectation of a rich, documentary texture such as that offered by Coleridge, Wordsworth, and Keats will come away disappointed. Keble is attached to his Gloucestershire landscapes, but only insofar as they offer an encoded theology. Stephen Prickett has articulated a crucial difference between his and Wordsworth's vision in this regard:

> "Nature," for Wordsworth, is neither outside man, nor is it the creation purely of his own mind: it is rather an interaction, an "ennobling interchange." In contrast, Keble's attitude is much more narrowly within the mediaeval and early Church's tradition of allegorical correspondences. There is a hidden allegorical system implicit in the workings of the material universe which gives it meaning and value, and which only the initiated Christian may read with accuracy and understanding.[48]

This narrow patristic vision contrasts unfavorably with the generosity and inclusiveness not only of Wordsworth's but also of Cowper's less developed ideas of the link between humankind and external nature. For Cowper is ready to view it as a divine index in only the most general aesthetic terms, not as a repository of "reserved" emblematic connections:

> ... the love of Nature's works
> Is an ingredient in the compound man,
> Infus'd at the creation of the kind.[49]

By the same token, his celebration of retirement manages to acknowledge the world even in the act of withdrawing—whereas Keble and
Newman harp perpetually on its wicked opposition to the Church:

> Hail, therefore, patroness of health, and ease,
> And contemplation, heart-consoling joys
> And harmless pleasures, in the throng'd abode
> Of multitudes unknown! hail, rural life!
> Address himself who will to the pursuit
> Of honours, or emolument, or fame;
> I shall not add myself to such a chase,
> Thwart his attempts, or envy his success.
> Some must be great. Great offices will have
> Great talents. And God gives to ev'ry man
> The virtue, temper, understanding, taste,
> That lifts him into life; and lets him fall
> Just in the niche he was ordain'd to fill.
>
> . . . .
>
> To me an unambitious mind, content
> In the low vale of life, that early felt
> A wish for ease and leisure, and ere long
> Found here that leisure and that ease I wish'd.[50]

The Task goes on to give as that low Bedfordshire vale in all its delight-
ful variety. Keble's watercolor sketches of Fairford fields, by contrast, are always being diagrammatized and cross- referenced as a
speculum humanae salvationis. And in the altogether more abstract
world of Newman's verse we hardly ever encounter the physical
pleasures of trees and flowers: he moves and has his being in rocky
landscapes of the mind. In their great battle against worldliness, the
Tractarians forgot the world.

2

Keble's *Christian Year*
Surveyed: I

AS I pointed out in the preceding chapter, G. B. Tennyson's appraisal of *The Christian Year* stresses its usefulness as a devotional aid above its value as poetry. Since devotion is frequentative in nature, it is easy to see how such an assessment would found itself on the repeated exposure of the worshipper to the material in hand. The proverb informs us that familiarity breeds contempt, and yet it is precisely those readers most familiar with *The Christian Year*— who have used it in the way that its author intended—who are least contemptuous of its achievement. People dipping into the volume with all their modernist and postmodernist prejudices intact will encounter an idiom apparently as faded and two-dimensional as floral keepsakes pressed in a book of Victorian album verse. And, not unsurprisingly, they will cast the volume aside with summary dismissals of its value. Repeated use, however, will to some extent habituate the reader to a style that, although it postdates the Wordsworthian revolution, has its roots in the Age of Sensibility. Keble was an archconservative. His social beliefs—envisioning a cryptofeudal utopia of docile peasants and paternal lords of the manor—were centuries out of date; his theology harked back through the seventeenth century to that of the church fathers, and he was ready to defend their least defensible fancies against the perceived "corruptions" of Hampden and Arnold. It comes as no surprise, therefore, that his poetic style should show a marked consistency with these other positions. His Oxford lectures on poetry, the *Praelectiones*, recall the battle of the books that had raged in the eighteenth century, awarding the laurel to the ancients and damning the moderns with comparatively faint praise and minimal coverage.

If I may for the moment be merely anecdotal, I began reading

The Christian Year some time ago and at first felt the revulsion that most readers might be expected to experience in the face of a style so unadventurous and unimpassioned, so dutiful and formulaic. I persevered, however, and tried to profit from the doctrine by disengaging it from its versification. As a result, I came more and more to appreciate the real qualities of the poetry, so modest as at first to escape notice. I had moreover the additional advantage of approaching the poems as a student of the Age of Sensibility, the imaginative powerhouse of Keble's diction and procedure. Anyone studying the poetry of Gray, Collins, and Goldsmith has to place in abeyance the *Preface to the Lyrical Ballads* and to disabuse himself or herself of all the Wordsworthian strictures about eighteenth-century diction that are still current in popular responses to poetry. (These are the more insidious for being invisible to those who stand by them.) Readers thus adjusted are more likely to respond to the quiet, undemonstrative merits of *The Christian Year* than those who implicitly or overtly share Wordsworth's irritation with his predecessors. Stephen Prickett has remarked that "to the modern reader, whatever his religious persuasion, the verses [of *The Christian Year*] seem mostly dull and above all insipid. Its Wordsworthian echoes seem shallow."[1] Taken in that order—Wordsworth to Keble—they would indeed. Haydn can seem insipid if we listen to him immediately after Beethoven, and Donizetti bland if we play him after Verdi. We need always to cleanse our palates and banish characteristic predispositions and expectations from of our minds.

If the Wordsworthian echoes in *The Christian Year* do indeed seem shallow, the reason, I believe, is that Keble's admiration for the great romantic was only nominal. Robert Pattison has pointed out that the Tractarians inoculated romantic art by rejecting its "demonic" elements:

> The Oxford Movement mounted an attack on the leading ideas of Romanticism—the religious awe of selfhood, the sacramental value of art, the divine inspiration of individual vision. This attack often borrows the language of its opponents, as Keble adapts the style of Wordsworth, but a similarity of language does not mitigate the underlying enmity.[2]

But that qualification itself needs qualifying. Keble *never* adapted the style of Wordsworth. His practice shows that, whatever his official lip service, he found it too harsh. It is surely significant that, formulating his beau ideal of the poet, he should have used a line from Gray's *Progress of Poesy*, though critics seem not to have remarked upon the fact:

> From their perfect parallelism they [the poems of the Old Testament] are the most artificial of all compositions, yet none ever so apt to relieve the deepest and most overflowing minds; exhibiting therefore by their very form, as compared with their matter, the perfection of that self-control which must itself be the perfection of a mixed creature like man; "thoughts that breathe and words that burn," exactly obeying a certain high law and shaped by it into perfect order.[3]

Gray's original describes how Dryden was inspired by "Bright-eyed Fancy":

> Hark, his hands the lyre explore!
> Bright-eyed Fancy hovering o'er
> Scatters from her pictured urn
> Thoughts that breathe and words that burn.[4]

It is Gray's aesthetic mode that dominates in *The Christian Year*, not Wordsworth's, for just as Gray had asserted that "The language of the age is never the language of poetry,"[5] so in a sense Keble claimed that the language of theology can never be the language of the age, having fixed its "true" self in a patristic mold. To break that mold, to seek "original" (in other words, liberal) alternatives to orthodox formulations, would be to flirt with heresy.

Returning to my anecdotal prelude, then, I can say that, with the right frame of mind created by a study of Gray and his fellows, I came at last, though by gradual and often reluctant stages, and from a theological position very different from his own, to concur with Housman that "Keble is a poet," and that "there are things in *The Christian Year* that can be admired by an atheist."[6] Trying to relay that experience to the reader, I have decided to read *The Christian Year* sequentially and to point to the many echoes of Gray that pervade it, hoping in this way to reproduce my slow conversion from qualified boredom to qualified admiration. Many sticking points remain, however, not least Keble's illiberal theological outlook, with which only the most unreconstructed fundamentalist can feel at home. Even so, these moments can be passed over for the sake of many real virtues in the collection, which I shall now begin to unroll poem by poem.

The circumstances that led to the collation and eventual publication of *The Christian Year* have been summarized by Walter Lock:

> It was while he was a Tutor at Oriel that the collection of poems began to grow, but it was the time of his curacies in Gloucestershire and Hampshire which was most prolific. . . . He had no idea of publication; he would have preferred that the poems should appear after his death, but they were shown among his friends. . . . Dyson pressed him to publish; Davison suggested that he should add the poems for the Occasional Services; his own father was anxious to see the work published before his death, and this was a pressure which he could never resist. Accordingly many poems were retouched to meet the criticism of obscurity, the last poems were written in the spring of 1827, and on May 30th the Preface was composed.[7]

And so *The Christian Year* was born after a long and irregular gestation. Before beginning the ecclesiastical cycle, Keble offered the reader two diurnal poems, "Morning" and "Evening." Because they are meant to be read each day, they provide a steady "figured bass" to offset the *idiomela* or special tunes associated with each distinctive feast. Humdrum though the business of daily living might seem, both poems urge a sacramental view of time, a self-renewing alertness and receptivity to the graces that address us at every moment.

"Morning" begins with references to the color, the breeze and the mist of a typical dawn. These vocative stanzas, having no syntactic resolution, create a pitch of expectancy that Keble then subverts:

> Hues of the rich unfolding morn,
> That, ere the glorious sun be born,
> By some soft touch invisible
> Around his path are taught to swell;—
>
> Thou rustling breeze so fresh and gay,
> That dancest forth at opening day,
> And brushing by with joyous wing,
> Wakenest each little leaf to sing;—
>
> Ye fragrant clouds of dewy steam,
> By which deep grove and tangled stream
> Pay, for soft rains in season given,
> Their tribute to the genial heaven;—[8]

Keble uses the syntactic potentiality of the unresolved stanzas to represent an unrealized aesthetic potentiality. It is as though he were saying with Coleridge—and the chronological relation of the poems permits the possibility of influence—"I see them all so excellently fair, / I see, not feel, how beautiful they are."[9] The animated and responsive dawn puts our insentience to shame: its colors are *taught* to swell in an action that portmanteaus the plumping of cloud and the welling of pigment, while the breeze itself becomes the medium of this vivifying presence and awakens "each little leaf" to sing. Keble has taken standard elements of the *reverdie* or spring song (elements of renewal and energy) and blent them with the cosmic praise of the *Benedicite*: "O ye Heavens, bless ye the Lord"; "O ye Winds of God, bless ye the Lord"; "O ye Dews and Frosts, bless ye the Lord."[10]

Another generic influence on the poem is that of the morning hymn, for which we might want to coin the term *eosphoron* to distinguish it from the erotic tradition of the aubade. *Jam lucis orto sidere* offers a paradigm of sorts. A translation of this hymn for the Office of Prime appeared in Keble's *Miscellaneous Poems*,[11] but its influence becomes visible only in the moralizing stanzas that form the midriff of "Morning." The ancient hymnist evokes the dawn in sketchy terms and offers only a blank ablative absolute to fix the time of day. A closer parallel for, and influence upon, Keble's poem must therefore be sought in Coleridge's "Hymn before Sunrise" (1802). Because this *eosphoron* also takes a landscape as its starting point, it more fully resembles Keble's poem than the Office hymn. Moreover, Coleridge anticipates Keble in claiming that to respond to physical nature is necessarily to respond to its informing Deity:

> Awake, my soul! not only passive praise
> Thou owest! not alone these swelling tears,
> Mute thanks and secret ecstasy! Awake,
> Voice of sweet song! Awake, my heart, awake!
> Green vales and icy cliffs, all join my Hymn.[12]

So far so good, but to move from Coleridge to Keble is at once to become aware of major differences in sensibility and diction. Coleridge presents a sublime landscape in a blank verse full of bardic interrogations and ritualizing patterns (a chiasmus, for example, tries to impose pattern but cannot wholly contain its materials against the surging repetition of "called you forth"):

> And you, ye five wild torrents fiercely glad!
> Who called you forth from night and utter death,
> From dark and icy caverns called you forth,
> Down those precipitous, black, jaggéd rocks,
> For ever shattered and the same for ever?
> Who gave you your invulnerable life,
> Your strength, your speed, your fury, and your joy,
> Unceasing thunder and eternal foam?[13]

Just as Coleridge's alpine splendors have little in common with the Fairford landscape of Keble's poem, so too his expression more obviously reflects the advance guard of romantic diction. Keble, by contrast, has modeled his on the gentler, more formulaic resources of the Age of Sensibility. On the one hand, he seems theoretically to have hailed the verbal simplification that Wordsworth's innovations brought in their wake, for in his essay on "Sacred Poetry" he censures poets whose style preserved the opposition between the poetic and the quotidian: "it is, indeed, greatly to be lamented that . . . writers . . . should have so little confidence in the power of simplicity, and have condescended so largely to the laborious refinement of the muse."[14]

The alternative, however, was revolution, and for Keble revolution presented a satanic option. This is how Willem Beek describes his outlook on those writers who drew attention to themselves by deviation, even if that deviation might have led to the refreshment of stock language and commonplaces: "What Keble understood by 'indulging one's own fancy' may appear from the fact that he thought it a shame to polish his own style, to study any worldly subject for its own sake. He criticized undue display of oratory or ingenuity in a preacher."[15] It is almost inconceivable that an acknowledged romantic like Keble should have so little regard for originality—but then Keble's romanticism was sui generis. Be that as it may, to change the course of poetry (as Wordsworth had changed it) might suit Wordsworth very well, but for Keble it would opened himself to charges of "undue display." Accordingly, if we are properly to adjust our perspective on his poetic heritage, it is to such poems as Gray's "Ode on the Spring" that we must turn:

> Lo! where the rosy-bosomed Hours,
> Fair Venus' train appear,
> Disclose the long-expecting flowers,
> And wake the purple year!

> The Attic warbler pours her throat,
> Responsive to the cuckoo's note,
> The untaught harmony of spring:
> While whispering pleasure as they fly,
> Cool zephyrs through the clear blue sky
> Their gathered fragrance fling.[16]

The periphrastic habit that converts nightingales to "Attic warblers" is precisely the habit that renders morning mist as "dewy steam" in "Morning." And it is to this linguistic conservatism that we must attribute the eclipse of Keble's reputation in our time. As the romantics became canonized and their innovations turned into norms, so poets who lagged behind them necessarily seem regressive. As Crabbe took his bearings from Augustan models, so Keble kept recurring to the poets upon whom he had formed his taste. Indeed as late as 1846, he felt no qualms about using "fleecy care"[17] to describe a flock of sheep. Surely—since there is no framing pastiche to exonerate it—this must be one of the most retrogressive archaisms in the history of poetry. Brian Martin has said that Keble "became a great admirer of Wordsworth as his poetry clearly shows,"[18] but it is difficult to decide how clearly in view of his subsequent observation that

> in the matter of diction Keble did not agree with Wordsworth, but looked backwards to the eighteenth century, and farther, especially to the language of Milton's minor poems. Almost everywhere in Keble's poetry the quality of diction is artificial and archaic: it is certainly not the sort of language which Wordsworth wanted to be used in describing nature . . .[19]

Any claim for a Wordsworthian influence must accordingly be modified—and modified to such an extent indeed that the initial claim becomes otiose. Even though *The Christian Year* appeared more than twenty-five years after the *Lyrical Ballads*, Keble's verse showed no sign of having profited by Wordsworth's example. The priorities of R. W. Church's assessment are more accurate than Martin's, stressing the primacy of the classics in Keble's poetic education, though acknowledging the impact of a "new school of poetry." What he fails to concede is that Gray and Collins, no less than Wordsworth, had both pioneered a "new" responsiveness to nature, and that when this is factored into Keble's classical training, his sympathies are better viewed as inclining toward the Age of Sensibility:

Born a poet, steeped in all that is noblest and tenderest and most beautiful in Greek and Roman literature, with the keenest sympathy with that new school of poetry which, with Wordsworth as its representative, was searching out the deeper relations between nature and the human soul, he found in poetical composition a vent and relief for feelings stirred by the marvels of glory and of awfulness, and by the sorrows and blessings, amid which human life is passed.[20]

I am by no means denying the value Keble set on Wordsworth in the abstract, but simply stressing that its practical impact was negligible. He undoubtedly admired the elder poet, but with an admiration like that of Haydn for Beethoven. The former clearly acknowledged his pupil's genius, and told Maximilian Franz that he would "in time fill the position of one of Europe's greatest composers."[21] Beethoven, however, distrusted his master, and as John Burk points out, if

jealousy did not color Haydn's opinion, there was always something grudging about his admiration. The free conception, a certain aggressiveness, were probably both distasteful and upsetting to his idea of where a reasonable trio should draw the line. [Haydn had advised Beethoven not to publish the C Minor trio of the Opus 1 set.] Haydn, experimental on his own account, could be hidebound when the innovations of another were in question.[22]

Whatever Haydn might have *said* about Beethoven's significance, he himself never incorporated, or profited from, the innovations of his pupil—a fact that speaks volumes. By the same token, Wordsworth's reservations about Keble provide proof of a similarly ambivalent relationship between the two poets. The most cutting of his criticisms was relayed to his nephew Christopher and centered on Keble's "vicious" diction, which, according to Wordsworth, was a consequence of his having "been seduced into many faults by his immoderate love of the ancient classics."[23] That Wordsworth applied the same epithet ("vicious")[24] to Cowper's diction and dismissed Gray's as being "curiously elaborate"[25] proves that he saw Keble as an epigone of the "school" against which he was reacting, not a co-equal poetic innovator.

When all this is taken into account, "admiration" strikes me as being altogether too strong a term for an attitude so patronizing and for praise so faint. We shall see in due course how echoes of Gray pervade the whole of *The Christian Year*, while the verbal influences of Wordsworth's poetry remain relatively slight. What Coleridge attacked as the ignis fatuus of the *Preface to the Lyrical Ballads*—the reproduction of "the real language of men"—would have struck Keble as doubly repellent, habituated as he was to a poetry of reserve and verbal guardedness. Far more restful and accommodating was the quiet *rifacimento* of familiar voices and habits of expression. Unlike Martin, George Saintsbury finds the similarity between Keble and Wordsworth in the general pronouncements they made about poetry. With regard to practice—decisions about diction and form—he is careful to stress the former's debt to the Age of Sensibility, Gray most especially. And even as he does this, he is generous enough to hail the worthiness of the achievements fathered from that source: "Nor should *Red o'er the forest peers the setting sun*—the only thing in the manner of Gray's *Elegy* that has come near the *Elegy* itself—be unnoticed."[26]

This detour has taken us a long way from "Morning," and it is to the fifth stanza of that poem that we must now return. It functions as a pivot, for, through a generalizing beatitude formula, Keble shifts focus from the sensuous proem to the abstract moralizing of the middle section:

> Oh! timely happy, timely wise,
> Hearts that with rising morn arise!
> Eyes that the beam celestial view,
> Which evermore makes all things new!

Usually Keble is eager to take up his descriptive material into the discursive sections that follow, but here he departs from his usual procedure of correlating outer and inner landscapes. Indeed the scenic opening is allowed to fade from view. More important than mere responsiveness to natural beauty, Keble implies, is the conformation of human to divine ways of seeing. To view the "celestial beam" is in a sense to align one's vision on its axis, to perceive that renovation of created nature recorded in Ps. 104:30 ("Thou sendest forth thy spirit, they are created: and thou renewest the face of the earth") and so participate in the spiritual renewal that St. Paul records in 2 Cor. 5:16 ("but though our outward man perish, yet the inward *man* is renewed day by day"). *Anadiplosis* supplies a transition into the central section of the poem, where Keble discreetly presents himself as someone able, through the desired alignment with the "celestial beam," to perceive how new the blessings of each day actually are.

The repetition of "new" in stanza 6 recalls the speed and urgency of a *stretta*, the point in a fugue at which the tempo quickens and the entries come thick and fast:

> New mercies, each returning day,
> Hover around us while we pray;
> New perils past, new sins forgiven,
> New thoughts of God, new hopes of Heaven.

The starting point for this stanza is a text from Lam. 3:22–23: "*It is* of the LORD's mercies that we are not consumed, because his compassions fail not. *They are* new every morning: great is thy faithfulness." The very fact of waking therefore recapitulates the miracle of creation, since it is predicated upon the mercy of God. Restating his belief that a mental disposition provides the key to the divinity locked away in everyday life, Keble once again uses a syntax of potentiality, choosing a conditional clause here ("If on our daily course our mind"), and, in stanza 12, a sequence of optative subjunctives:

> O could we learn that sacrifice,
> What lights would all around us rise!
> How would our hearts with wisdom talk
> Along Life's dullest dreariest walk!

It is this sense of contingency that differentiates Keble's *eosphoron* from hymns like *Jam lucis orto sidere*. There the format is intercessory, and the initiative transferred to God:

> Jam lucis orto sidere,
> Deum precemur supplices,
> Ut in diurnis actibus
> Nos servet a nocentibus.
>
> Linguam refraenans temperet
> Ne litis horror insonet:
> Visum fovendo contegat,
> Ne vanitates hauriat.[27]

Keble would have sensed from *Tintern Abbey* that the romantic ethos of the times required a posture altogether less passive than that taken up by a huddle of fearful monks—hence his stress on a participatory response, on the believer's *correspondence* with graces bestowed:

"both what they half create / And what perceive."[28] Keble's, after all, is not wholly a "fugitive and cloistered virtue." He is writing long after the closure of Little Gidding, and decades before the establishment of Anglican orders, for an audience to whom the monastic ideal would have seemed remote and "popish":

> We need not bid, for cloister'd cell,
> Our neighbour and our work farewell,
> Nor strive to wind ourselves too high
> For sinful man beneath the sky:
>
> The trivial round, the common task,
> Would furnish all we ought to ask;
> Room to deny ourselves; a road
> To bring us, daily, nearer God.

Such cheerful adaptability and temperateness are the notes of Anglicanism in the early nineteenth century. We sense Keble's caution about Baroque devotionalism in his use of "wind," which hints at the writhing Solomonic pillars of Bernini's *Baldacchino* at the same time as it condemns a self-induced, "cranked-up" emotionalism.

This use of "wind" goes back to Herbert, who also conceived Anglicanism as an Aristotelian mean between the extremes of excess and nudity. Here, as in Keble, "winding" suggests the taint of baroque self-display: "Is there in truth no beautie? / Is all good structure in a winding stair?"[29] And of course "The Elixir" supplies a precedent for "the trivial round":

> A servant with this clause
> Makes drudgerie divine:
> Who sweeps a room, as for thy laws,
> Makes that and th' action fine.[30]

This Herbertian color persists into the penultimate stanza, where "rest," conceived as the attribute of divinity, recalls the priorities of "The Pulley." In that poem, Herbert contrasts a fatal "rest in Náture" against resting in "the God of Nature."[31] Finally, we must note how Keble also follows Herbert in using petitionary prayer as terminal device, braking the frequentative rhythm of the middle section with an upward-thrusting appeal:

> Only, O Lord, in Thy dear love
> Fit us for perfect Rest above;
> And help us, this and every day,
> To live more nearly as we pray.

Here Keble repeats his belief in aligning human and divine perspectives, and tries to incorporate prayerfulness into the actual business of living.

We have seen how the poet's diction derives for the most part from the Age of Sensibility and how it lags behind the pioneering efforts of Wordsworth and Coleridge. In "Evening," pendant to the poem above, the conservatism extends even to the subject matter. Gray and Collins had both explored the poetry of twilight—indeed they may be said to have invented it—but Keble offers no evening scene to balance the dawnscape of "Morning." Rather he starts with an ending, and anxiously notes the disappearance of the sun:

> 'Tis gone, that bright and orbèd blaze,
> Fast fading from our wistful gaze;
> Yon mantling cloud has hid from sight
> The last faint pulse of quivering light.
>
> In darkness and in weariness
> The traveller on his way must press,
> No gleam to watch on tree or tower,
> Whiling away the lonesome hour.[32]

Given Keble's attunement to the full range of natural beauty, it seems probable that his horror of darkness springs not so much from Augustanism as from doctrinal orthodoxy. Whereas "Morning" shows little resemblance to its corresponding office hymn, there can be no doubt that "Evening" and *Te lucis ante terminum* share a common outlook, and that that outlook itself ultimately takes its bearings from the psalms, notably the 91st, prescribed for the office of compline. Night here is associated with terror and with pestilence.

However, whereas almost all the nocturnal psalms are sedentary, starting in composure and settlement, Keble's poem is a sort of *hodoiporikon* or journey poem. Thus while the speaker of Psalm 91 offers the assurance of dwelling and stability—"Whoso dwelleth under the shadow of the most High: shall abide under the shadow of the Almighty," Keble offers the distressful image of a benighted traveler. Evening brings no respite for pilgrims; it simply compounds the difficulty and the danger of their undertaking.

Having established gloom and despondency, Keble projects a fine mental sunburst in the third stanza, where the presence of God, irradiating earthly sorrow, anticipates the *lux perpetua* of eternity: "Sun of my soul! Thou Saviour dear, / It is not night if Thou be near." Placing the journey metaphor in abeyance for the time being, he acts as if a real light had indeed flooded the world that, after the sunset of the opening stanzas, had been plunged into darkness. The light of God confers a preternatural insight on believers, enabling them to penetrate behind physical surfaces and perceive their informing divinity—the "Wisdom, Power, and Love" to which they testify. This light also enables believers to detect a purpose and pattern beneath the contingencies of time. Like a summer sun, it fosters fruition, so that "all the flowers of life unfold." Finally, it ignites the human heart with its own principle of *caritas* and guarantees the mutuality of Creator and creature.

Even though the poem ranges far and wide, a modulatory chain of images anchors and guides the line of thought. Thus we move from physical features ("earth or sky . . . stream or grove") to their metaphysical translation ("Time's full river as it flows"; "flowers of life"), while Keble adjusts the light to foreground the whatever properties (heat or brilliance or warmth) are relevant to his purpose. In 1836 he would contribute his fine translation of the Φῶς ἱλαρον to *Lyra Apostolica*, and almost certainly had the Greek hymn in mind when he wrote "Evening." John K. Hale has spoken about the "impassioned odelike transitions" of the original, and noted how much "of the ecstatic circling of thought *is* regained by Keble."[33] "Evening" reveals a comparably seamless progression from topic to topic. But whereas the ancient hymn records the ceremony of *epiluchnion*, a ritual lighting of lamps, Keble's poem in *The Christian Year* interiorizes that symbolic light and, like many Protestant lyrics, turns ritual into metaphor. (In *Miscellaneous Poems*, on the other hand, we encounter a whole suite of lyrics concerned with one or other fire ritual: "Lighting of Lamps," "Lights at Vespers," "Lights in the Upper Chamber" and "The Churchman and His Lamp.")[34]

The epigraph alludes to Emmaus, but Keble also seems to have the earlier events of Maundy Thursday in mind when he recalls how the Beloved Disciple rested on the breast of Christ: "Be my last thought, how sweet to rest / For ever on my Saviour's breast." That

is the first point (after six discomfited stanzas) at which Keble introduces an image of repose—repose conceived, moreover, as death.
Not surprisingly this strikes a mortal chord, and the poem develops
a fine plangency as it relays the poet's "night thoughts." The temporal night blends ineluctably with the night of extinction:

> Abide with me from morn till eve,
> For without Thee I cannot live:
> Abide with me when night is nigh,
> For without thee I dare not die.

If we compare this with H. F. Lyte's "Abide with me" we at once
perceive how much more intense and anguished Keble's utterance
is. Lyte uses the quotation as a comforting frame, and the *inclusio*
places the speaker in the center of God's presence:

> Abide with me; fast falls the eventide:
> The darkness deepens; Lord, with me abide:
> When other helpers fail, and comforts flee,
> Help of the helpless, O abide with me.[35]

Perhaps an essential difference between Catholic and Protestant
mind-set is highlighted in the urgency of Keble's stanza, where unable confidently to proclaim his salvation, the poet recalls the angst
of the *Libera me: Tremens factus sum ego et timeo.*[36] Lyte disjoins the
phrase and sets it in place; Keble seizes it by the hem and will not let
it go. The symmetrical repetitions, far from balancing and stabiliz-
ing the design, evoke cries of alarm and panic. There is no calm
alternative to the absolute verbs of "cannot" and "dare not."

The disquiet persists through the remainder of the poem, for
Keble discards the restfulness of "kindly sleep" and "Saviour's
breast" almost as soon as he introduces them. The journey is now
recast as that most horrific nineteenth-century nightmare, a winter
voyage (cf. Dickens's *American Notes*), though it is turned to safe
harborage by the presence of God. An enharmonic modulation via
a pun on the *Gubernator* who steers in stanza 9 and who rules in
stanza 10 takes us from the sea to the seat of government, while a
logical shift from temporal to spiritual power invokes the journey
of the *Via Dolorosa* as a paradigm for priests. Sea voyages and the
path of atonement are, for all the accompanying distress, journeys
with a purpose. For a contrasting sense of purposeless travel Keble

now moves to the rudderless drift of the undevout, hinting (in the light of the earlier tempest imagery) at the legend of the Flying Dutchman: "If some poor wandering child of Thine / Have spurn'd, to-day, the voice divine." Nor do Christians collectively escape a comparable fate. Keble's sober coda recalls the banishment of Adam and Eve in *Paradise Lost*. Compare

> The World was all before them, where to choose
> Thir place of rest, and Providence thir guide:
> They hand in hand with wand'ring steps and slow,
> Through *Eden* took thir solitary way[37]

with a similar bleakness in Keble's strophe:

> Come near and bless us when we wake,
> Ere through the world our way we take;
> Till in the ocean of Thy love
> We lose ourselves in Heaven above.

That is the imaginative resolution to all the distressful elements in the poem—to transpose the distress of an ocean voyage into the key of Divinity. Here Keble refers not to the loss of direction (for God is omnipresent), but rather to the loss of self, drowned in the transcendent will of God.

So much for the diurnal (that is to say recurrent) poems of *The Christian Year*. "Advent Sunday" is the first to take us into the cycle of the ecclesiastical calendar. Keble effects the transition with a clarion call that contrasts with the sleep imagery of "Evening." The poet has a special waking in mind, however, the waking of soldiers to the reveille. He reconceives St. Paul's image for the diffusion of the Gospel—"Their sound is gone out into all lands"—as a cumulative dress rehearsal for the *tuba mirum spargens sonum*:

> Awake—again the Gospel-trump is blown—
> From year to year it swells with louder tone,
>   From year to year the signs of wrath
>   Are gathering round the Judge's path,
> Strange words fulfill'd, and mighty works achiev'd,
> And truth in all the world both hated and believ'd.[38]

Keble urges the "liegeman of the Cross" to respond to the reveille and to gather for battle at the "eastern mount," the messianic mountain of Zion. Since its "eastern" placement will be apparent only to people in the west, most readers would think that Keble had a contemporary audience in mind and that the poem's temporal setting is 1823, the date of its composition. However, in a strange dreamlike warping of historical sequence, he takes us back to the triumphal entry into Jerusalem and Christ's weeping at the fate of that city:

> Nor wonder, should ye find your King in tears,
> E'en with the loud Hosanna ringing in his ears.
>
> Alas! no need to rouse them: long ago
> They are gone forth to swell Messiah's show:
>   With glittering robes and garlands sweet
>   They strew the ground beneath His feet:

Then, having taken us into an immediate historic present, Keble at once cuts away with a steep temporal recession like that at the end of *The Eve of St. Agnes*: "And they are gone: aye, ages long ago / These lovers fled away into the storm."[39] In Keats the recession is elegiac, and stresses the irrecoverability of happiness; in Keble its function is recapitulative. The fickleness of the crowd in Jerusalem is not unique, and the transition from third- to second-person pronouns implies that Keble's contemporaries would be quite as capable of defection: "They strew the ground beneath His feet: / All but your hearts are there." History, viewed providentially, is not so much a sequence of discrete moments as a set of typological connections, of *protasis* and *apodosis* fused in the timeless apprehension of God. That is why the time scheme of the poem is so mysterious and fluid, and why the poet's references keep lacing together a specific past with a frequentative present. Christ's progress through Jerusalem is superimposed upon the image of Christ in glory as he monitors the course of time:

> Meanwhile He paces through th' adoring crowd,
> Calm as the march of some majestic cloud,
>   That o'er wild scenes of ocean-war
>   Holds its still course in Heaven afar:
> E'en so, heart-searching Lord, as years roll on,
> Thou keepest silent watch from Thy triumphal throne:

Back again in the frame of Passion Week, Keble views Jerusalem through the eyes of Christ, prophetically conscious that the acclaim he is receiving amounts to nothing and picking out scenes of past happiness, not least the home of Mary and Martha. Even that historical detail soon gives way to suprahistorical truth as Keble blends the personalities of the protagonists into an austere, absolute personification:

> And fast beside the olive-border'd way
> Stands the bless'd home, where Jesus deign'd to stay,
> The peaceful home, to Zeal sincere
> And heavenly Contemplation dear,
> Where Martha lov'ed to wait with reverence meet,
> And wiser Mary linger'd at Thy sacred feet.

Just as the tragedy of Passion Week is doomed to repeat itself through time, so the faithful remnant remains dissociated from that betrayal. Poetical *conspecti* of history (as in Gray's "Progress of Poesy") tend to be very selective—and Keble's poem reveals the same omissive sweep as its predecessors. Even as Arianism betrays the divinity of Christ, there remain pockets of Catholic truth in Palestine; even as Palestine falls to Islam, Crusaders arise under St. Louis's leadership in 1248. And in the Age of Reason, brilliantly imaged as an unrelieved glare ("and age of light, / Light without love, glares on the aching sight"), the piety of Izaak Walton identifies him as yet another avatar of the "faithful remnant." Such a juxtaposition might at first blush seem eccentric in the extreme, but it is clarified by Keble's belief in the invisible unity of the Church and by his Herbertian sense of unheroic holiness. A national, public hero like St. Louis has in these terms no greater claim to sainthood than a retiring Anglican biographer.

Having made his selective tour through history, Keble returns in the final stanzas to the eschatological topic of Advent, and tries to order its materials as a catalog of signs and portents. Just as Mary and Martha had taken marmoreal form as Contemplation and Zeal, so the poet presents himself as a statuesque personification of Faith, alert to a parousia that will come like a thief in the night: "Lord, ere our trembling lamps sink down and die, / Touch us with chastening hand, and make us feel Thee nigh."

"Advent Sunday" turns repeatedly to the events of Palm Sunday, odd though the dislocation might seem in a cycle so closely knitted to the sequence of the Christian calendar. Be that as it may, "Second Sunday in Advent" presents a different kind of dislocation:

the disharmony between external and ecclesiastical season. Such disparities occur because, after the Conference of Whitby, a southern authority (Rome) imposed its own liturgical design upon the northerly section of the Continent. Newman himself acknowledges that the English May sometimes fails to strike a festive Marian note: "A man may say, 'True; but in this climate we have sometimes a bleak, inclement May'. This cannot be denied; but still, so much is true that at least it is the month of *promise* and of *hope*."[40] In "Second Sunday in Advent," Keble likewise attempts to rationalize the discrepancy between natural phenomena and the feast they accompany:

> Is she less wise than leaves of spring,
> Or birds that cower with folded wing?
> What sees she in this lowering sky
> To tempt her meditative eye?

That of course is the question—the *quaestio* for an inner debate. Christian eschatology has always prophesied natural derangements of one kind or another, and Keble offers the unsympathetic weather of an English November as the type of these portents, set out in a grand anaphoraic catalog:

> By tempests, earthquakes, and by wars,
> By rushing waves and falling stars,
> By every sign her Lord foretold,
> She sees the world is waxing old,[41]

There is something oddly Shelleyan about the last of those four lines, recalling as it does the millenarian expectancy of the Choruses from *Hellas*: "The world's great age begins anew, / The golden years return, / The earth does like a snake renew / Her winter weeds outworn."[42] But of course the poets are ideological worlds apart— Shelley's snake image, half recalling the *ouroboros*, is one of secular self-renewal; Keble envisages a world transfigured and divinized. Thus whereas the Radical recoils from the carnage and turmoil so central to eschatological visions—"O cease! must hate and death return? / Cease! must men kill and die"[43]—the High Churchman welcomes them as an assurance of the Second Coming: "And through that last and direst storm / Descries by faith her Saviour's form." Such phantasmal and indistinct apprehensions are well and good, but Keble also suggests that atmospherics are a consequence of atmosphere. All sublunary existence will de facto be clouded by uncertainty because the earth is enveloped in haze. Only by the clarified light of heaven will the full purpose of God be discerned:

> But chiefly ye should lift your gaze
> Above the world's uncertain haze,
> And look with calm unwavering eye
> On the bright field beyond the sky,

The nineteenth-century conception of angels tended, as John Carey has pointed out, to be sentimental and ineffectual: "The deterioration of the angel is a further sign of Victorian religion ebbing into sentiment."[44] Nothing, however, could be further from this and from the pious domesticity of Patmore's "Angel in the House" than Keble's vision of angels in "Second Sunday in Advent." In the sixth stanza he translates that clear vision "bright fields beyond the sky" into correlative human action. Recovering the etymological root of "angel" in *angelos* or messenger, he declares that a prophetic vision must issue in prophetic office, the resolute proclamation of the Gospel: "Angels He calls ye: be your strife / To lead on earth an Angel's life."

It would seem from "Third Sunday in Advent" that Keble knew something about Jesuit spirituality, for the poem is a *compositio loci*, that amplification of Gospel narratives recommended by St. Ignatius in his *Spiritual Exercises*. Here, by way of sample, is a directive for Day 1 in contemplating the Incarnation: *"The second is the composition, seeing the place. Here it will be to see the great extent and circuit of the world, where so many and such diverse nations dwell: in like manner afterwards to behold in particular the house and chamber of our Lady, in the city of Nazareth, in the province of Galilee."*[45] Many poems in *The Christian Year* offer *compositiones loci* to flesh out an otherwise vague grasp of biblical narratives. In the case of "Third Sunday in Advent," Keble takes his epigraph from the relevant lectionary reading—Matt. 11:7–9: "What went ye out into the wilderness to see?"—where Christ follows the rhetorical procedure of *expeditio*. Through it he offers his audience three possible motives for their excursion into the desert, viz., scenic pleasure, the sight of worldly riches ("soft raiment"), and the encounter with a prophet. The figure is designed to eliminate the wrong reasons in order to give prominence to the right one. In his poetic expansion, however, Keble manages to work over each element of the *expeditio* before discarding it. His projection of the

Wilderness reveals a truly vivid topographical imagination, a capacity to project landscapes very different from those of Fairford and Hursley. In "Second Sunday in Advent" we have already encountered the imaginative glimpse of a "tender gem / Set in the fig-tree's polish'd stem"; here he offers us oleanders rustling on Galilean hills.

Because of these flights, I would want to take issue with Elbert Thompson when he claims that in *The Christian Year* "the descriptive passages . . . are so often lacking in precision that they are not less sure on places which the poet had never seen than on those familiar to him."[46] While this might seem a backhanded way of saying that Keble's Palestinian landscapes are as vivid (or as pale) as his English ones, what Thompson is really objecting to is the decorative scrim imposed by the diction of Sensibility, a diction that tends to denature and generalize rather than to specify:

> What went ye out to see
> O'er the rude sandy lea,
> Where stately Jordan flows by many a palm,
> Or where Gennesaret's wave
> Delights the flowers to lave,
> That o'er her western slope breathe airs of balm?
>
> All through the summer night,
> Those blossoms red and bright
> Spread their soft breasts, unheeding, to the breeze,
> Like hermits watching still
> Around the sacred hill,
> Where erst our Saviour watch'd upon His knees.[47]

Keble begins by replicating the question format of Christ's *expeditio*, but he soon breaks with the tone of his source. Where the reed shaken by the wind in the Gospel account functions as a red herring, Keble's scenic data, like St. Ignatius's *compositiones loci*, provide a clew that will ultimately lead to an encounter with God Incarnate. The recreation of space issues in an abridgment of history, and the contemplative returns in spirit to the time of Christ himself:

> Here may we sit, and dream
> Over the heavenly theme,
> Till to our soul the former days return;

> Till on the grassy bed,
> Where thousands once He fed,
> The world's incarnate Maker we discern.

Sitting is of course a posture associated with spatial memory—the Hebrews, recalling the beloved country during their exile, sat beside the Euphrates ("By the rivers of Babylon, there we sat down, yea, we wept, when we remembered Zion"—Ps. 137), and Goldsmith, contemplating the mysterious bond between space and spirit, takes up a similar position in *The Traveller*: "Even now, where Alpine solitudes ascend, / I sit me down a pensive hour to spend."[48]

However, having created this spatial immediacy, Keble returns to his epigraph and takes up its pattern of systematic dismissal. His gratuitous reference to crossing the main (hardly appropriate to Jordan) makes it clear that he is allegorizing the false options of reed and soft raiment as the trappings of British imperial power. These are false choices, choices of transience and luxury, that must be subordinated to the nonimperial landscapes of Bethlehem, Carmel (scene of Elijah's contest with the prophets of Baal), and Gethsemane. At this point he would seem to have switched from noetic to actual travel and to be advocating literal pilgrimage as a vehicle for *compositio loci*: "Then rise at dawn of day / And wind thy thoughtful way, / Where rested once the Temple's stately shade." The contemplative would have no difficulty in imaging the temple; it is the pilgrim physically there who must contend with absence and deletion. Keble seems to play with old belief in Jerusalem as the omphalos or navel of the world when he suggests that movement in the Holy Land occurs, as it were, about the axis of a still center: "Their heart untravell'd still adores the King of kings." He then inverts this conceit and claims that the stay-at-homes who do not otherwise enjoy the privileges of pilgrims will have imaginative access to Palestine as long as they exercise the right mental discipline. The reed and the soft raiment of Matt. 11 recur now in allegorical form as items likely to deflect the contemplative from the right objects of contemplation. This is Keble's own version of the *expeditio* employed in his epigraph. Object after object is set aside as the believer approaches the ineffable presence of the Creator, a presence that, being omnipresent, finally makes all movement seem otiose. Keble puns on the adjective "homeliest," suggesting fitness for God's habitation on the one hand, and an unpretentious, untraveled regionalism on the other:

"Blesséd be God, Whose grace / Shews Him in every place / To homeliest hearts of pilgrims pure and meek." Once again we hear the accent of Herbert in that final sentence—a beatitude colored by the content of the poem from which it emerges. Compare the conclusion to "The Church-floore": "Blest be *Architect,* whose art / Could build so strong in a weak heart."[49] Nor should we neglect the influence of Milton. It is clear that Keble has partly replicated the stanza form of his hymn "On the Morning of Christ's Nativity"—trimeter couplet and pentameter "promontory" repeated twice over. The reason lies in the content of Milton's poem, for just as the Incarnation localizes and materializes the Deity, so too does the spatial emphasis of *compositio loci* give a habitation and a name to the abstract tenets of dogma.

Looking over the shifts, realignments, and interchange of physical and mental space throughout this poem, many readers would reject Thompson's stricture about the poet's sense of design. Poems like "Third Sunday in Advent" are by no means as ploddingly expository as he implies: "Keble's poems, furthermore, have a progress such as one might find in a sermon. Beginning as they do with Biblical incident or natural scene, they move on from thought to thought."[50] We ought to recall that, distinguished classicist though he was, Keble thought that Sir Walter Scott's ignorance of Greek literature was actually a providential blessing, which "tended to keep his style exclusively and unaffectedly *romantic,*" and secured its "frank military artlessness"[51]—artlessness not only of style but also of structure, as this celebration of agglutinative Gothic buildings shows: "Who would wish the architect of Canterbury Cathedral to have been deeply versed in the proportions of the four regular orders of Greece?"[52] While there can be no denying that foursquare homiletic poems *do* occur at intervals throughout *The Christian Year,* they are nonetheless intercalated with generous, bardic utterances like "Third Sunday in Advent." Keble's way of contrasting the abbeys of Tintern and Fountains provides a topographic parallel for the distinction I am drawing. In a letter to Thomas Keble he remarked that "from this very circumstance you have a mixture of impressions, whereas at Tintern everything conspires to produce one single effect—add to this that the ground plan of Tintern is much more simple."[53] There are poems in *The Christian Year* with a Tinternesque concinnity and clarity, others less assimilable in one glance, full of turns and slippages and redirections—lyrics in the Fountains mould.

Even though Advent traditionally invites the believer to peni-

tence and preparation for the Second Coming, only the second of
Keble's suite for the season addresses the passing of the world and
the imminence of a new moral order. In the final poem from this
segment of *The Christian Year*, he transposes the apocalypse from a
secular to a personal plane and writes a long verse meditation on a
private advent—the arrival of the soul in paradise. "Fourth Sunday
in Advent" begins with an admission of failure:

> Of the bright things in earth and air
>   How little can the heart embrace!
> Soft shades and gleaming lights are there—
>   I know it well, but cannot trace.
>
> . . . .
> I cannot paint to Memory's eye
>   The scene, the glance, I dearest love—
> Unchanged themselves, in me they die,
>   Or faint, or false, their shadows prove.[54]

This is Keble in an uncharacteristically Platonic frame of mind. Creation is too a vast a proposition for the creature to absorb; the artist
is defeated by his material. As our sense data can only shadow the
ontology of the metauniverse, efforts to convey it are inadequate
either by virtue of their feebleness or—worse—their untruthfulness
to the Truth: "faint, or false, their shadows prove." Once again Keble
invokes the sublunary, murky atmosphere of "Second Sunday in
Advent," his version of the Pauline glass that distorts and clouds
our apprehension both of Deity and design: "'Tis misty all, both sight
and sound."

Heaven by contrast enables art to reveal its subject instead of
betraying it. To establish his point, Keble recurs to an old topos—
the music of the spheres—but he is sufficiently a man of his time to
feel some caution about its tenability in 1822. So it is that he "mists"
his affirmation with a subjunctive:

> But patience! there may come a time
>   When these dull ears shall scan aright
> Strains, that outring Earth's drowsy chime,
>   As Heaven outshines the taper's light.

We would be wrong, however, to see in this caution the prototype
of Tennyson's irresolute hopefulness in "Crossing the Bar": "I hope
to see my Pilot face to face."[55] *His* tentative verb has an agnostic

color, whereas Keble's misgivings center on the obsolescence of the image in hand. When it comes to confirming the point at which the creature sees its Creator, he borrows the emphatic form of the future tense from his source (Isa. 23:17):

> These eyes, that dazzled now and weak,
>   At glancing motes in sunshine wink,
> Shall see the King's full glory break,
>   Nor from the blissful vision shrink:
>
> In fearless love and hope uncloy'd
>   For ever on that ocean bright
> Empower'd to gaze; and undestroy'd,
>   Deeper and deeper plunge in light.

Keble does not specify the exact nature of that ocean. On the one hand it seems to refer to the sea described in the book of Revelation, but it also functions as a metonym for the vast, illimitable nature of Deity. It is almost as if he were inverting and irradiating a moment from Gray's "Bard." There closure is effected by suicide ("Deep in the roaring tide he plunged to endless night"),[56] whereas in Keble's poem closure is supplanted by a sense of infinite accession, a plunging towards, not away from, the center of things. Frederick Faber's comparatively passive conception of eternal life will serve to measure the exuberance and progressiveness of Keble's:

> Father of Jesus, love's reward,
>   What rapture will it be,
> Prostrate before thy throne to lie,
>   And gaze and gaze on thee![57]

Reassured by this destiny, the poet is able now to review the despondency recorded in the opening stanzas of the poem. The landscape thus revisited no longer causes despair at the imagination's failure to encompass the full range of experience. Keble's chastened tone also shows that he does not regret his failure to transcribe it: he is confident that the ability will come with the alignment of creature and Creator in Paradise. Indeed, he is even able to rejoice in his limitation: omniscience without omnipotence would prove intolerable. There is something providential in human incapacity: "Yet are there saddening sights around, / Which Heaven, in mercy, spares us too." The poem ends with a reminiscence of Herbert's "Jordan (I)." The signifier of the "winding stair" is recalled by the maze, its signified; the aureate style is displaced by the simple enunciation of truth: "Content thee with one simple strain"—which is how Keble paraphrases Herbert's final lines ("Nor let them punish me with losse of rime, / Who plainly say, *My God, My King*").[58]

Advent past, we move to Christmas Day and its satellite festivals. Like St. Thomas in *Murder in the Cathedral*,[59] Keble seems to have sensed the interconnectedness of these feast days, and has chosen not to tuck away his poems on St. Stephen, St. John, and the Holy Innocents amongst the other hagiological pieces at the end of *The Christian Year*. Since he appends a note from Charles Wheatly's *Rational Illustration of the Book of Common Prayer* to "St. Stephen's Day," we can be fairly certain, even though he does not admit the influence, that Wheatly also prompted his retention of the Christmas cycle, for, again like St. Thomas in *Murder in the Cathedral*, the eighteenth-century divine also stresses the interrelatedness of the Incarnation and martyrdom: "The placing of them immediately *after Christmasday*, was to intimate, as is suppos'd, that none are thought fitter attendants on Christ's Nativity, than those blessed Martyrs, who have not scrupl'd to lay down their lives for him, from whose Incarnation and Birth they received life eternal."[60] Having cited Wheatly as a source for the arrangement of the lyrics, we need to stress that these poems are not themselves cross-referential. Nor do they exploit the scenery associated with Christmas verse. So carefully indeed does "Christmas Day" avoid the traditional pageantry (say, of Milton's hymn for the season) that it actually breaks with tradition. Having seen how readily Keble offers *compositiones loci* in other poems, one is struck by the analytical way in which he approaches the Nativity. The interrogative opening would seem at first to place us alongside the shepherds of Bethlehem, but they enter the poem only at stanza 7. Keble chooses rather to write as an astronomer might write in recording a supernova or a brilliant comet:

> "Glory to God!" from yonder central fire
> Flows out the echoing lay beyond the starry quire;
>
> Like circles widening round
> Upon a clear blue river,
> Orb after orb, the wondrous sound
> Is echoed on for ever:[61]

Keble liked to image God's presence as oceanic light and would later, in *Lyra Innocentium*, conceive baptism by sprinkling as the type of total immersion: "We plunge thee in Love's boundless sea."[62] That same sea figures here in the synesthesia of flowing fire and "starry quire," which blends the ineffable nature of music with the ineffable nature of light. Even though the poet dissociates the two elements later in the poem, he nonetheless stresses their suitability as vehicles for the divine: "In music and in light Thou dawnest on their prayer." This dazzled interchange of light and music is only one aspect of the poem's analytic bias, however. More striking still is the way Keble construes the elements of St. Luke's narrative. Unlike Milton's angels in *Paradise Lost*, *his* seem not to have been apprised of the Atonement until the very last minute:

> Yet stay, before thou dare
> To join that festal throng;
> Listen and mark what gentle air
> First stirr'd the tide of song;
> 'Tis not, "the Saviour born in David's home,
> "To Whom for power and health obedient worlds should come:"—
>
> 'Tis not, "the Christ the Lord:"—
> With fix'd adoring look
> The choir of Angels caught the word,
> Nor yet the silence broke:
> But when they heard the sign, where Christ should be,
> In sudden light they shone and heavenly harmony.

Keble converts what is merely temporal sequence in the original Gospel story to a pattern of causation. Because the proem of the angel's speech centers on the standard messianic prophecy ("For unto you is born this day in the city of David a Saviour, which is Christ the Lord"), the host shows no response. Only when God discloses a new development in the economy of salvation does the chorus break forth, not least because its "gentle air" subverts the triumphalism conventionally associated with the Messiah.

There is a curious pleasure to be had from Keble's weaving biblical phrases into his meter in this and in other poems. He had reservations about the procedure in secular prose and condemned Walter Scott for quoting Scripture in everyday contexts: "the irreverent introduction of Scripture phrases in familiar talk and corespondence [*sic*], which, it is too plain from Scott's letters and still more from some of those addressed to him, was practised among them as a matter of course."[63] Be that as it may, the more reverent circumstances of sacred poetry provided a proper occasion for plaiting of divine text into ad hoc contexts. We need to distinguish Keble's practice from that of mere paraphrase, however. The procedure in Brady and Tate and in Sternhold and Hopkins is to dissolve the original unmetrified material and reconstitute its essence (but not its verbal form) in regulated meter—an effect little different from that of a verse translation, where formal priorities take precedence over accuracy. In the case of Keble, however, the shape of the original prose remains intact to a large degree, and with a few minimal adjustments (some smoothing, inlaying, clipping, and fitting—to borrow terms from Keats), it is then slid into the line. The effect is much closer to collage, where discrete items retain their identities even while they are being assembled in a new contextual frame. So it is that we contemplate the dissonant substitution of "home" for "city" in "the Saviour born in David's home," and appreciate the theological foregrounding secured by the displacement—the unsecular, intimate version of the Messiahship upon which Christianity bases itself.

While this sort of metrical but accurate quotation testifies to the literal aspects of "Christmas Day," the poem is, as I have said, just as striking for the abstraction of its theological analysis. Cutting to the functions behind the local personalities, Keble allegorizes the human participants in the drama—Mary, the shepherds, the Magi:

> Thee, on the bosom laid
> Of a pure virgin mind,
> In quiet ever, and in shade,
> Shepherd and sage may find;
> They, who have bow'd untaught to Nature's sway,
> And they, who follow Truth along her star-pav'd way.

Even though, in the words of the *Prayer Book*, Keble views the Incarnation as "full, perfect and sufficient," he nonetheless opens up its finite historicity, suggesting that it can replay itself in the minds both of simple rustics and scholars. The conditions for that reenactment are Kebelian in the extreme—quietude and retirement—and exemplify the poles of his own spirituality, the concerns and commitments of a country priest, on the one hand, and those of a cloistered scholar, on the other.

The conclusion of "Christmas Day" has an interest of its own if we bear in mind that the greater part of *The Christian Year* was written primarily for personal catharsis and not for publication. I therefore question Thompson's claim that "the poet's self does not intrude in his work as it does in Herbert's."[64] While Keble allegorizes the Nativity as a pattern of descent and fulfillment to give it as wide an application as he can, he ends on a personal note. It is to himself as country parson that he turns, not to Christians at large:

> O faint not ye for fear—
>   What though your wandering sheep,
> Reckless of what they see and hear,
>   Lie lost in wilful sleep?

In due course we shall see that these highly personal "intrusions" do in fact color and shape a number of poems in the collection—the same sort of guardedly confessional impulse that we find in poems by Gray, to whose influence (not Wordsworth's "egotistical sublime") we must attribute Keble's strategy.

"St. Stephen's Day," as we have already seen, takes a passage from Wheatly's *Rational Illustration of the Book of Common Prayer of the Church of England* as its starting point—that and also, perhaps, some iconographic conventions current in quattro- and cinquecento painting. That Keble had a love of Italian devotional art can be gathered from an essay in which Newman attempts to depict him as being *catholique malgré lui*: "while other college rooms were ornamented with pictures of Napoleon on horseback, or Apollo and the Graces, of Heads of Houses lounging in their easy chairs, there was one young man, a young and rising one, in whose rooms, instead of these, might be seen the Madonna di Sisto or Domenichino's St. John—fit augury for him who was in the event to do so much for the revival of Catholicism."[65] It is virtually impossible to say what engravings might or might not have been available to Keble, but we can be reasonably certain he would have known Raphael's *Disputation of the Holy Sacrament*, one of the murals in the Stanza della Segnatura.[66] The focal point of the design is a seated figure of Christ encased in a semicircular halo, and at the outer rim of the halo, itself a fan of stylized rays, is a border of angel heads with red and blue wings, respectively. These represent divine love (seraphim) and divine wisdom (cherubim). Counterpoising the semicircular frame is an inverted semicircle with broader ribs, while six full-bodied angels hover along the zone between golden radiance and blue sky.

The chief constituents in this design are the representations of celestial radiance, formalized versions of the rising sun, its zones mapped out by angelic markers.

Taken together, they provide Keble with the rough material for "St. Stephen's Day":

> As rays around the source of light
> Stream upward ere he glow in sight,
> And watching by his future flight
>   Set the clear heavens on fire;
> So on the King of Martyrs wait
> Three chosen bands, in royal state,
> And all earth owns, of good and great,
>   Is gathered in that choir.[67]

The opening periphrasis once more indicates Keble's aesthetic and emotional allegiance to the Age of Sensibility. Instead of this gentle riddling dalliance with "the source of light," a full-blooded romantic would name the sun as Brünnhilde names it in *Siegfried*—"Heil dir, Sonne." But the obliquity serves Keble well, since he is working in an iconic rather than a descriptive mode. Even the apparent solecism of upward streaming (rather than upward beaming) rays can be explained by his habitually conceiving God in oceanic terms, while the Nicene Creed defines Christ as *Lumen de Lumine*. At dawn the disposition of rays is often semicircular (like the halo in the *Disputation*), and the sky frequently divides into different bands of color. Thus when Keble speaks of "chosen bands," the noun acquires a double charge—"zones" and "assemblages." With this iconographic register firmly in place, Keble can paraphrase the three modes of martyrdom set out in Wheatly's *Rational Illustration of the Book of Common Prayer*. He uses the gnomic present to show that the three types of martyr provide a taxonomy valid for all time: "One presses on, and welcomes death: / One calmly yields his willing breath, . . . And some, the darlings of their Lord, / Play smiling with the flame and sword." St. Stephen, eternally before Christ and therefore out of time, has been incorporated into his own dying vision—a cue to shift temporal frames and return us to the relevant moment in Acts: "Well might you guess what vision bright / Was present to his raptur'd sight, / E'en as reflected streams of light / Their solar source betray." This is a view of the opening image, but taken from a different angle. There we moved from vehicle to tenor, here from vehicle back to tenor. And just as Keble scumbles the division between fact and iconic stylization, so here he blurs the boundaries between heaven and earth as St. Stephen makes the crossing through his death. *Anadiplosis* provides a perfect image for that seamless transition:

> He sees them all; and earth's dull bounds
> Are melting fast away.
>
> He sees them all—no other view
> Could stamp the Saviour's likeness true,
> Or with His love so deep embrue
> Man's sullen heart and gross.

And so Keble effects another of his smooth modulations. St. Stephen now functions as the paradigm of humankind, rather as the Blessed Virgin did in "Christmas Day," and a theological analysis is super-imposed on the physical moment of martyrdom.

"St. John's Day" takes the enigmatic text of John 21:21–22 as its epigraph. In 1864 Browning would take the same words as a start-ing point for *A Death in the Desert*, and yet nothing could be further removed from Keble than the long sermon on evolutionary faith that the former places in the mouth of *his* St. John—even though St. Jerome tells us that in old age he used to utter only two sentences: "Love one another. That is the Lord's command: and if you keep it, that by itself is enough."[68] Far from offering a psychological portrait of St. John, Keble's lyric focuses rather on the misplaced anxieties of St. Peter. Moreover, he conceives St. Peter not so much as a histori-cal individual as a paradigm of all those people who bother offi-ciously about the fate of their fellows. Even though the AV transla-tion of his question presents itself as an iambic tetrameter ready-made, it does not inspire Keble to reconstruct the scene from which it issues; he moves instead into the gnomic present, the eternally recurring tense of moral discourse. That discourse is simple—the individual will, once harmonized with God's, will, in addition to its own self-concern, give up all fretful and envious concern for others. *En la sua volontade è nostra pace.* To persist in questioning the disposi-tions of Providence is to trench on impiety—hence the vigorous com-mand twice repeated: "Leave it in his Saviour's breast" and "Leave it all in His high hand."[69] Answers lie in the firm seizure of faith, or so the emphatic anaphora of stanza 1 would seem to imply—its con-fidence made doubly tangible and foursquare by the gestures of rev-

elation, as though St. John's achievements were being adduced as
evidence for the claim:

> If his love for Christ be true,
>> Christ hath told thee of his end:
> This is he whom God approves,
> This is he whom Jesus loves.

But even though Keble sidesteps the historical circumstances of John
21:21-22, they nonetheless haunt "St. John's Day" like *pentimenti*.
We cannot read "Leave it in his Saviour's breast" and *not* think of
the beloved disciple's lying on the breast of Christ during the Last
Supper. Similarly, having quoted Wheatly on St. John as the type of
all those who embrace martyrdom in will (if not in deed), Keble
gives his plea for Christian resignation a tense undertone. It is, after
all, a martyr—St. Peter—who has asked the question to which the
lyric presents a response. Here is John Marsh's commentary on this
passage from which the poem has sprung:

> Peter was evidently walking with Jesus, and chanced to turn round
> and saw the beloved disciple following them. . . . He had behaved
> very differently on the night of the trial and the day of the crucifix-
> ion. . . . He was now "following" Jesus. But would "following" in his
> case also mean a tragic destiny? It may well be that there was some
> uncertainty in Peter's own mind about his position *vis-à-vis* the be-
> loved disciple. . . .[70]

Since discipleship can entail extreme personal suffering, Keble modi-
fies his resolute, dismissive tone and allows a sense of frailty to humanize its vigor: "Only, since our souls will shrink / At the touch of
natural grief, / When our earthly lov'd ones sink, / Lend us, Lord,
Thy sure relief."

   If "St. John's Day" seems abstract and hortatory, in "The Holy
Innocents" Keble opts for a physical realization of the massacre. Indeed, remembering the putti in Nativity paintings, he provides his
own fanciful enlargement of the Gospel story. A sort of theological
X-ray reveals the palace beneath the stable:

> Say, ye celestial guards, who wait
> In Bethlehem, round the Saviour's palace gate,
>> Say, who are these on golden wings,
> That hover o'er the new-born King of Kings?[71]

A precedent for this interrogation, marked by deference for an addressee more potent and knowledgeable than the speaker, can be found in Gray's "Ode on a Distant Prospect of Eton College": "Say, Father Thames, for thou hast seen."[72] We can also trace the ventriloquial response of Keble's angels to the *Elegy Written in a Country Churchyard*. Compare:

> Ask, and some angel will reply,
> "These, like yourselves, were born to sin and die,
> "But ere the poison root was grown,
> "God set His seal, and mark'd them for His own["]

with the "remote control" of Gray's swain:

> If chance, by lonely Contemplation led,
> Some kindred spirit shall inquire thy fate,
>
> Haply some hoary-headed swain may say,
> "Oft have we seen him at the peep of dawn
> "Brushing with hasty steps the dews away
> "To meet the sun upon the upland lawn ["][73]

"Mark'd them for his own" likewise echoes the phrasing of the Epitaph—"*And Melancholy marked him for her own*."[74] While Keble's marking refers chiefly to the seal of baptism, it also recalls the exemptive mark of the Passover, though that repelled the attention of an angel, whereas the Christian sign attracts it.

Given the generalizing temper of *The Christian Year*, it comes as no surprise that "The Holy Innocents" should meditate on infant mortality, always a difficult subject for theologians to tackle. And since the Augustinian Keble believed that original sin made corruption inevitable, it also comes as no surprise that he should guide his theodicy along these lines. He finds Platonic reinforcement for this Christian conviction in Wordsworth's "Intimations Ode," clearly the origin of the ocean image in Stanza 5. (He would reemploy it in a later collection—"Was it from heaven's deep sea a gleam / Not faded quite on earth's dim shore"):[75]

> Then, as each fond unconscious child
> On th' everlasting Parent sweetly smil'd,
>   (Like infants sporting on the shore,
> That tremble not at Ocean's boundless roar,)

> Were they not present to Thy thought,
> All souls, that in their cradles Thou hast bought?

Compare Wordsworth:

> Our souls have sight of that immortal sea
> Which brought us hither,
> Can in a moment travel thither,
> And see the Children sport upon the shore,
> And hear the mighty waters rolling evermore.[76]

Even though the compressed typology in the finale of "The Holy Innocents" places Rachel's bereavement in the light of the Resurrection, the confidence is humanized and even subverted by Keble's sense that ordinary feeling cannot be wholly banished, no matter how strong the intellectual assent of the faithful mind: "She dares not grieve—but she must weep."

"First Sunday after Christmas" shows a similar oscillation between statements of faith and a more hesitant, questioning acceptance, as witness the change from stanza 1 ("'Tis true of old th' unchanging sun / His daily course refus'd to run")[77] to stanza 2 ("But can it be, one suppliant tear / Should stay the ever-moving sphere?"). The conflict carries through to the image patterns as well, pitting the brilliance of fire against the overwhelming force of water, or (if we read these as metonyms), the permanence of Heaven against the transience of Earth. Keble sets the "mystic dance" performed by "wanderers of the sky" against the "waves of Time, / That now so swift and silent bear / Our restless bark from year to year." Half-alluding to Canute's enacted parable, the poet calls on God to reverse the course of those waves and retrieve for us the innocence of Eden. That is the hope; the reality is a stormy landscape in the style of Salvator Rosa, where the light seems intermittent and feeble and the water overwhelming: "These, and such faint, half-waking dreams, / Like stormy lights on mountain streams, / Wavering and broken all, athwart the conscience glare." Keble claims, however, that hearts should not be stained and dimmed by tears, but should rather glow like the polished metal of thuribles, thuribles dropped, as in a memory of some Flemish reredos, from a cluster of upward-soaring angels. The convex shape of the heart (thurible-like) renders the conceit more plausible. In addition, an upward-beaming glow replaces the earthward gravitation of the tears, a reversal restated in the last stanza but one. Although at first the metaphors seem tangled, it is possible to unravel the deep structure of Keble's thought:

> O Thou, who keep'st the Key of Love,
> Open Thy fount, eternal Dove,
>   And overflow this heart of mine,
>   Enlarging as it fills with Thee,
>   Till in one blaze of charity
> Care and remorse are lost, like motes in light divine;

Keble's starting point must have been the stanza in Gray's "Progress of Poesy" in which Shakespeare enters the "apostolic succession" of great poets:

> ["]Thine too these golden keys, immortal boy!
> This can unlock the gates of joy;
> Of horror that and thrilling fears,
> Or ope the sacred source of sympathetic tears."[78]

God, who entrusted the keys of Heaven and Hell to St. Peter, likewise holds the key to a miraculous fountain, or, in Gray's words, a "sacred source." Gray was antiquarian enough to have known that the mother of Henry VII had enclosed St. Winifred's well in a stone building,[79] and Keble also seems hint that the right of admission is reserved for penitents only. The transition from "fount" to "font" is easily made and would explain the invocation of the Holy Spirit in the guise of a dove (as in Matthew's baptism narrative—3:16) and in Herbert's "Whitsunday": "Listen sweet Dove unto my song / And spread thy golden wings in me; / Hatching my tender heart so long."[80] But Keble's "fount" also retains its sense of a fountain with basins to direct the overflow, hence the "enharmonic" modulation to the overflowing heart. An earlier stanza had imaged the heart as a censer glowing with the light of "accepted love," countervailing the downward course of water with upward blaze of love. Although the cultus of St. Philip Neri had to await the founding of the two oratories before it arrived in England, it is not improbable that Keble had heard of the miracle (an enlarged heart) associated with that saint: "He spent much time in prayer, especially in the catacomb of St Sebastian, where in 1544 he experienced an ecstasy of divine love which is believed to have left a permanent physical effect on his heart."[81] Be that as it may, Keble ends his poem with the elements into which Cleopatra melts in Shakespeare's play—"I am fire, and air":[82]

> Till, as each moment wafts us higher,
> By every gush of pure desire,
> And high-breath'd hope of joys above,
> By every secret sigh we heave,
> Whole years of folly we outlive,
> In His unerring sight, who measures Life by Love.

Thus Keble brings us back to the tentative account of Hezekiah and the power of a "suppliant tear" over the "wanderers of the sky"—converting that hesitancy to a triumphant affirmation. Time indeed has no bearing on the timelessness of divine love.

"The Circumcision of Christ" correlates the beginning of the year—the feast falls on January 1—with the beginning of Christ's redemptive work. In a curious intra-Christian adaptation of typology, Keble suggests that the blood that flowed at the Circumcision prefigures the blood of the Atonement:

> The year begins with Thee,
> And Thou beginn'st with woe,
> To let the world of sinners see
> That blood for sin must flow.[83]

But, following the more usual cross-Testament lines of typology, Keble also takes the event as a sort of hinge for the two covenants: the Savior's submission to the Law images the continuity between them. So great is his humility that it is not enough to have submitted to a humbling incarnation: he must also submit himself to institutions that acknowledge the sinfulness of the flesh he has assumed:

> Thine infant cries, O Lord,
> Thy tears upon the breast,
> Are not enough—the legal sword
> Must do its stern behest.

The result is great concourse of Christian and Jewish witnesses, imaged, as in "First Sunday after Christmas," through the reversal of waters, only here they seem to flow from the Red Sea. The Incarnation has in fact abolished the sequential flow of history and disclosed a static, meaningful pattern beneath the flux. Keble laces up Old and New Testaments in a chiastic pattern projecting stability and perfection (perfection in the sense of completedness and fulfillment):

> Both theirs and ours Thou art,
> As we and they are Thine;
> Kings, Prophets, Patriarchs—all have part
> Along the sacred line.

The poem ends with a series of questions and gestural statements that, *salva reverentia*, can be traced back to pedlars' songs. In Anthony Munday's *Downfall of Robert Earl of Huntingdon* (1601), for example, we find the following cry: "What lacke ye? what lacke yee? what wil ye buy? / Any points, pins, or laces, any laces, points or pins?"[84] Nanki-Poo's *aria di sortita* in *The Mikado* ("A wandering minstrel I")[85] likewise establishes a lack, creates a corresponding desire and offers to satisfy that desire with the relevant items; and so does J. M. Neale's "Art thou weary, art thou languid."[86] Perhaps the Ur-Pedlar's song is Isa. 55:1: "Ho, every one that thirsteth, come ye to the waters, and he that hath no money; come ye, buy, and eat; yea, come, buy wine and milk without money and without price." Keble has also divinized this genre. He asks, for example, "Wouldst thou a poet be?" and then, half paraphrasing the priestly invitation in the Communion service, calls would-be poets to their consummation in Christ: "Come here thy soul to tune, / Here set thy feeble chant." Similarly, he enquires "Art thou a child of tears, / Cradled in care and woe?"—following this enquiry with a cletic stanza:

> Look here, and hold thy peace:
> The Giver of all good
> E'en from the womb takes no release
> From suffering, tears, and blood.

The poem comes full circle when the final stanza repeats the temporal reference of the first, turning the seasonal into an anagogic metaphor: "So life a winter's morn may prove / To a bright endless year."

Unlike its predecessor, "Second Sunday after Christmas" makes no metaphoric play on the freezing winters of northern Europe, but tries instead to project the anguish of a Mediterranean drought. Keble takes as his starting point the evocation of thirst in Isa. 41:17, and, as so often, recasts the image in mental terms. He conveys the agony of a parched and desolate spirit with interrogatives of disbelief and then resolves them in a list of biblical thirst-quenchings. The procedure is not new, for many collects in the *Book of Common Prayer* correlate some divine action with the petition at hand, offering a kind of surety for God's response. In Keble's poem, the contingency of intercession is replaced by a rock-solid credal format:

> Thou wilt—for Thou art Israel's God,
>   And Thine unwearied arm
> Is ready yet with Moses' rod,
>   The hidden rill to charm
> Out of the dry, unfathom'deep
> Of sands, that lie in lifeless sleep,[87]

But the poem is more subtle than this rather brassy mode might at first suggest. While Keble presents a God of providential refreshment, he also shows that, in view of his omnipresence, we should perceive him as fully in the crisis as in the solution: "These moments of wild wrath are Thine— / Thine too the drearier hour." And of course it is the knowledge of the human agony entailed by the Incarnation that connects the subject's suffering with the God whose own Passion makes sense of it. Here Keble comes close to paraphrasing a stanza from the *Dies Irae*, one which likewise takes comfort from, and gains confidence through, the miseries of Christ (*Quaerens me, sedisti lassus; / Redemisti crucem passus; / Tantus labor non sit cassus*):[88]

> Thou, who didst sit on Jacob's well
>   The weary hour of noon,
> The languid pulses Thou canst tell,
>   The nerveless spirit tune.
> Thou from Whose cross in anguish burst
> The cry that own'd Thy dying thirst,
> To Thee we turn, our Last and First,
>   Our Sun and soothing Moon.

Making the sun stand for the Son is of course a standard topos; altogether more original is the invocation of the moon—a luster suited to the dark night of the soul. (On another occasion, Keble uses the moon to emblematize a Church which can only *reflect* the radiance of the Son until the parousia—"Christ in the Font became our Noon, / The Holy Church, our Moon."[89]

"The Epiphany" also attempts to take stock of loss and dereliction, but from an entirely different perspective. Here the trial cannot be ascribed to God's providential testing but rather to adult hardenings and fallings away from childhood grace—the failures Wordsworth lamented in the *Intimations Ode*. In a way time-honored since the Sphinx's riddle, Keble compares the life cycle of humankind to the three segments of the day. He renovates the cliché, however, by considering the effect of sunlight on our perception of other heavenly bodies. Whereas in "Evening" he had imaged night as occlusion, here he falls back on postures more typically associated with the Age of Sensibility: daylight figures as something crude and glaring, rather like the harshly luminous rationalism projected in "Advent Sunday" ("Light without love, glares on the aching sight"):

> Star of the East, how sweet art Thou,
> > Seen in life's early morning sky,
> Ere yet a cloud has dimm'd the brow,
> > While yet we gaze with childish eye;
>
> . . . .
>
> Too soon the glare of earthly day
> > Buries, to us, Thy brightness keen,
> And we are left to find our way
> > By faith and hope in Thee unseen.[90]

In Keble's adaptation of the day/life trope, sunset once again reveals the star, present all along (though unperceived). The star itself is a compound symbol. Keble's uppercase pronouns throughout the poem point to its function as a figure of Christ, a function pointed to by the oblique allusion to Num. 24:17 towards the end of the poem. Here Balaam, a representative of what Keble calls the "Gentile Church" in stanza 10, applies the star to the Messiah: "I shall see him, but not now: I shall behold him, but not nigh: there shall come a Star out of Jacob, and a Sceptre shall rise out of Israel." Christ, imaged by this prophetic star, is actually present in the Nativity scene. St. Mary and St. Joseph, on the other hand, figure as Chastity and Reverence—another instance of Keble's "extractive" personification, personification that X-rays the human personage to find the abstract quality within. The analytical phase of Ignatian method might have contributed something to this sublimation, but whereas the *Spiritual Exercises* recommend the contemplative to reflect on the *actions* of the Holy Parents—"*The third point is to behold and consider what they are doing, as, for example, the journey and the toils they undergo in order that our Lord may be born in extreme poverty*"[91]—Keble moves up a rung on the ladder of abstraction and offers us images of what they *are*. So the poem resolves itself into a simple *sicut/ita* design. Just as humankind begins and ends its life with a strong capacity for faith (i.e., sight of the starry Christ), so the Gentile church began well in Balaam's prophecy and ended well in the visit of the Magi, though it lost direction in the noonday of its existence—a line of thought as strange as it is original.

   "First Sunday after Epiphany" is much less adventurous than its predecessor. One of Keble's moralizing nature poems, half didactic, half observed, it reads as though some careful botanical plates had been interleaved *en face* with the woodcuts of an emblem book. As if he himself were aware of his closeness to, and distance from, the emblem poems of Herbert, Keble begins in ontological uncertainty, a procedure more typical of romantic poems. He seems indeed to be imitating the stylized hesitation at the start of Wordsworth's cuckoo poem: "O Cuckoo, shall I call thee Bird, / Or but a wandering Voice?"[92] Hence the wavering between instinct (natural theology) and inspiration (divine revelation) in the opening stanza:

> Lessons sweet of spring returning,
>   Welcome to the thoughtful heart!
> May I call ye sense or learning,
>   Instinct pure, or Heaven-taught art?[93]

Epiphany falls in the dead of winter, but Keble has found a seasonal escape into April through the window of his epigraph and has a fine time evoking the sights and sounds of a Fairford spring. In reaction (whether conscious or unconscious) to Wordsworth's retirement to Rydal, he implies that the romantic sublime does not provide the only route to divinity. (We might recall that in "Morning" he renounced the "glamor" of monasticism for its humdrum Anglican alternative—"We need not bid, for cloister'd cell, / Our neighbour and our work farewell.")[94]

> Needs no show of mountain hoary,
>   Winding shore or deepening glen,
> Where the landscape in its glory
>   Teaches truth to wandering men:

> Give true hearts but earth and sky,
> And some flowers to bloom and die,
> Homely scenes and simple views
> Lowly thoughts may best infuse.

This sort of minimalism, a reaction to the baroque spendors of the eighteenth century, had already manifested itself in the verse of Sensibility. A line of development connects the moderate desideratum in Gray's *Elegy*—"*He gained from Heaven ('twas all he wished) a friend*"[95] with the *magnum in parvo* at the end of the *Intimations Ode*—"To me the meanest flower that blows can give / Thoughts that do often lie too deep for tears."[96] What gives an added luster to Keble's claim is its validation by his own simple life, his real renunciation of grandeur when he gave up Oxford. Of course this sort of temperate spirituality did not appeal to the more flamboyant temperaments of second-generation Tractarians. Dean Church records that if "in England there flourished the homely and modest types of goodness, it was in Rome that, at that day at least, men must look for the heroic,"[97] and goes on to relate W. G. Ward's secession to his impatience with Anglican caution and reserve: "English piety and goodness at its best, in such examples as George Herbert and Ken and Bishop Wilson, seemed unambitious and pale and tame."[98] It is not surprising, given the extremes of Continental Catholicism, that Keble should call the standard tropes of the sublime a "show," for this outlook influenced the whole tenor of the Oxford Movement. Church points out that he made Isaac Williams "an old-fashioned High Churchman, suspicious of excitement and 'effect'."[99]

However, the minimalism that contents itself with a tame, unglamorous landscape has as compensation a sharply focused eye, a readiness to detect the significance of details that might otherwise be lost in an alpine vista or in the crags and dales of the Lake District. Indeed it would be fair to say that Keble's picture of the willow tree embodies some of his finest verse. Its energy can be attributed in part to the fact that, according to Charlotte Yonge, the tree had a real-life original, growing on the road between Fairford and Coln St. Aldwyn.[100] But the description differs from comparable moments in Wordsworth's poetry in being dislocated and transposed into the mental space of emblem. So whereas in *Michael*, for example, the reader encounters a set of spatial directives ("If from the public way you turn your steps / Up the tumultuous brook of Greenhead Ghyll"),[101] Keble "uproots" his Fairfood willow to enhance its typicality—a point of difference, perhaps, between proto-Tractarian reserve and the "egotistical sublime." Indeed it is worth remarking that Keble's idea of regionalism did not reach to the specificity with which the great romantics invested it. His allegiance to eighteenth-century standards of diction, essentially generalizing, excluded anything too gutsy and guttural. So attenuated is his sense of regionalism that he even finds it in stanzas by Scott ("The elfin harp, his neck around") simply because they name places: "Would it not be true to say, that this passage is but the expression, in sad truth and real life, of the same deep local attachment, which gives the tone to the following tender stanzas, occurring among the earliest which Scott ever published."[102] And here are those "tender stanzas":

> Then forth he went—yet turn'd him oft
>   To view his ancient hall;
> On the grey tower, in lustre soft,
>   The autumn moonbeams fall.
>
> And Leader's waves, like silver sheen,
>   Danc'd shimmering in the ray,
> In deepening mass, at distance seen,
>   Broad Saltra's mountains lay.

Turning from these (offered as specimens of strong "local attachment") to the willow on the road between Fairford and Coln St. Aldwyn, we are able to appreciate how Keble's register has to some extent supervened between the real tree and the type into which he has turned it:

> See the soft green willow springing
>   Where the waters gently pass,
> Every way her free arms flinging
>   O'er the moist and reedy grass.
> Long ere winter blasts are fled,
> See her tipp'd with vernal red,
> And her kindly flower display'd
> Ere her leaf can cast a shade.

The debt to Gray is obvious: we are reminded of the *Ecce* which starts the "Ode on the Spring," while the willow's animizing "arms" recall the oak trees in "The Bard": "O'er thee, oh king! their hundred arms they wave."[103] The debt, however, has been supercharged

with additional energy—"flinging" catches the tug and dash of a
gale force wind. There is also a specificity that the Age of Sensibility,
too close to the doctrine of "general nature," could not fully encompass. Those red-tipped buds anticipate the Pre-Raphaelite attentiveness we find in Rossetti's "Woodspurge" much more than they recall the stylized, swelling gems of Gray's "Alliance of Education
and Government."[104] Likewise the magical evocation of the nightingales at the end of the lyric. Where Gray chooses *brunus* (a classical
epithet) to convey a similar experience in the "Ode on the Spring"
("Where'er the oak's thick branches stretch / A broader browner
shade")[105] the lived-through green of Keble's tree more fully suggests the "submarine" leafiness of an English summer:

> Where the thickest boughs are twining
>   Of the greenest darkest tree,
> There they plunge, the light declining—
>   All may hear, but none may see.

That the nightingales represent a beatific state can be gathered as
much from Keble's choice of an aquatic metaphor as from the surface statement of his poem: again and again in *The Christian Year*
God's love figures as an immeasurable tract of water.

The opening stanza of "Second Sunday after Epiphany" once
more combines the accents of the two poets most influential on *The
Christian Year*—Gray and Herbert. The idea of a childhood sealed
off from human suffering derives from the *sententia* at the end of the
"Eton College Ode"—"where ignorance is bliss, / 'Tis folly to be
wise"[106]—while Keble's actual phrasing recalls the provisional exemption from grief set down in the first stanza of "The Flower"—
"Grief melts away / Like snow in May, / As if there were no such
cold thing":[107]

> The heart of childhood is all mirth:
>   We frolic to and fro
> As free and blithe, as if on earth,
>   Were no such thing as woe.[108]

Gray and Herbert acknowledge that such beliefs are illusory, while
Keble regards their persistence into adulthood as evidence of an
immature hedonism. It is the soft voice of the serpent that utters the
carpe florem theme in stanza 2. Half recalling the macabre festivity in

Gray's "Bard" ("Fill high the sparkling bowl, / "The rich repast prepare, ... Fell Thirst and Famine scowl / "A baleful smile upon their
baffled guest"),[109] Keble presents this febrile pleasure-seeking as a
suicidal quest for poison:

> And still, as loud the revel swells,
>   The fever'd pulse beats higher,
> Till the sear'd taste from foulest wells
>   Is fain to slake its fire.

Not surprisingly, the poet then invokes the decorum and quietude
of the messianic banquet as foil to this distress, recalling his epigraph (the miracle at Cana) to suggest enrichment instead of degradation. The three theological virtues provide the key to this
meliorism; Hope gives the impetus to Faith, while Faith provides
the confirmation of Hope in words that recall the flight of Milton in
"The Progress of Poesy." Compare "He passed the flaming bounds
of place and time"[110] with Keble's lines:

> ... but Faith
> Her daring dreams will cherish,
> Speeding her gaze o'er time and death
>   To realms where naught can perish.

Just as in "The Epiphany" he reconnected the faith of infancy with
the faith of old age, so here Keble stresses the continuity between
childish innocence and the intimations of immortality that (in his
view more than in Wordsworth's) tell more with the onset of age.
And just as Gray's Bard loses his vision "in long futurity,"[111] so too
does Keble's representative Christian. A dramatic aposiopesis and
syntactic dislocation suggest the breakdown of language as it moves
toward the ineffable:

> Ever the richest tenderest glow
>   Sets round th' autumnal sun—
> But there the sight fails: no heart may know
>   The bliss when life is done.

Tidying up after this collapse of vision, Keble inserts the poem's tail
into its mouth and paraphrases his epigraph. In this way he crystal-
lizes the spiritual meliorism at the center of the lyric: "And keep our
best till last."

"Third Sunday after Epiphany" once again reveals a structural virtuosity with which Keble is seldom credited. It seems at first to have little relevance to the feast of the Epiphany, but as the design unspools, its components all harmonize and interconnect. Like many other poems in *The Christian Year* it opens with a seasonal dissonance and recalls the vision of a rainbow in a stormy autumn sky. This Salvatorian sublime is followed by a subtler, blanker kind of sublimity such as we might find in a Northern master like de Koninck or Ruisdael:

> Light flashes in the gloomiest sky,
>   And Music in the dullest plain,
> For there the lark is soaring high
>   Over her flat and leafless reign,
> And chanting in so blithe a tone,
> It shames the weary heart to feel itself alone.[112]

These are motifs expounded but kept in reserve for later development, as in a symphonic design. For the moment, the poet simply uses them as a source of imaginative nurturing, as in Wordsworth's "I wandered lonely as a cloud" ("They flash upon that inward eye / That is the bliss of solitude"),[113] or in Coleridge's "Kubla Khan" ("Could I revive within me her symphony or song, / To such a deep delight 'twould win me"):[114]

> It was a gleam to Memory dear,
>   And as I walk and muse apart,
> When all seems faithless round and drear,
>   I would revive it in my heart,

A steep modulation leads us away from this particular train of thought, however, for the rainbow and the lark song are now adapted to the trope of *expeditio*, stages to be crossed out in our progress to a fuller and better grasp of the truth. The comparative phrases of this section might well have been inspired by Reginald Heber's great Epiphany hymn, "Brightest and best of the sons of the morning": "Richer by far is the heart's adoration, / Dearer to God are the prayers of the poor."[115] In Keble's version, the metaphors, dramatic and arresting though they might be, also fall away as they approach a humble absolute, one drawn from the experience of his curacy:

> Brighter than rainbow in the north,
>   More cheery than the matin lark,
> Is the soft gleam of Christian worth,
>   Which on some holy house we mark;
> Dear to the pastor's aching heart
> To think, where'er he looks, such gleam may have a part;

—a part in the angelic choir before the throne of God.

Having established the primacy of humble prayer, Keble must also allow equal opportunity to intellectuals. He does this by reviving rainbow and birdsong as emblems of visual and musical art, respectively—the highest offerings of the human spirit that, however inadequate in absolute terms, have been rendered acceptable in the sight of God by the Incarnation and intercession of the Son, whose grace also enhances the offerings of rustic and peasant. These offerings allow Keble to allude directly to those of the Magi, and to present them as the recurrent offerings of the "Gentile Church": "Risen, may embalm His sacred name / With all a Painter's art, and all a Minstrel's flame."

Many poems in *The Christian Year* set up a polar contrast between the dispensations of the Old and New Testaments or between different but complementary aspects of the Deity, using symmetrical patterns to throw the antithesis into relief. One of these is "Fourth Sunday after Epiphany," where the first and second stanzas both begin with the sentence "They know x." Power (imaged by a storm) and love (represented by a grove that rebuffs the wind) accordingly develop a binary tension. But it is equally typical of Keble to move from outer to inner landscape, and to internalize and spiritualize the materials of his exposition. He is helped on this occasion by the sequence of St. Matthew's narrative, moving as it does from the stilling of the tempest to the healing of the demoniac Gergesenes. The middle section of the poem accordingly presents a spirit that can set its perturbations aside and respond to God's grace. A characteristic spatial slippage takes us from Fairford to Roman Galilee. The selectiveness of the metonymy renders the sketch more plausible, and so does the unusual choice of "green" for the lake (either indicating reflected hills or a chemical element in the water), which offsets the generalizing diction of Sensibility ("dewy tresses"): "Green lake, and cedar tuft, and spicy glade, / Shaking their dewy tresses now the storm is laid."[116] Such shifts are as much thematic as structural and recall the imaginative flight and union recorded in Keats's "Ode to a Nightingale." By taking us to the morning after the storm, Keble seems to be saying "Already with thee," and thereby dramatizing a heart and soul fully attuned to Christ's. The alternative locus of the soul—and here Keble alludes to the lectionary reading, the exorcism of the Gergesenes who had haunted burial sites—would be the self-entrapment and claustrophobia of the tomb, or, cast in contemporary language, the sensationalism of the gothic:

> And wilt thou seek again
> Thy howling waste, thy charnel-house and chain,
>   And with the demons be,
> Rather than clasp thine own Deliverer's knee?

Keble might well have Byron in mind when in the coda to the poem he suggests that, properly responding to restorative landscapes, demonic minds will slough their violence and choose instead to sing the *Sanctus*.

"Fifth Sunday after Epiphany" begins *in medias res* with a dramatic intercession—a device clearly borrowed from Gray's "Bard." Without any authorial control on our responses, we might at first assent to the values that prompt this cry. However, Keble has profited from the example of Herbert's poetry, where again and again an opening position, specious and plausible, is probed and rejected for a better one—a procedure that Helen Vendler has examined at length in her book on the poet.[117] Since the Christian idea of the Messiah is as much humble as it is glorious, the Church is wrong to cry "Now for Thy glory's sake, / Saviour and God, arise."[118] To drive this point home, Keble takes the story of St. Philip and the Ethiopian, and turns it into a parable. The African, who is the member of a worldly court, learns the meaning of Messiahship from the prophecies of the Suffering Servant, and carries these new values of humility and submission into his old milieu ("No storm can now assail / The charm he wears within"). And, given this new disposition, the worldliness of the opening cry is shown up for what it is, something "hard" and resistant that penitential tears must dissolve away. "Sixth Sunday after Epiphany" shares the same dual shape, the same before and after, the same improper and proper disposition of spirit. Here Keble examines the false desire for certitude, the sort of coercive miracle that Christ rejected in his second temptation. Such irritable reaching

after fact and reason cannot (in his book) be squared with the tenets
of faith. To shore up his belief that true commitment can be born
only of incertitude and trial, he cites examples from human experience, using that stanzaic parallelism often associated in his poetry
with incontrovertible statements—"'Tis so in war"; "'Tis so in love"—
opposing activities in which the antithetic elements resolve in a
single-minded tenacity of purpose. Keble would probably have re-
sented any comparison with the "fleshly school" of Keats, but he
does indeed strike a note of negative capability in the last stanza.
Since his subtheme, derived from the intangible bases of faith, is the
inexpressibility of heaven—it is fitting that he should have drama-
tized this incapacity of language with an aposiopesis. The "peace"
with which he effects the interruption suggests both silence and the
tranquility of a mind properly disposed:

> But peace—still voice and closèd eye
> Suit best with hearts beyond the sky,
> Hearts training in their low abode,
> Daily to lose themselves in hope to find their GOD.[119]

Thus does he exorcise the false quest for certainty set out in the opening stanza, while hinting at the *via negativa* through which mystics
have found God's presence.

"Septuagesima Sunday," like "Morning," has found its way into
Anglican hymnals, but so logical and symmetrical and general is its
design that it has required far fewer adjustments to suit it to the
task. The ballad stanza (common meter) has no doubt had something to do with its appropriation—many of Keble's stanza patterns
are too complex to be wholly suitable for congregational use. Also,
no doubt, the compilers of *Hymns Ancient and Modern* appreciated
the simplicity and the stanzaic self-containment of each thought.
Verse after verse begins with a definite article and noun, as though
inventorying the full range of creation to illustrate its theme—the
right way to read the book of nature. Even so, the anthologists have
made one or two significant changes in *Hymns Ancient and Modern*,
in contrast to the compilers of *The English Hymnal*, who leave the
text intact. Keble's sense of the indivisibility of Godhead is so intense that he perceives "light and heat" as a hendiadys, a singular
entity that calls for a singular verb, but the text in *Hymns Ancient
and Modern* regularizes the grammar to read "The Saviour lends the

light and heat / That crown the holy hill."[120] More importantly, they have cut out a quirkish but interesting moment in the poem where Keble mimics the interrogations of a catechism:

> The saints above are stars in Heaven—
> What are the saints on earth?
> Like trees they stand whom GOD has given,
> Our Eden's happy birth.[121]

The metaphoric equation of stars and saints likewise seem to have struck the compilers as being too primitive and animistic a notion, for they supplanted it with a more cautious simile. All these modifications have the effect of constraining and regulating the freedom with which Keble laces in and out of different keys. One of the casualties is the pastiche that recalls the naïve deictic gestures of emblem poetry: "Faith is their fix'd unswerving root, / Hope their unfading flower." This naïveté presents a stumbling block to contemporary readers, perhaps, because they are more accustomed to evidential claims. Keble's "there is" formula serenely begs the questions that will enter even "pure minds and Christian hearts." Writing about the analogical structures in this and in other poems of *The Christian Year*, Walter Lock has remarked: "Some of these illustrations may seem fanciful, but the analogy underlies all our Lord's teaching by parables, and if we do not take Nature as the *adequate* type of man with his free will, it must be true."[122] The question is, Did God make the analogies, or have they been imposed by the mechanism of the fancy? In a poem such as "Septuagesima Sunday" we tend to resist Keble's readiness to offer problematic parallels as though they were transparent. Since he revered Bishop Butler, it is surprising that he should have forgotten an important caveat sounded by his mentor and by Origen before him: "Hence, namely from analogical Reasoning, *Origen* has with singular Sagacity observed, that *he who believes the Scripture to have proceeded from Him who is the Author of Nature, may well expect to find the same sort of difficulties in it, as are found in the Constitution of Nature.*"[123] If, as "Septuagesima Sunday" implies, God created the moon to signify the reflected luster of the Savior in the Church, why did he pock it with craters, and why did he permit the apparent instability of its waxing and waning cycle? These contradictions, which would provide fodder for *In Memoriam* some twenty years later, seem never to have crossed Keble's mind.

If Herbert's voice can be heard echoing through stanzas of "Septuagesima Sunday," then the start of "Sexagesima Sunday" has a decided touch of Donne. Recalling the bold and defiant arraignment of Death in "Death be not proud," Keble addresses Satan at the start of his poem, placed at the actual evening of the fall, as though he had been an angelic spectator of the events:

> Foe of mankind! too bold thy race:
> Thou runn'st at such a reckless pace,
> Thine own dire work thou surely wilt confound:
>   'Twas but one little drop of sin
>   We saw this morning enter in,
> And lo! at eventide the world is drown'd.[124]

It is not Keble's habit to fix his poems in time and space, however, and in the next stanza he has swept through the intervening aeons to his own arraignment by an angry God. But since those aeons have witnessed the advent of the second Adam, he is able to take comfort from the fact that justice has been tempered by mercy. The poem then moves into a parabolic mode. Mothers who are subject to the pangs of childbirth—according to Genesis, a consequence of the Fall—nonetheless draw comfort from the fact that those pangs have since been sanctified by the Incarnation; marriage offers no exemption from suffering, and yet it adumbrates the love of Christ for the sinner, and so on. An interesting formal consequence flows from Keble's dogged efforts at putting a brave face on things—the relentless symmetry of the syntax which places the Fall in the *protasis* and the redemption in the *apodosis* of each conditional structure. So rigidly does the poem persist with this pattern that it almost seems to have embraced it as a penitential straitjacket, a sort of stanzaic anaphora that blinkers and curtails the potentially willful movement of the imagination.

"Quinquagesima Sunday" likewise sticks to a single design in its opening strophes, a triad clearly inspired by Herbert's "Vertue" ("Sweet day . . . Sweet rose . . . Sweet spring.")[125] It is also likely that Keble had the invocation of "Whitsunday" in mind—"Listen sweet Dove unto my song."[126] Here, however, he does not follow the trim *articulus* of Herbert's poem but treats those three invocations as so many dabs of pigment on a palette—the raw materials from which a poem on salvation will be fashioned. Once again he shows the resourcefulness and flexibility of his structural method, ready in one stanza to move from homely analogy (Noah is like a nineteenth-century sailor leaving ship) to his anagogical sense of God as an ocean:

> So home-bound sailors spring to shore,
>   Two oceans safely past;
> So happy souls, when life is o'er,
>   Plunge in th' empyreal vast.[127]

This is to compress two distinct stages of Ignatian devotion—*compositio loci* and *colloquium*—into a single moment. Although the rainbow had long been taken as a type of the messianic promise, Keble here gives it a personal twist. He suggests that, by refracting the invisible radiance of God into colors that humankind can see, it points to the Incarnation. In this regard he seems to have remembered but deliberately inverted the Neoplatonic lines in *Adonais* ("Life, like a dome of many-coloured glass, / Stains the white radiance of Eternity"):[128]

> What but the gentle rainbow's gleam,
>   Soothing the wearied sight,
> That cannot bear the solar beam,
>   With soft undazzling light?
> . . . .
> The Son of God in radiance beam'd
>   Too bright for us to scan,
> But we may face the rays that stream'd
>   From the mild Son of Man.

The intimacy and affection of the opening invocations thus "prove" that we are able to approach God by virtue of his having taken human form.

"Ash-Wednesday" is a dialogic poem, starting, like "Fifth Sunday after Epiphany" with an unidentified outcry. Even though the poet eventually corrects the values embodied in that cry, the procedure renders him more sympathetic, and so wins the reader's trust. When the corrective judgments are finally set in place, they do not seem to issue ex cathedra from a remote, inhuman judge for Keble seems to have worked through the crisis with the confessor. The crisis in question centers on the privacy of guilt and the anguish of a soul that cannot externalize its remorse. Although Keble would later complain to Judge Coleridge that he had been unable to convince all his parishioners about the benefits of auricular confession, *The Christian Year* views it only as an option:

> Thus oft the mourner's wayward heart
>   Tempts him to hide his grief and die,
> Too feeble for Confession's smart,
>   Too proud to bear a pitying eye;[129]

The solution offered here is domestic rather than auricular confession ("to fall / On bosoms waiting to receive / Our sighs"), or, failing that, an austere, undemonstrative penance that will align the subject with Christ in the Wilderness and so earn access to the mercy-seat. Keble has taken the conventional instruments of Catholic penance—what Scott in *The Heart of Midlothian* calls "the dogmata of a religion, which pretends, by the maceration of the body, to expiate the crimes of the soul"[130]—and sublimated them into types and figures rather as the author of Hebrews gives a metaphoric reading to the Temple cultus.

In "First, Second and Third Sundays in Lent" (if I may be permitted so to glue their titles together) we confront the first of several poems in *The Christian Year* where our theological distance from Keble demands a greater-than-usual effort of adjustment. He wrote his poetry before the advent of the higher criticism in England, and even when it came, he maintained an obstinate fundamentalism in the face of its challenge, having earlier rebuked Pusey for doubting the idea of plenary inspiration. Not that the latter's attitude to the matter was any way progressive: he remarked that Keble "published *The Christian Year* while Newman was just emerging from Evangelicalism and I was busy with Arabic in the hope of counter-working, with God's help, German rationalism on the Old Testament."[131]

Since Keble's belief in the literal truth of the Bible was unconditional, it led him to embrace many distressingly narrow and tribal elements in the Old Testament. Indeed, Beek has commented on his penchant for relating it to contemporary events: "Keble was particularly fond of setting forth the importance of the Old Testament. He thought it 'confirms authoritatively the plain dictates of conscience in matters of civil wisdom and duty'). He always turned to it when public duties, errors and dangers were in question, as was so often the case during his life-time."[132] There is no sense here of evolution—Keble's was a static rather than dynamic mind, and he put off reading Newman's *Essay on the Development of Christian*

Doctrine for years. Accordingly, the Old Testament incidents and actions that Thomas Paine had had every reason to deplore, he accepts as the true notes of Divinity. In *The Age of Reason*, Paine had observed that

> Moses was not, because *he could not be*, the writer of them [the books of the Pentateuch], and consequently there is no authority for believing that the inhuman and horrid butcheries of men, women and children, told of in those books, were done, as those books say they were, at the command of God. It is a duty incumbent on every true Deist, that he vindicate the moral justice of God against the calumnies of the Bible.[133]

We can scarcely expect Keble to have responded to the gauntlet thrown down with such glittering confidence at the end of that paragraph, but we might have expected him at least to show some sort of apologetic caution in the selection of his materials from the Old Testament. He seems, however, to have felt no need. The destruction of the Cities of the Plain, the treacherous denial of Esau's birthright, the genocides upon which the occupation of the Promised Land was predicated—he saw all these as the data of faith, to be accepted unqueryingly or justified. As further instance of this attitude, we could cite the poem in *Lyra Innocentium* which takes the hideous story of Elisha, the boys, and the bears, and turns it into a cautionary tale in the tradition of *Struwwelpeter* ("Disrespect to Elders").[134] Even Lock, a sympathetic High Church commentator, sounds a Pained note at such fundamentalism. In his assessment of Tract 89 he remarks that Keble "makes no attempt to screen fanciful uses of the method [patristic exegesis], but selects the examples most likely to startle and scandalize the modern reader; he goes near to shocking the moral sense by his unwillingness to condemn immoral actions in the Bible."[135] Hence "Third Sunday in Lent" views the Greek War of Independence as a religious conflict (not as a struggle for political liberty), and provides "justifying" instances of brutal and immoral spoliation from the Bible without so much as a tremor of distress. Keble remembers the "fearful joy" associated with illegitimate adventure in Gray's "Eton College Ode" ("They hear a voice in every wind, / And snatch a fearful joy"),[136] but in his adaptation, the fearfulness functions much more as an index of awe than of guilt:

It was a fearful joy, I ween,
    To trace the Heathen's toil,
The limpid wells, the orchards green,
    Left ready for the spoil,
The household stores untouch'd, the roses bright
Wreath'd o'er the cottage walls in garlands of delight.[137]

The temptation to take over the exclusive note of preexilic Judaism was one to which Tractarians succumbed with as much readiness as their Evangelical counterparts. Keble claimed to individuate and personalize the tribal collectivity of the Old Testament: "It seems clear to me, on reading over the Old Testament, that the example of the Jews *as a nation*, is there held out in such a way as to regulate and correct the religious conduct of Christians as *individuals*."[138] Clearly there is no sense here of any major qualitative difference in the perspective of the two dispensations—and it was easy enough for Evangelicals, on the one hand, and Tractarians, on the other, to appropriate the status of a chosen people, and damn all those who fell outside the compass of their particular "covenant." Newman, conditioned no doubt by his early exposure to Evangelicalism, was forever constructing strained typological relations between the situation of the British Church and various figures and events in the Old Testament. Shortly before his conversion to the Roman Catholic Church he compared Anglicanism to the Kingdom of Israel, schismatically severed from Judah, and later still suggested that the Church of England was a Zoar in his pilgrimage toward Rome—an ironic recollection of Keble's typological efforts in "First Sunday in Lent," where the universal Church functions as the Zoar in our pilgrimage to God.

A corollary of believing in this special privilege and tribal sanctification is an uncharitable view of the "enemy," a view most notoriously embodied in the Psalmist's instruction to dash the little ones of Babylon against the stones. Both the Tractarian and Evangelical parties rejected the Broad Church tendency toward universalism and its concomitant denial of hell; both would later prove vocal in their condemnation of F. D. Maurice. We must trace the root cause of such attacks to the fundamentalism shared by both groupings, and so discomfitingly expounded in the first three Lenten poems of *The Christian Year*. "Second Sunday in Lent" argues for a divine justice untempered by mercy:

> But where is then the stay of contrite hearts?
> Of old they lean'd on Thy eternal word,
> But with the sinner's fear their hope departs,
> Fast link'd as Thy great Name to Thee, O Lord:
>
> That Name, by which Thy faithful oath is past,
> That we should endless be, for joy or woe:—
> And if the treasures of Thy wrath could waste,
> Thy lovers must their promis'd Heaven forego.[139]

Keble would have done well to remember a hymn of the seventeenth century, *O Deus, ego amo te.* Here is the first stanza, Englished by Edward Caswall: "My God, I love thee, not because / I hope for heaven thereby, / Nor yet because who love thee not / Are lost eternally."[140] Yet even as we recoil from the theology of fear plaited like a dark ribbon through Keble's Lenten verse, we can applaud the imaginative energy of its conception. There is something impressive in the staid, formal colloquy between Justice and Mercy at the start of "First Sunday in Lent," as though he had animated the figures of an allegorical ceiling by Veronese, and in the vivid *compositio loci* in "Third Sunday in Lent." Presumably without having seen them outside a conservatory, he brilliantly conveys the heavy, reluctant movement of palm fronds in the wind: "A gale from bowers of balm / Sweep o'er the billowy corn, and heave / The tresses of the palm."[141]

 "Fourth Sunday in Lent" is one of those paradoxical poems (like the palinode) that defies its own precepts in the process of articulating them. Keble takes the inscrutability of natural processes as an instance of reserve and fashions two types of the kind set forth in "Septuagesima Sunday." In Keble's view, the actual blossoming of a rose and the first glimmering of a star at sunset defy our observation, and so inscribe "reserve" in the book of nature. But even as he describes he realizes, much as Gray imparts a Berkeleian reality to rose and gem in the famous deprivation stanza of the *Elegy.* In the same way, by describing the post-Resurrection appearance of Christ to his mother, Keble is forced to fill in what the Gospels have expressly omitted, and so simultaneously to deconstruct his belief that some information is almost too sacred to impart. But the poem's paradoxical nature extends still further—a specious "so" leads Keble from an omission in the Gospels to the presentation of Joseph as the "truest image of the Christ":

> So, truest image of the Christ,
>   Old Israel's long-lost son,
> What time, with sweet forgiving cheer,
> He call'd his conscious brethren near,
>   Would weep with them alone.[142]

The logic—if indeed it deserves that name—suggests that because the Holy Ghost inspires Scripture, omissions of crucial data indicate that Christ himself practices reserve: the doctrine of *circumincessio* enables anything predicated of one person of the Trinity to be predicated of another. That being so, the fact that Joseph wept for his brethren in private makes him the truest image of the Christ, and this despite the fact that Christ *asked* for companionship in Gethsemane and that Isaac has always been taken as the standard patriarchal type of Christ. Keble is reputed to have distrusted originality, as witness this anecdote relayed to us by Newman: "I recollect his borrowing a friend's sermon, which had been preached before the University and, I suppose, had been well spoken of to him. When he returned it he whispered into his friend's ear, 'Don't be original'."[143] The same outlook informs his sense that "Ingenuity in argument should always put us on our guard, because it is in some sort an appeal to our vanity."[144] Yet again and again in *The Christian Year* we find moments like these, readings and constructions so personal and uncanonical that they seem eccentric. Keble is also not averse, as Herbert before him, to baptizing the tropes and procedures of secular verse. Take for instance these stanzas from "Fourth Sunday in Lent":

> Who ever saw the earliest rose
>   First open her sweet breast?
> Or, when the summer sun goes down,
> The first soft star in evening's crown
>   Light up her gleaming crest.
>   . . . .
> But there's a sweeter flower than e'er
>   Blush'd on the rosy spray—
> A brighter star, a richer bloom
> Than e'er did western heaven illume
>   At close of summer day.[145]

The advance by comparative stages beyond the data of rose and star to a datum more perfect than they occurs in many amorous poems, not least Jonson's "Her triumph": "Have you seene but a bright Lillie grow . . . Ha' you mark'd but the fall o' the Snow . . . O so white! O so soft! O so sweet is she!"[146]

On "Fifth Sunday in Lent" we need not dwell at length—its attitudes and outlook make it rebarbative to a century that has seen them conclude in the Holocaust. Deep-dyed reactionary that he was, Keble would have opposed Jewish relief as an engine of Whiggery— and he is too complacent to see that the state of the Jews after the Diaspora had much more to do with Christian oppression than providential edict: "God will not quench nor slay them quite, / But lifts them like a beacon light / Th' apostate Church to scare."[147] Like the defense of the Irish bishoprics in 1833, such attitudes show Tractarianism in a very unflattering light. We find the same fault in Newman, the same readiness to make theological capital out of suffering produced by human persecution—as witness his treatment of the Jews in *A Grammar of Assent*.

"Palm Sunday" is unusual among the poems of *The Christian Year* insofar as it makes no effort to glance at the biblical narrative associated with the feast. Rather it offers itself as an esthetic manifesto—one that, like the *Praelectiones* that was later to follow it, presents a wholly Christian conception of the poet as a celebrant of God. Martin imagines him to have had Byron and Shelley in mind when he rebukes the "idol-hymns" of bards: "[I]t may be well to regard Keble's poem in *The Christian Year*, written for Palm Sunday, as a direct reference and prayer for these two lost souls."[148] The reference does not, however, strike me as being time-specific: it could as easily take in past and future ages. Keble, like Gray in *The Progress of Poesy*, is conscious of being the unworthy inheritor of a great tradition, for he claimed his canonical "primary poets" all shared his sense that poetry celebrated God. But what, he asks, would happen if even an epigone like himself should yield the stage to godless poets? His answer, swooping tangentially off his epigraph about the crying stones, is that God would move down the entire chain of being to ensure the continuity of his praise.

As we approach the central mysteries of the Atonement and the Resurrection, Keble lays down a carpet of poems across the whole of Holy Week. "Monday before Easter," eager to fill in the interstices of the Gospel narrative, imagines that Christ spent Tuesday to Thursday of Passion Week contemplating, one by one, the souls who would later benefit from his Crucifixion—an idea derived, perhaps, from the ghostly pageants *Richard III*, *Julius Caesar*, and *Macbeth*.

"Tuesday before Easter" also "fills in," rather like a Franciscan contemplation on the Seven Last Words, the circumstances surrounding the statement "Sitio." Here the Roman soldiers speak with the accents of Gray, for Keble wishes to allude to the mocking banquet of deprivation in "The Bard" ("Fill high the sparkling bowl"):[149]

> "Fill high the bowl, and spice it well, and pour
> "The dews oblivious: for the Cross is sharp,
>   "The Cross is sharp, and He
>   "Is tenderer than a lamb.["][150]

This kind of florid cantata-esque writing fails to suit the gravity and poignancy of the occasion, as eighteenth-century language often fails to do. Anyone who, delighted by Handel's *Messiah*, has gone on to sample the other oratorios, bewigged in Augustan diction, will have experienced disappointment at a style less compelling than the AV's. It is not, however, the elaborate diction but rather a metrical flaw that I wish to censure here. The offending line is a versification of the *kenosis* by which Christ was "Made heir, and emptied of Thy glory' awhile." The elision of "glory' awhile" is distressingly clumsy and supports Battiscombe's reservations about the poet's metrical expertise: "Keble's poetry is nothing so much as a piece of music written by someone who is a master of the technical side of harmony but yet tone-deaf. It marches forward with a perfectly accurate and sickeningly regular beat."[151] That the poetry marches is true enough—there is insufficient flexibility in the placing of the caesura and a poor acoustic sense in the combination of vowel and consonant, but I disagree that the problem lies wholly with Keble's regularity—something desired, when you come to think of it, by almost all his contemporaries, bar the iconoclastic Byron and the consciously informal Hunt. I think the readers of Keble are also to blame. Conditioned by his diction and the content (both redolent of staple items in *Hymns Ancient and Modern*), they tend to impose a straitjacketing hymnal gestalt on the poems, a relentlessness that bends each strophe to the outline of the tune. How many of us, when singing "Morning" in its hymnically filleted version, have not flinched at the mercies that "Hover around us while we pray"?

"Wednesday before Easter," one of the best poems in the collection, does not court this danger because, like some of Herbert's poems, it can be termed bistrophic. Two quite different stanza patterns differentiate a "heart" from a contrasting "rind." In the first stanza a sestet of couplets reinforces the Herbertian feel of the poem, for the asymmetrical distichs *(5a2a5b2b5c2c)* recall the earlier poet's prefer- ence for this design principle—a principle to which A. M. Hayes has given the dubiously useful name of "counterpoint."[152] In Keble's adap- tation, the counterpoint tends to align the roomy pentameter with God, and the humble dependent dimeter with the human subject:

> O Lord my God, do Thou Thy holy will—
>   I will lie still—
> I will not stir, lest I forsake Thine arm,
>   And break the charm,
> Which lulls me, clinging to my Father's breast,
>   In perfect rest.[153]

This is the proem, a series of adjustments and exorcisms. When the mind is properly disposed, a different pattern is established: ten- line units of tetrameter couplets in which a newfound mental bal- ance registers in the alignment of the members. The first stanza takes the form of a cletic hymn, an invocation to self-devotion and resig- nation, respectively; the next paraphrases a sentiment from Jeremy Taylor; and the third corrects any misconceptions that might arise. This summary, partial though it is, alerts us to yet another Kebelian characteristic—we might call it (in mock-neoclassical fashion) dis- unity of person. The three unities derived from Aristotle were of course the unities of time, place and action. Augustan theorists seem to have taken a fourth unity for granted, viz., that any literary utter- ance will be governed by a consistently developed point of view. However, anyone who has read the Prophets, will have been struck by the fluid modulations from first to second to third person in the course of any one oracle. Here, for instance, is an extract from Isa. 49:

> 11 And I will make all my mountains a way, and my highways shall be exalted.
> 12 Behold, these shall come from far: and, lo, these from the north and from the west; and these from the land of Sinim.
> 13 Sing, O heavens; and be joyful, O earth; and break forth into singing, O mountains: for the LORD hath comforted his people, and will have mercy upon his afflicted.

In much the same way, the focus and consciousness of "Wednesday before Easter" keeps shifting, rotating the object under scrutiny so as to examine it from all conceivable angles. Hence the opening para-phrase of Luke, which the poem attributes to the speaker, not to Christ in agony; hence the banishment of fancy (like the banishment of "vain deluding joys" in Milton's *Il Penseroso*)[154] and the summons to self-devotion and "Resignation, spirit meek," avatars likewise of Milton's Melancholy: "Come pensive Nun, devout and pure."[155] The next stanza couches some received wisdom in the third person, and Keble casts the one after that as a second-person address. A species of *inclusio* at the start of the final strophe returns us to Gethsemane but now gives the verse its proper attribution.

"Thursday before Easter"—more unusual even than "Palm Sun-day" (which at least made oblique use of Christ's entry into Jerusa-lem)—says nothing about the Last Supper but chooses rather to fo-cus on ideas of foresight and prophecy. Keble's conception of Holy Week seems to have centered on the idea that Christ kept rehears-ing the Passion in his mind—hence, perhaps, his need to dwell on Daniel, an association prompted by the prophecy of Jerusalem's fall. In stanza 1 we find Daniel praying toward the ruins of his beloved city, and, with the frailty of empire and earthly power thus embod-ied for us in a *sic transit* tableau, Keble turns to the state of imperial England and dreads a similar punishment for its godlessness and sensuality. While the land might be free of the specious externalities of Romanism (which is how I interpret the phosphoric waves of line 3), its moral state will not bear scrutiny:

> 'Tis true, nor winter stays thy growth,
> > Nor torrid summer's sickly smile;
> The flashing billows of the south
> > Break not upon so lone an isle,
> But thou, rich vine, art grafted there,
> The fruit of death or life to bear,
> Yielding a surer witness every day,
> To thine Almighty Author and His stedfast sway.

> Oh! grief to think, that grapes of gall
> Should cluster round thine healthiest shoot![156]

There speaks the defender to the bitter end of the *via media* as the most healthful branch of the universal Church. Even as he quails at the prospect of judgment upon these "grapes of gall"—proleptic image of the vinegar and gall associated with the Crucifixion—Keble submits to the counsels of Providence, and, content with glimmerings and uncertainty as Daniel himself had been, no longer strains to decipher the future. (Judgment was indeed at hand in the form of the Reform Bill, but Keble, blinkered by his Tory vision, failed to perceive this when it came and preached about national apostasy instead of hailing the just suppression of the Irish bishoprics in 1833.) Battiscombe has complained about the sobriety of *The Christian Year*, remarking that "the reader begins to wonder whether Keble had ever known the poet's fine frenzy, or the exultation of the mystic, inebriated, as the author of the *Anima Christi* prays to be, with the blood of Christ."[157] One can concede the general truth of this statement and point at the same time to the extraordinarily explicit conclusion to "Good Friday":

> Lord of my heart, by Thy last cry,
>   Let not Thy blood on earth be spent—
> Lo, at Thy feet I fainting lie,
>   Mine eyes upon Thy wounds are bent,
> Upon Thy streaming wounds my weary eyes
> Wait like the parchéd earth on April skies.
>
> Wash me, and dry these bitter tears,
>   O let my heart no further roam,
> 'Tis Thine by vows, and hopes, and fears,
>   Long since—O call Thy wanderer home;
> To that dear home, safe in Thy wounded side,
> Where only broken hearts their sin and shame may hide.[158]

Where, one may justly ask, is that vaunted Tractarian reserve, that clamped emotion, that horror of showy, conceited language? Seeking a reason for the outburst, one might guess that reserve has been swallowed up in grief, so much so that the very prayer that Battiscombe invokes as the measure of Kebelian dryness has clearly shaped the conduct of the poem. Compare the "streaming wounds" with this line from the *Anima Christi*: *Aqua lateris Christi, lava me;* and the conceit that stows the sinner in the side of Christ derives from another clause of that prayer: *Intra vulnera tua absconde me*. Keble might in theory have recoiled from the baroque emotionalism of the Roman Catholic Church and one of its chief Franciscan vectors, the stations of the cross. He might by the same token have averted his face from the emotionalism rampant in an entirely different quarter—Lutheran Germany. Yet, as Pusey found out, Protestantism made emotional capital of the Passion in ways very similar to those of "Good Friday." Faber has this to say about Schleiermacher, one of his German mentors: "He *felt* towards the person of Christ the kind of mystical devotion which the Moravians practiced—the desire to dwell in imagination upon the Five Wounds of the Lord, upon the Bloody Sweat, and the Piercing of His Side."[159] No wonder, then, that Christians of such different theological color should all converge at the point of the Crucifixion and acknowledge a common basis of salvation, whether expressed in medieval conceit or in the chaster eighteenth-century diction of Watts when he surveys the "wondrous cross."

"Easter Eve" takes us into the sepulchre with the buried Christ, and speculates freely (like the pseudepigraphal *Gospel of Nicodemus*) about the harrowing of hell. In a way typical of the poet, a space is cleared within the Gospel narrative to admit the reader into the experience and to allow participation in the Resurrection at first hand— a technique Keble learned from the collaborative phrase ("with thee") sprinkled throughout the poetry of Herbert:

> Each on his cross, by Thee we hang a while,
>   Watching Thy patient smile,
> Till we have learn'd to say, "'Tis justly done,
> "Only in glory, LORD, thy sinful servant own."
>
> Soon wilt Thou take us to Thy tranquil bower
>   To rest one little hour,
> Till Thine elect are number'd and the grave
>   Call Thee to come and save:[160]

A further Metaphysical touch can be detected in the quiet, domesticating conceit that turns the tomb into a bower, as Herbert had earlier turned the grave into a bed: "Therefore we can go die as sleep, and trust / Half that we have / Unto an honest faithful grave; / Making our pillows either down, or dust."[161]

A touch of Herbert can also be detected also in acclamatory structure of "Easter Day," where each stanza functions as the calyx for a self-contained triumphal image, and a broad appositional rhythm keeps the poem together. Compare Keble's opening strophe:

> Oh! day of days! shall hearts set free
> No "minstrel rapture" find for thee?
> Thou art the Sun of other days,
> They shine by giving back thy rays:[162]

with Herbert's own "minstrel rapture" in "Easter" ("Rise heart; thy Lord is risen. Sing his praise / Without delays"),[163] and such lines as these from "Sunday": "The couch of time; cares balm and bay: / The week were dark, but for thy light: / Thy torch doth show the way."[164]

What we could term the "arthrosis" or stanzaic articulation of the poem later abandons this tidy image-containment, however, and relays a dialogue between the "world" and the Christian believer trapped by Keble's archaic poeticizing in a Ptolemaic universe: "Our crown, our treasure is not here, / 'Tis stor'd above the highest sphere." In "Monday in Easter Week" we find another instance of this comic conservatism. The Nonjurors so revered by the Tractarians retained a belief in a sacral kingship at a time when the *Instauratio Magna* had all but reduced the Great Chain of Being into a heap of broken links. In the aesthetic sphere Keble can often seem antediluvian, tenaciously retaining materials that his contemporaries had discarded in their quest for new matter.

Thus while the poem begins with a strikingly observed datum, the vivid moss of a stream set against the dun green of the surrounding heath, a later stanza versifies a Poussin canvas. Compare:

> Go up and watch the new-born rill
> Just trickling from its mossy bed
> Streaking the heath-clad hill
> With a bright emerald thread[165]

with

> Or canst thou guess, how far away
> Some sister nymph, beside her urn
> Reclining night and day,
> 'Mid reeds and mountain fern,

That is stylistic schizophrenia—near Wordsworthian simplicity and observation followed by the most frigid Augustan artifice. Yet the poem survives its blemish, making pretty use of its terraced stanza (like the declivities of a fountain) and a neatly handled emblem that relates a confluence of waters to a confluence of prayers.

Equally assured is the image articulation of "Tuesday in Easter Week," where the snowdrop offers an intimation of immortality. Keble here makes use of the rhetorical trope of *occupatio*, which introduces material while appearing to pass over it. Emblem poems (of which "Tuesday in Easter Week" is a late example) have always had to diagrammatize and denude the image-vector so as to focus on the moral without any distracting detail. In this mode there can be no numbering the streaks of the tulip. But Keble clearly loves snowdrops as much as he does the *moralitas* extracted from them, and he attentively details the physical aspects of the flower while pretending to discount them:

> Thou first-born of the year's delight,
>   Pride of the dewy glade,
> In vernal green and virgin white,
>   Thy vestal robes, arrayed.
>
> 'Tis not because thy drooping form
>   Sinks graceful on its nest,
> When chilly shades from gathering storm
>   Affright thy tender breast:[166]

'Tis not for this and other things besides—but because they witness to the perennial resurrection of the spring. Yet even though he has dismissed the sensuous data of the snowdrop, Keble quietly appropriates its drooping form as an emblem of reverence, and its early appearance (snowdrops are preceded only by aconite in the cycle of flowers) as a sign of courage. From these arresting qualities he moves on to describe his rural parishioners, human embodiments of the snowdrop's self-effacing confidence.

"First Sunday after Easter" also draws on personal experience: a meditation, like Herbert's "Aaron," on the priestly speaker's sense of unworthiness. Equally Herbertian is the personalized typology that relates the loss of Temple furniture to the loss of hieratic purpose, the Babylonian exile to a comparable secular episode in the speaker's life:

> Upon Thine altar's horn of gold
> Help to lay my trembling hold,
>   Though stain'd with Christian gore;—
> The blood of souls by Thee redeem'd,
> But, while I rov'd or idly dream'd,
>   Lost to be found no more.[167]

It might at first be tempting to find a proto-Tractarian note in the sacerdotalism of the poem, but reflection will show us that much of the typology had been sanctioned and institutionalized by the Epistle to the Hebrews, and was therefore as viable a poetical resource for Protestant as for Catholic writers. (As proof of this widespread tendency, one could mention that in 1859 the American evangelist Joseph Seiss delivered some lectures subsequently published as *Holy Types; or, The Gospel in Leviticus*.)[168] In any case, Keble makes it clear that his rich sacerdotal images, bearing no relation to the surplice with which even the highest churchman of 1827 was content, are simply a figure of speech ("'To heap the censer's sacred fire, / 'The snow-white Ephod wear?'"). And, what is more, the pride associated with the priestly cultus is arraigned in a finale that brings us back to "the trivial round, the common task" of a country parson: "Around each pure domestic shrine / Bright flowers of Eden bloom and twine, / Our hearths are altars all." There is something distinctively Kebelian about that substitution of "hearths" for the expected "hearts."

Keble devotes "Second Sunday after Easter" almost exclusively to *tableaux vivants* of Balaam's prophecy and makes his visual purpose clear at the start:

> O for a sculptor's hand,
> That thou might'st take thy stand,
> Thy wild hair floating on the eastern breeze,
> Thy tranc'd yet open gaze,
> Fix'd on the desert haze,
> As one who deep in heaven some airy pageant sees.[169]

Much of the imaginative effort in this and in the following stanzas had already been anticipated by Gray's "Bard," to which Keble clearly owes a debt—compare "Loose his beard and hoary hair / Streamed, like a meteor, to the troubled air."[170] The originality of the poem inheres in its cunning stanza, where after all the statuesque prophecy, a cumbersome alexandrine "drags its slow length along."[171] These heavy six-footers are often trammeled with worldly reservations and unholy desires, and ready us for a finale in which Keble takes over the images of Balaam's prophecy ("Sceptre and Star divine") and calls on God to integrate vision and soul, an integration of which the prophet was obviously incapable. The "heavenly" upward tug of the enjambment helps lift and lighten the coils of the terminal hexameter: "O teach our love to grow / Up to Thy heavenly light, and reap what Thou hast sown."

"Third Sunday after Easter" dramatizes a disharmony between

inner and outer weather. Its elegiac color derives in part from Ps. 137 ("By the rivers of Babylon, there we sat down") and from a hint of Keatsian Thanatos (the line about easeful death in "Ode to a Nightingale"): "I sit me down beside the hazel grove, / And sigh, and half could wish my weariness were death."[172] Keble makes sense of this springtime melancholy not in the traditional way of being too happy in others' happiness but through a chiasmus that crosses labor pains (the start of parenthood) with flowers on a grave (the end of parenthood). Joy and sorrow, he claims, are woven inseparably into the fabric of life:

> She joys that one is born
>   Into a world forgiven,
> Her Father's household to adorn,
>   And dwell with her in Heaven.
> So have I seen, in Spring's bewitching hour,
>   When the glad Earth is offering all her best,
> Some gentle maid bend o'er a cherish'd flower,
> And wish it worthier on a Parent's heart to rest.

That somberness is only temporary, however. Keble has placed human suffering *sub specie aeternitatis* and inverted the meaning of Caliban's poignant lines ("when I waked / I cried to dream again"):[173] "Like a sad vision told for joy at morn, / For joy that we have wak'd and found it but a dream."

"Fourth Sunday after Easter" also comes to terms with *rerum lacrimae*, using the blank between Ascension and Pentecost to show how blessings withdrawn can turn into blessings compounded. It begins as a colloquy rather like Herbert's "Dialogue"—a note of incredulous interrogation links Keble's opening ("My Saviour, can it ever be / That I should gain by losing Thee?")[174] with Herbert's ("Sweetest Saviour, if my soul / Were but worth the having").[175] But, in a way typical of his inventive, unpredictable structures, Keble cuts from intimacy to grandeur, and versifies the Ascension in terms that bring a Correggian fresco to mind:

> When Heaven's bright boundless avenue
> Far open'd on their eager view,
> And homeward to Thy Father's throne
>   Still lessening, brightening on their sight,
> Thy shadowy car went soaring on;
>   They tracked Thee up th' abyss of light.

There is something very impressive and painterly about the visualization of this scene, not least the matching of diminution and intensity that recalls the vanishing points of trompe l'oeil ceilings and the oxymoronic "abyss of light." Darkness and negation are the items more usually found *dans l'abîme*. Once this dazzling parenthesis has run its course, the intimate dialogue resumes its course, and the soul admits that deprivation can often issue in fulfillment. We noted earlier that Battiscombe regrets the "sickeningly regular beat"[176] of Keble's metrification, but I wonder what she would make of the final line of the lyric. In every other stanza Keble has ended with a tetrameter. Here he gives it an extra foot, a heart-stopping clumsiness that enacts the idea of how literal gain can engender an actual loss of grace: "Else we should all sin on or sleep / With Christ in sight, turning our gain to loss."

A striking feature of "Fifth Sunday after Easter" is the free (almost cavalier) way in which Keble reshuffles and cross-refers discrete biblical images—a sort of holy mix 'n match. He begins by dramatizing the pause before the breaking of the seventh seal, as though it were an imminent and not a remote apocalyptic event, and then reinvents that pause as the space between the Resurrection and the Ascension. It is not enough that the "Conqueror now / His bonds hath riven"[177]—humankind must be instructed in the meaning of the Atonement: "Yet hath not man his lesson learn'd, / How endless love should be return'd." But, having projected an awe-inspiring silence, Keble immediately breaks it with the sound of a turtledove. St. Paul's Epistle to the Ephesians presents the Church as the bride of Christ, and the majority of patristic commentators, unlike Theodore of Mopsuestia, applied the Song of Songs to that doctrine. "Dove" figures among the metaphoric endearments of that book, and so the ground is prepared for Keble to image the Church as a turtledove, "widowed" by the ascension of her Lord. The dove then displaces the sparrow of Ps. 102 and merges through scriptural double-exposure with the second bird sent out by Noah. At this point the ecclesiological metaphor slides from dove to ark: "Chiefly for Aaron's seed she spreads her wings, / If but one leaf she may from Thee / Win of the reconciling tree." The reconciling tree is of course the cross, and so the almost surreal meltings and reformings proceed, an elaborate development of the sort of fusion represented by a line from the previous poem: "The Dove must settle on the Cross." One of the chief supplications made on Rogation Sunday (the fifth after Easter) calls for an increase in vocations. It is not surprising, therefore, that the relevant poem should ultimately focus on the sons of Levi and end with an invocation of Christ as the dual fulfillment of Moses and Aaron, abrogating the types of teacher and priest. An anxiety about the state of the Anglican Church also provides an undertow to this stanza—even in 1824 Keble seems to perceive the signs of a national "apostasy":

> Teacher of teachers! Priest of Priests! from Thee
> The sweet strong prayer
> Must rise, to free
> First Levi, then all Israel, from the snare.
> Thou art our Moses out of sight—
> Speak for us, or we perish quite.

And as if to bring the poem full circle, those vocatives echo the cry in Revelation—"King of Kings, and Lord of Lords."

"Ascension Day" provides a sort of metafictive commentary on the imaginative effort behind such poems as "Fourth Sunday after Easter," tracing as it does the actual process of *compositio loci*. We start with a May sky in England and follow the line of the poet's vision as, in a sudden collapse of time, he gazes at the ascending Christ. The graduated upward movement finds its resolution, as we might expect, in the image of an oceanic deity that engulfs the speaker's selfhood:

> Sure, when I reach the point where earth
> Melts into nothing from th' uncumber'd sight,
> Heaven will o'ercome th' attraction of my birth,
> And I shall sink in yonder sea of light:[178]

There are fascinating strains and paradoxes in this exercise, which speaks of how the soul defies gravity, the "attraction of my birth," and yet, in a sort of antimeric inversion, sinks *downward* in the sea of light, until it rests (as though on an ocean bed) beside its Lord. Keble nonetheless marries the becoming of earth with the being of Deity, and so avoids that passivity upon which traditional images of heaven have always trenched. I admire Faber's "My God, how wonderful thou art," but have always felt its last two lines have a touch of the proverb that permits a cat to look at a king: "Prostrate before thy throne to lie / And gaze and gaze on thee."[179] By stressing God's continued involvement with his creation, Keble imparts a greater energy to *his* version of the beatific vision. Indeed, it is possible to read a sort of purgatorial progression into the final stanza of "Ascension Day," where the Catholic *disciplina arcani* would allow like-minded readers to construe "worthier" as "progressively worthier," while the Evangelical readership would take "worthier" in comparison with an unworthy world:

> Then shall we see Thee as Thou art,
> For ever fix'd in no unfruitful gaze,
>   But such as lifts the new-created heart,
> Age after age, in worthier love and praise.

Even the fixity of God's eternal presence permits of development, the *process* of fructification.

"Sunday after Ascension" is a most curiously assembled poem, revealing, as it does, a sort of Siamese twin design. It begins with the transparent *sicut/ita* pattern typical of emblem verse—just as the earth receives seed and renders it fruitful, so should we receive the gifts of God and multiply our talents like faithful stewards. Keble fixes the analogy in a fine anaphoric stanza that promises resolution and closure. The *traductio* thrums relentlessly on gifts and giving:

> Largely Thou givest, gracious Lord,
> Largely Thy gifts should be restor'd;
> Freely Thou givest, and Thy word
>   Is "Freely give."
> He only, who forgets to hoard,
>   Has learn'd to live.[180]

After this the poem takes an entirely new turn, commenting first on the inscrutable silence with which God and his agent Charity work their purposes out. Charity, indeed, fulfills the messianic prophecies of Isaiah and leads the gaze of the believer towards a sky left blank after the Ascension. It is here that the significance of the stanza pattern becomes apparent, its sense of effortlessness and continuity sharply interrupted. (A tetrameter tercet is pulled up short by a dimeter, allowed to extend to four feet again, and then reined in once more.) In the light of such felicities, we can dissent from Thompson's regret that "in 'Sunday after Ascension'. . . [Keble] employed the more distinctive 'Burns stanza,' whose peculiar lilt hardly suited his theme."[181]

The ten-day intermission between Ascension and Pentecost held a special fascination for Keble, for almost all the poems clustered round this feast advert to it in one way or another. Perhaps he found in it a poignant emblem for the expectancy of the Christian, from whom Christ is as physically absent as he was for the apostles and for whom the consolation of the Holy Spirit often seems a distant rather than an immediate possibility. Even so, when he addresses the feast of Pentecost in "Whitsunday," he certainly rises to the occasion. As Battiscombe has observed, it is "a poem so logical and symmetrical as fairly to deserve to be called majestic."[182] However, it worth pointing out that the symmetry (evident in the oscillating movement between Sinai and Pentecost) is qualified in an important way. At first the dispensations embodied by each event are contrasted in traditional images of wrath and mercy. An adversative "but" hinges the comparison:

> But when He came the second time,
>   He came in power and love,
> Softer than gale at morning prime
>   Hover'd His holy Dove.
>
> The fires that rush'd on Sinai down
>   In sudden torrents dread,
> Now gently light, a glorious crown,
>   On every sainted head.[183]

It is clear from the definite article, moreover, that "*the* fires" are qualitatively identical; they differ only in their physical manifestation, for the second theophany is closer to the beautiful than the sublime. Indeed, the delicacy and ethereality of that second "coming" show that Keble might well have known the famous medieval lyric "I sing of a maiden," a lyric that treats the Incarnation in the same tender way:

> He cam also stille
> To his moderes bowr,
> As dew in Aprille
> That falleth on the flowr.[184]

Be that as it may, the pattern of contrast secured by "but" gives way to one of analogy, stressing the continuity rather than the difference between the two events:

> So, when the Spirit of our God
>   Came down His flock to find,

> A voice from Heaven was heard abroad,
> A rushing, mighty wind.

There is no cause for complacency; the wind stresses the sublimity of the dispensation and its exacting moral demands—more demanding still than those of Mosaic law—and parallels (instead of displacing) the trumpet that thrilled on Sinai. At Pentecost as much as at Moses' theophany, Keble implies, conscience must give back "th' appalling tone." And what had initially seemed the antithetic emotions of terror and tenderness now present themselves as commutable equivalents: "Save, Lord, by Love *or* Fear." "Monday in Whitsun-week" likewise dwells on continuity, the paradoxical continuity of flux. Taking *sic transit gloria* as his central theme, Keble begins with an English landscape and acknowledges that Britain belongs to a succession of empires and is doomed like them to pass away. All he can ask is that the dissolution should be gradual rather than apocalyptic: "With lulling spell let soft Decay / Steal on, and spare the giant sway, / The crash of tower and grove."[185] After surveying the imperial cycle expounded in the book of Daniel, Keble rebukes the national pride of England, which ought to see its own fate prefigured in the ruin of Babylon. Reactionary though he was, Keble recalls Gray's forensic address to a heartless political elite in the *Elegy*. Compare "Nor let Ambition heartless mourn; / When Babel's very ruins burn" with "Let not Ambition mock their useful toil."[186] The paths of glory . . .

"Tuesday in Whitsun-week" has that multiple focus, that plurality of persons, which characterizes the more adventurous poems of *The Christian Year*. Addressed as it is to "Candidates for Ordination," it obviously draws on Keble's own vocational crises and misgivings, and tries to generalize them for the benefit of his audience. The opening stanzas convey the priest's resentment toward the secular and godless world he has to serve. As in Herbertian dialogue poems, an answer to this hostility comes from God, though the tone is brusquer and more challenging than that of Herbert's Deity:

> What? wearied out with half a life?
> Scar'd with this smooth unbloody strife?
> Think where thy coward hopes had flown
> Had Heaven held out the martyr's crown.[187]

At stanza 5, Keble takes over the poem *in propria persona*, and stresses the humiliations and setbacks suffered by Christ. But to counterbalance the stripping of divine privileges entailed in *kenosis*, he urges his priestly audience to find divinity in the ordinariness of their lives, using the tradition of Constantine's labarum to image the discoveries they will make: "How bright, in Heaven, the marks will glow / Of the true cross." Keble resolves the bafflement and resentment with a deictic often used in the Bible—in 1 John, "this is the message" and "this is the promise"; in Herbert, "This is the famous stone"[188] and "These are thy wonders, Lord of Love."[189] By letting the demonstratives focus on the object, Evangelist and poets alike offer a key, there, as it were, for the grasping: "This is Thy pastoral course, O LORD, / Till we be sav'd, and Thou ador'd." From that triumphal discovery it is easy to move to a coda that combines the earlier allusion to Constantine (*In hoc vinces*) with a reference to the quest in *The Faerie Queene*, book 1: "Ye lift, for Him, the red-cross shield."

The tercets of "Trinity Sunday" are obviously emblematic, but the images that move through them prove less blatant. Their scumblings and shifts and paradoxes enact the efforts of the mind to grasp the most difficult dogma in all the creeds. Keble controls his design by means of *inclusio*, bracketing the start and finish with an invocation to each of the persons in turn: "Creator, Saviour, strengthening Guide."[190] It is worth remarking in this regard that Keble saw poetry as an occasion for the unfolding of difficult ideas: "But is it not the very office of poetry to develop and display the particulars of such complex ideas? in such a way, for example, as the idea of God's omnipresence is developed in the 139th Psalm?"[191] "Trinity Sunday" could be said to assay the same task, registering the essential mystery of its subject by moving in and out of unrelated images. For example, in stanza 4 the Church figures as a temporal structure, paved with the weeks of the ecclesiastical year:

> Along the Church's central space
> The sacred weeks, with unfelt pace,
> Have borne us on from grace to grace.[192]

But Keble then concretizes the abstract Church as a Gothic structure, using the standard metaphor of the stone forest to effect the transition:

> As travellers on some woodland height,
> When wintry suns are gleaming bright,
> Lose in arch'd glades their tangl'd sight;—

Keble's Trinitarianism declares itself in that plural, for, as anyone familiar with another *Winterreise* knows, an optic phenomenon can "triplicate" the winter sun without compromising its essential unity, as witness Müller's *Nebensonnen*: "Drei Sonnen sah ich am Himmel stehn, / Hab' lang und fest sie angesehn."[193] But no sooner does Keble place us in a woodland setting than he immediately returns to his architectural conceit:

> Such trembling joy the soul o'er-awes
> As nearer to Thy shrine she draws:—
> And now before the choir we pause.
>
> The door is clos'd—but soft and deep
> Around the awful arches sweep
> Such airs as soothe a hermit's sleep.

Keble's punctuation here is dramatically hesitant, those intersective pauses giving the effect of sketchy, incoherent notations. Even the syntax begins to fall apart in the succession of the pronouns: "she" to "we." Nor is there any architectural coherence in the idea of a choir with a door, though the door of an Orthodox iconostasis offers an approximation of sorts. And if it does, what are we to make of the arches, carvings, and frettings, none of which can be reconciled with the smooth, continuous surfaces of Byzantine architecture? The answer lies of course in the fluid shifting of the metaphor, for Keble has by this time forgotten about his physical church and imaged the choir as the Real Presence of paradise. The melodies that soothe a hermit also furnish a Trinitarian image, their three-part harmonies heard as an aural unity. Having served that purpose, they fall away to admit the notion of "one safe nest," which modulates back, through the hermit's sleep, to the "arch'd glades" initially set before our eyes. These enharmonic movements from key to key eventually overlap in the pun that superimposes the architectural meaning of "dome" upon its Latin root (*domus* = "home"). Keble might also have been aware that the German *Dom* can mean an entire cathedral:

> What echoes from that sacred dome
> The selfish spirit may o'ercome
> That will not hear of love or home!

But that dome is also the dome of Hebraic cosmogony, what in "Septuagesima Sunday" Keble calls "The glorious sky embracing all"—for the preceding tercet has shifted outdoors:

> Alas! for her Thy opening flowers
> Unheeded breathe to summer showers,
> Unheard the music of Thy bowers.

It is odd that Keble should so closely duplicate a passage from Keats, a poet he did not admire—or, if he admired, felt theological scruples about hailing. In *Sleep and Poetry* Keats had had much the same thing to say about the Augustans: "Ah dismal soul'd! / The winds of heaven blew, the ocean roll'd / Its gathering waves—ye felt it not."[194] However, the trouble about the book of nature (its *Nebensonnen* notwithstanding), is that it does not prove the doctrine of the Trinity. That is why Keble felt constrained to add the artificial image of the church building so as to mention the "Three solemn aisles" that "approach the shrine."

"First Sunday after Trinity," like Herbert's "The Bunch of Grapes," personalizes the impersonal structures of typology and applies them to the circumstances in which the poet finds himself. Both make rather querulous use of the *ubi sunt* topos. Herbert cries "But where's the cluster? where's the taste / Of mine inheritance? / Lord, if I must borrow, / Let me as well take up their joy, as sorrow,"[195] while Keble likewise begins on a note of whining deprivation: "Where is the land with milk and honey flowing, / The promise of our God, our fancy's theme."[196] The key to his dilemma is to found in the elision of God's promise and poet's fancy, an apposition that confuses Providence with wish fulfillment. And so Keble banishes the imaginative play he holds so dear in the poets of Sensibility—the faery-lore, say, of a Collins ode—and utters a stern palinode like that at the start of Marvell's "Horatian Ode": "These are not scenes for pastoral dance at even, / For moonlight rovings in the fragrant glades." What makes this adapted typology more immediate even than Herbert's is the fact that Keble has done what St. Ignatius recommends we do: relive the advent in the promised land. We could borrow a term from Tom Mozley and call this "introversial" typology, "that is, entering into and describing states of mind, struggles within."[197] But a land promised is not a land gained, and Keble, like Herbert before him, has to admit his false construction and substitute the true—it is not on earth but in heaven

that the promised land will be found. Inverting Wordsworth's famous aphorism about the child and the man, and also half alluding
to visionary conception of childhood in the "Intimations Ode," he
acknowledges his failure of vision ("The Man seems following still
the funeral of the Boy") and realigns his demonstratives—"These"
in stanza 2; "that glorious world of Thine" in the final strophe—a
realignment that dramatizes his new state of mind.

We saw in "First Sunday after Trinity" how cautious, even dismissive, Keble's attitude to the fancy was. Something of the same
distrust carries over into "Second Sunday after Trinity," a poem seem-
ingly based on the readings he had advocated in "Septuagesima
Sunday." However, having run and read, Keble repeatedly stresses
the subjective nature of his interpretations: "To Fancy's eye their
motions prove / They mantle round the Sun for love."[198] To say this
is in effect to elide devout Christian readings in the book of nature
with primitive animism—but that seems less surprising when we
recall that both Keble and Newman believed that God had scattered
seeds of his truth among the Gentiles and so inspired them with
crypto-Christian impulses. What Keble is trying to do, however, is
to show that the animizing tendencies of the imagination indicate a
right disposition, a readiness to detect love in all the workings of
creation. Hence the triumphal paraphrase of Wordsworth's salute
to the rainbow:

> But he whose heart will bound to mark
>   The full bright burst of summer morn,
> Loves too each little dewy spark,
>   By leaf or flow'ret worn:

It is precisely this ability to render God's love through animistic fancy
that will bring an additional insight—the baptismal regeneration
beneath the evidences of sin.

"Third Sunday after Trinity" provides further testimony to
Keble's skill in graduating the development of his images and us-
ing those graduations to redirect and canalize the line of thought.
He begins with an allegorical tableau in the mode of Gray and
Collins: Memory personified to represent the consciousness of sin.
As in Gray's "Ode to Adversity" a passive participle establishes her
character by recording her impact on those around her. Here is Gray:
"Scared at thy frown terrific, fly / Self-pleasing Folly's idle brood,"[199]
and here is Keble: "Chill'd at her touch, the self-reproaching soul /

Flies from the heart and home she dearest loves."[200] Underneath the
Gray surface of the diction, we find a sentiment of Horace, for Keble,
like his classical forebear, is stressing the futile efforts of people who
try to escape the self: *Caelum, non animum, mutant, qui trans mare
currunt.*[201] Before long, however, Memory has softened into an angelic presence. (Angels are metonymns for the omniscience of God
and for the comprehensiveness of the *liber scriptus.*) This development leads in turn to a fanciful passage in the manner of Berkeley,
which, while it attempts to divinize the fanciful fairy lore of Collins,
seems hesitant about the whole enterprise: "but what if purer
sprights / By moonlight o'er their dewy bosoms lean / To' adore
the Father of all gentle lights?" Having thus subsumed the consciousness of sin into the greater consciousness of God, Keble refocuses
the poem in the breast of the penitent and offers a dual solution
both transitive and intransitive: "O turn, and be thou turn'd!" The
tears that spring from sorrow will purify the heart, as a river washes
away the dirt over which it moves and so clarifies itself. A new,
unterrified sense of God's omniscience enables the soul to make a
final turning, which will issue in steadfastness and fixity instead of
the craven flight described at the start of the poem:

> O turn, and be thou turn'd! the selfish tear,
>   In bitter thoughts of low-born care begun,
>
>   . . . .
> Then fearless turn where Heaven hath set thy part,
>   Nor shudder at the Eye that saw thee stray.

3

Keble's *Christian Year* Surveyed: II

FOURTH Sunday after Trinity" belongs to the tradition of the Augustan night piece and of the liturgical nocturnals from which that genre evolved. The mediators of the line are of course the poets of Sensibility, as witness the distinct echo of Collins's "Ode to Evening" in stanza 3 of Keble's poem:

> Which bids us hear, at each sweet pause
> From care and want and toil,
> When dewy eve her curtain draws
> Over the day's turmoil.[1]

Keble has followed the countess of Winchelsea in associating night with innocence, though her "Nocturnal Rêverie" not does not allude quite so explicitly to the idea of regeneration:

> When a sedate Content the Spirit feels,
> And no fierce Light disturbs, whilst it reveals;
> But silent Musings urge the Mind to seek
> Something too high for Syllables to speak;
> Till the free Soul to compos'dness charm'd,
> Finding the elements of Rage disarm'd,[2]

The "free soul" is not an idea that Keble's notions of original sin can readily accommodate, but the poems otherwise have a great deal in common, not least their sense of turmoil and rage associated with the day, and of night as a time of spiritual release. Collins also defines Evening (following a tradition established by Bottom in *A Midsummer Night's Dream!*) as an absence of daylight; and it is from

Collins that Keble has taken the idea of an occluding curtain: "and marks o'er all / Thy dewy fingers draw / The gradual dusky veil."[3] With human noise thus deleted from the sound track, the primal innocence of nature re-asserts itself in a quiet, nocturnal paraphrase of Ps. 19:

> 1 The heavens declare the glory of God; and the firmament sheweth his handywork.
> 2 Day unto day uttereth speech, and night unto night sheweth knowledge.

Remembering, perhaps, the vocal nature of those psalmic days and the silent demonstration of the nights, Keble stresses the quietude of night thoughts:

> In the low chant of wakeful birds,
>   In the deep weltering flood,
> In whispering leaves, these solemn words—
>   "God made us all for good."

None of these sounds has any penetration; their being heard depends on the suppression of the noise that would otherwise blot them from consciousness. Parallels could be drawn with a minor German lyric made great by Schubert's music: Johann von Pyrker's "Die Allmacht." Here the reader is likewise learns that God speaks in *des Waldstroms laut aufbrausenden Ruf* and as well as in *des grünenden Waldes Gesäusel*,[4] analogues of Keble's "deep weltering flood" and "whispering leaves." And both of course find a common heritage in the experience of Elijah, to whom God does not appear as wind, earthquake, or fire but as the "still small voice" (1 Kings 19:11–12).

The message conveyed by Keble's quiet nocturnal chorus—that, *pace* Milton, external nature has escaped the fall—yields a pun at the start of the following stanza, where "true" in the musical sense of being in tune also gathers up the opening line, which affirmed a truth by negating idle fancy. Reversing the elements on this occasion, a further pun connects the intellectual affirmative of "consent" with musical "concent" in "one consenting voice." Following an established thematic route of the Augustan nocturnal, Keble claims that because sin comes with consciousness itself, the dawn will recapitulate the Fall:

> Sin is with man at morning break,
>   And through the live-long day
> Deafens the ear that fain would wake
>   To Nature's simple lay.

From this point on the poem develops a parabolic color, for Keble rehearses the story of the Atonement and shows how it inverted and therefore redressed the downward motion of sin, and sanctified the "meanest things below"—a clear verbal echo of the flower at the end of the *Intimations Ode*—with "a seraph's robe of fire." Just as in Winchelsea's "Nocturnal" the mind sought "Something, too high for Syllables to speak," so the Incarnation, by humbling divinity, divinizes the humble. Keble now turns his twilight opening to good use and connects the messianic prophecy of Isa. 60:1 with the darkness-banishing radiance of the Incarnation: "For, behold, the darkness shall cover the earth, and gross darkness the people, but the LORD shall arise upon thee, and his glory shall be seen upon thee." Compare:

> The rod of Heaven has touch'd them all,
>   The word from Heaven is spoken;
> "Rise, shine, and sing, thou captive thrall;
>   "Are not thy fetters broken?["]

This light cannot blaze for long, however, for free will presupposes the existence of evil. And so the poem loses its exaltation and curves back to its epigraph ("the whole creation groaneth and travaileth in pain together until now") which it ends by paraphrasing: "Hence all thy groans and travail pains."

In "Fifth Sunday after Trinity" Keble opens up the historical specificity of an utterance in the Bible, and, by showing how it typifies an eternal human attitude, gives it a frequentative force. We have already encountered the device in "St. John's Day," where the poet attributes St. Peter's words to his immediate audience and so establishes the recurrence of the error: "'Lord, and what shall this man do?' / Ask'st thou, Christian, for thy friend?"[5] "Monday before Easter" uses a quotation from the *Iliad* in a comparable way, extracting an eternal present out of a time-bound instant: "'Father to me Thou art and Mother dear, / 'And Brother too, kind Husband of my heart'."[6] "Fifth Sunday after Trinity" resembles both these poems by virtue of its start—a paraphrase of St. Peter:

"The live-long night we've toiled in vain,
  "But at Thy gracious word
"I will let down the net again:—
  "Do Thou Thy will, O Lord!"[7]

Keble then elides the saint and the contemporary Christian (or, more specifically, the Christian priest):

So day by day and week by week,
  In sad and weary thought,
They muse, whom God has set to seek,
  The souls His Christ hath bought.

Jesuit spirituality requires that *compositio loci* draw the contemplative into closer union with the object of contemplation. Not so in this poem, though. The poet lavishes his imagination on the various sense data associated with the event—a sea-chantey and other night sounds:

Where rippling wave and dashing oar
  Our midnight chant attend,
Or whispering palm-leaves from the shore
  With midnight silence blend

—and having done that, dismantles the scenery so carefully set in place. By canceling this effort, Keble stresses its remoteness from the reader's situation in 1821:

Sweet thoughts of peace, ye may not last:
  Too soon some ruder sound
Calls us back from where ye soar so fast
  Back to our earthly round.

While the disciples braved the storm in the *physical* presence of Christ, their nineteenth-century successors have only his spiritual attendance to fall back upon: "Full many a dreary anxious hour / We watch our nets alone." Even so, faith ought to acknowledge that attendance and create a trust that will subordinate human desire to the dictates of Providence. The perseverance entailed in that surrender registers in the insistent patterning of the verse at this point:

Cast after cast, by force or guile
  All waters must be tried:

> By blameless guile or gentle force,
>   As when He deign'd to teach
> (The lode-star of our Christian course)
>   Upon this sacred beach.

Here the *epanorthosis* retracts the phrase "force and guile" thrown down in the initial statement, qualifying its parts as "blameless guile" and "gentle force." And for the first time we are given a sense of safe haven through the close-up gesture of "this beach" and a sense of purposeful navigation by the lodestar. Keble footnotes Habakkuk as a source for a coda in which he stresses the insignificance of the instrument and the power of the Deity behind it—"To our own nets ne'er bow we down." He also seems to have had 2 Cor. 12:9 in mind: "My grace is sufficient for thee: for my strength is made perfect in weakness."

"Sixth Sunday after Trinity" expands the rubric to the Fifty-first Psalm (which refers to David's adultery) and marries it with the relevant passage in 2 Sam. 12. Whereas in other poems Keble usually begins with a historical matrix and works outward toward his contemporary readers, here he reverses the sequence, and begins with the universal experience of guilt before moving to the case of David. Indeed, the opening stanza gives no hint of the subsequent line of development and simply sets down the parallels of inner and outer life that Keble's Book of Nature lyrics have by now made familiar. If the opening of "Sixth Sunday after Trinity" differs at all from this established precedent, it is in the comparative subtlety of its procedure, for instead of clipping tenor and vehicle together with a simile, Keble simply places his images alongside each other and allows the current to leap the gap:

> When bitter thoughts, of conscience born,
>   With sinners wake at morn,
> When from our restless couch we start,
> With fever'd lips and wither'd heart,
> Where is the spell to charm those mists away,
> And make new morning in that darksome day?
>   One draught of spring's delicious air,
>   One steady thought, that GOD is there.[8]

On closer inspection we realize that the nature imagery is not transcriptive, since the recurrent force of "When . . . when" cancels the idea of a specific season and turns "spring's delicious air" into a metaphor. This gains value from the following stanza, however, where Keble explains that the spiritual life has a seasonal cycle peculiar to itself, full of sudden reversals, upliftments, and fallings away. Not surprisingly, he bases his interpretation on a stanza in Herbert's "Flower" that records similar peripeties in our spiritual life: "These are thy wonders, Lord of power, / Killing and quickning, bringing down to hell / And up to heaven in an houre."[9] Keble's version collapses external and internal time ("thought") into each other by predicating both on God. It bears the same sort of relation to Herbert's original as one of Liszt's operatic paraphrases to its source material in turn: "These are Thy wonders, hourly wrought, / Thou Lord of time and thought, / Lifting and lowering souls at will." The point is doubled in the figurative use of "wintry" later in the stanza, and the antonomasia that makes "May" stand for any kind of regenerating brilliance, no matter what the actual month of the year may be.

Having established God's instant remission of physical and metaphysical storms, Keble can now show his equally swift way of remitting sins, and he does so by recalling the "Comfortable Words" and priestly invitation of the *Prayer Book* and by nudging the poem toward its "historical" basis. Following the philosophy of "Septuagesima Sunday," most readers would imagine that the page set open for our inspection and profit is another page from the Book of Nature (though the miraculous ink of the inscription—"balm"—recalls a line in Herbert's "Sunday"—"Th' indorsement of supreme delight, / Writ by a friend, and with his bloud"):[10]

> Would'st thou the pangs of guilt assuage?
> Lo! here an open page,
> Where heavenly mercy shines as free,
> Written in balm, sad heart, for thee.

By this time Keble's page has become a literal one bearing the text of Ps. 51. The dull, hard stone of David's heart not only melts at his absolution but also nourishes those wretches with "fever'd lips and wither'd hearts" mentioned in the first stanza. Hence he inverts the type of the cleft rock (which nurtured the Israelites in the Wilderness), and suggests that the tears of David's penitence offer refreshment to all who have sinned and wish for God's forgiveness: "The rock is smitten, and to future years / Springs ever fresh the tide of holy tears."

Of course, by its very nature Scripture superimposes the eternity of God upon the transience of human experience—that is the key to its relevance. Typology has developed as a means to regulating the application, acknowledging the fulfillment of specific Old Testament types in the Gospels. However, some of the most original poems in *The Christian Year* involve the construction of a *personal* typology. "Seventh Sunday after Trinity" offers an example of this innovative practice. Its very opening is unusual. Most hymns offer a summons to attend the scene the hymnist is celebrating, whether it be the *Adeste* of "O come, all ye faithful"[11] or the *Ite* of J. Montgomery's "Go to dark Gethsemane."[12] Here, however, Keble commands that we stay and conquer our dislike for a desolate scene: "Go not away, thou weary soul: / Heaven has in store a precious dole / Here on Bethsaida's cold and darksome height." This austere word-painting continues into the next stanza as well, one of those moments when *The Christian Year* flairs into brilliance:

> And far below, Gennesaret's main
> Spreads many a mile of liquid plain,
> (Though all seem gather'd in one eager bound,)
> Then narrowing cleaves yon palmy lea,
> Towards that deep sulphureous sea,
> Where five proud cities lie, by one dire sentence drown'd.[13]

Here, for once, the abstract generalities of Keble's eighteenth-century diction enhance (rather than neutralize) the vividness of his description. The spare chorographic data receive neither color nor texture from the language (if we except the "palmy lea"), and the scenery is furthermore sobered by an imaginative shadow superimposed by the mind—the drowned cities of the plain. A giddy vantage point reduces miles of water to a single outline and places the speaker high up the mountain. (It is on mountains, far from human dwelling, that theophanies occur.)

Hence the relief and reassurance supplied by stanza 3: "Landscape of fear! yet, weary heart, / Thou needs't not in thy gloom depart, / Nor fainting turn to seek thy distant home." Bethsaida, of course, was where the loaves and fishes were miraculously multiplied, and it is to this event that Keble now turns, setting its humble details in opposition to the more grandiose food miracles of the Old Testament. It is not the literal meal, however, but rather the desolateness that followed the departure of the multitude that seizes

Keble's imagination. This solitude, however bleak and lonely it might seem to worldly eyes, can in fact nurture the soul. Retirement, as many other lyrics of *The Christian Year* assert, brings one into the presence of God: "So when the tones of rapture gay / On the lorn ear, die quite away, / The lonely world seems lifted nearer heaven." As in the stories of Elijah and St. John the Baptist, the Wilderness becomes the vector of God's providence, except that the barren stoniness of Bethsaida itself becomes a miraculous meal rather than the setting for one: "Nor fear to seek Him farther in the wild / Whose love can turn earth's worst and least / Into a conqueror's royal feast." This takes considerable license with the traditional alignments of typology, focusing as it does on frames and borders rather than on the subjects they enclose. Even though Keble distrusted originality, his imagination sometimes made him an original *malgré lui*.

"Eighth Sunday after Trinity" is altogether more straightforward—perspicuous even to the point of dullness. The subject is apostasy and the double wickedness of an apostate priesthood. The chief interest of the poem is its programmatic stanza—two tetrameters followed by two trimeters—which offers a sense of falling off and depletion, a metrical "apostasy." It also it shows Keble trying to humanize the repulsive Old Testament narrative from 1 Kings 13, in which a prophet of Judah is trapped into a sort of apostasy by false assurances and put to death. The Judaic prophet is instructed not to retrace his steps, but then is inveigled into doing so by another who assures him: "I *am* a prophet also as thou *art*; and an angel spake unto me by the word of the LORD, saying, Bring him back with thee into thine house, that he may eat bread and drink water." For Keble, however, the forbidden return journey is not an unfair test of fidelity, but rather a return to scenes renounced by the prophet's calling, or rather (to slip a Christian key into the typological lock) the priest's vocation and the renunciation of world, flesh, and devil. He takes the traditional tableau of *Et in Arcadia ego* (depicted by Poussin as a group of distressed and puzzled shepherds about a tomb) and substitutes a pastor for Virgilian *pastores*, and the slain prophet for the figure of *Mors*: "Alas, my brother! round thy tomb / In sorrow kneeling, and in fear, / We read the Pastor's doom / Who speaks and will not hear."[14]

"Ninth Sunday after Trinity" takes similar imaginative liberties with its biblical source, in this case the appearance of God to Elijah and his failure to declare himself in the magisterial aspects of the natural world. Once again Keble has taken an arbitrary element of folklore—the trial of a prophet whose expectancy is undimmed by disappointment—and moralized it with meanings that the writer chose to withhold, or, much more probably, never entertained. If we were to seek a precedent for this sort of reading, we would find it in patristic hermeneutics, in such exercises as St. Augustine's reading of the Good Samaritan as an allegory of the Church. Keble's admiration for the Fathers' way of going about their business would later be attested by his tract about their mysticism, but "Ninth Sunday after Trinity" testifies quite as vividly to this fondness. It is also worth noticing that he takes extraordinary liberties with the lead-up to his allegory, providing an orthodox metrical version of Elijah's cry in the Wilderness but forging God's answer from Elihab's reproach to David. What the Bible fails to report, Keble eagerly supplies, since he has in any case conceived Elijah's despair as an eternal condition, one to which God will always respond: "Perhaps our God may of our conscience ask, / 'What doest thou here, frail wanderer from thy task? / 'Where hast thou left those few sheep in the wild?'"[15] And we should as often address him with Elijah's words: "Then should we plead our heart's consuming pain, / At sight of ruin'd altars, prophets slain, / And God's own ark with blood of souls defil'd." This is to move from time-specific history into the timeless world of allegory, a mode which allows Keble to present a patristic reading of wind, earthquake, and fire. A reference to Sinai superimposes Moses upon Elijah, detaching separate figures from the cycle of history to demonstrate their continuity. Even the Wilderness to which Elijah retired and into which the poem has earlier taken us now turns out to be metaphor for the dark night of the soul, a soul that ignorantly sets a false construction on its experience: "Nor deem thyself upon a desert shore, / Because the rocks the nearer prospect close." Indeed, arriving at one of those tangential conclusions to which the opening stanzas give no index whatever, Keble suggests that faith and sight are at cross purposes: "Choose to believe, not see."

As if to endorse the austere priorities of this judgment, "Tenth Sunday after Trinity" begins with a visual tableau—Christ's weeping over Jerusalem—and uses *expeditio* to discount the various readings that might rise in the minds of spectators. Unlike Xerxes at Abydos, Jesus does not weep because he senses the mortality of the crowds before him, nor does he weep in anticipation of his Passion, which Keble registers in one of the arresting "strong lines" that spring so naturally from the paradoxes of Christianity. (It is tempting to think that Newman recalled "Our God in agony" in one of his sermons on the Passion: "Now I bid you recollect that He to Whom these things were done was Almighty God".)[16] Having dismissed all likely readings, Keble claims that the sorrow is inscrutable, and all our speculation beside the point:

> But hero ne'er or saint
>   The secret load might know,
> With which His Spirit waxeth faint;
>   His is a Saviour's woe.[17]

Failing to penetrate that mystery, all the poet can do is relay the speech beneath which the sorrow lies. He does so in one of his deft paraphrastic stanzas that slots almost all of Luke 19:43–44 into metric form. Keble manages to "improve" the AV, however, as when in "Christmas Day" he ran the Vulgate and the King James versions together and offered us "love to men of love."[18] Although the original Greek verb in Luke 19:44— ἐδαφίζειν —can mean "to level" or "to dash," the Jacobean translators opted for the first, giving us "And shall lay thee even with the ground, and thy children within thee." Keble, however, combines the idea of leveling with the idea of physical violence, building in an allusion to Ps. 137 ("that taketh and dasheth thy little ones against the stones") to show that Jerusalem will suffer the same fate it once wished on Babylon:

> "Now foes shall trench thee round,
>   "And lay thee even with the earth,
> "And dash thy children to the ground,
>   "Thy glory and thy mirth."

That is the oracle, and that, in a sense, it is "all ye need to know." But Keble has one more surprise in store. We have already noted the moment at the end of *The Eve of St. Agnes* where past events (in which the reader has so eagerly and intensely participated) are shown to be irretrievably past: "And they are gone: aye, ages long ago / These lovers fled away into the storm."[19] At the end of "Tenth Sunday after Trinity," Keble does the same thing, but in reverse. Whereas up till now the events of Palm Sunday have been contained within the historical frame of the Gospel narrative, the final stanza uses the present tense to throw the icon of the weeping Savior forward in time and inculpates the readers who have hitherto looked on passively:

> Ye hearts, that love the Lord,
>   If at this sight ye burn,
> See that in thought, in deed, in word,
>   Ye hate what made Him mourn.

Keble implies that those tears will only cease flowing if we do not ourselves recapitulate the indifference and hard-heartedness of Jerusalem. Our burning, while it might suggest an ardent, generous indignation, can also imply a sense of shame.

It is hard to warm to poems like "Eleventh Sunday after Trinity," which have that prim, hard, defiant, self-immolating tone that characterizes the masochistic elements in the Oxford Movement, where discipline signifies not so much a healthy self-control as the penitential scourge. Given the self-cossetings of the Anglican establishment, Newman was no doubt right to prefer holiness above comfort, but the holiness of Christ seems far removed from the holiness of Wordsworth's stern daughter of the voice of God and of Keble's ferocious palinode:

> No—rather steel thy melting heart
> To act the martyr's sternest part,
> To watch, with firm unshrinking eye,
> Thy darling visions as they die,
> Till all bright hopes, and hues of day,
> Have faded into twilight gray.[20]

If, as Oscar Wilde has claimed, men kill the things they love, there is murder of sorts in the harsh, lapidary stanzas of this poem. Their insistent renunciations trample Keble's love of the countryside and the gentle reveries of the Age of Sensibility to which he clearly felt drawn—the "shadowy toys" of fancy recall the "shadowy car" in the "Ode to Evening,"[21] while the substitution of a hard metallic texture for a soft, emollient one ("steel thy melting heart") subverts a line in Gray's "Ode to Adversity": "What sorrow was thou bad'st her know, / And from her own she learned to melt at others' woe."[22] In much the same way, the demarcation of "No" and "Yes" at the start of stanzas 3 and 4, and the systematic *adjunctio*, supplying as it were a shopping list of renunciations and miserable moods ("To act"; "to watch"; "And if the world seem dull and dry" "If long and sad")—these features mechanize the utterance, so that, all passion spent, it sounds dead and hollow. This *contemptus mundi* represents a reaction to what Keble perceived as the worldliness of the Augustan Anglicanism. Walter Lock has pointed out that the "'Anglo-Hanoverian' Church tone of the eighteenth century repelled him with its utilitarian *cui bono* principles, its presumptions in favour of liberty and against self-denying faith, its preference for external evidences of religion, its excessive and easy-going toleration, its want of a charitable austerity."[23] If the "Anglo-Hanoverian" Church, like Jack Sprat's wife, could eat no lean, then the Tractarians resembled Sprat himself in their intemperate renunciation of fat. "Self-denying faith" can easily issue in self-admiring self-denial, and "charitable austerity," as "Eleventh Sunday after Trinity" attests, can all too easily slough its "charitableness." Sooner "excessive toleration" than the unfleshed intolerance of a Desert Father.

"Twelfth Sunday after Trinity" begins with the familiar tense-swing of a typological structure, the "was" of history and the "shall" of its moral application:

> The Son of God in doing good
>   Was fain to look to Heaven and sigh:
> And shall the heirs of sinful blood
>   Seek joy unmix'd in charity?[24]

If that sounds familiar, it is because Keble has adapted the argument of Herbert's "Pulley"[25]—Providence ordains a deprivation so that the deprived soul, having savored the insufficiency of the creature, will throw itself upon its Creator. Having contemplated the world's intermixture of joy and sorrow for several stanzas, Keble ends his poem with the *prozeugma* of a litany, clause upon clause strung out in advance of the terminal verb to illustrate, as it were by a parable of syntax, the speaker's dependence on God.

Like "Whitsunday," "Thirteenth Sunday after Trinity" sets up a polar contrast between Old and New Testaments, but, unlike that poem, fails to resolve them in continuity. We begin with Moses on Sinai, where the priestly materials that the postexilic compilers placed in the Pentateuch are rendered as a visionary pageant—one clearly borrowed from Gray's "Bard." Even despite their closeness, God remains invisible to Moses, and Keble, never one to question the internal contradictions of Scripture, makes no mention of the contradictory Yahwist element in Exod. 24:10–11—"And they saw the God of Israel." Such visual deprivation is for him a feature of the Mosaic dispensation—a note of its incompleteness:

> Yet monarchs walk'd as pilgrims still
>   In their own land, earth's pride and grace;
> And seers would mourn on Sion's hill
>   Their Lord's averted face.[26]

An inverted possessive structure—"Canaan was theirs"—recalls a similar effect in Gray's "Ode on a Distant Prospect of Eton College," where a sense of incompleteness also registers in the inert, ascriptive complement (rather than an energetic transitive verb): "Gay hope is theirs by fancy fed"; "Theirs buxom health of rosy hue."[27] Completeness comes, however, when the face of God is revealed in the Incarnation. Keble's veil of cloud that curtained Sinai is also the veil of history, literally rent by the apocalypse: "But He their aching gaze repress'd / Which sought behind the veil to see." Once again the "private" annexation of typology enables Keble to read back into the partial glimpses and intimations of the Mosaic dispensation— the "basons" of ox blood (Exod. 24:6), the "clift" in which Moses hides when God passes over him in Exod. 33:22)—and find their abrogation in the full (and their sacramental continuance as the real) presence of Christ.

We can gather from a comment by Judge Coleridge that some nineteenth-century readers were puzzled by occasional "opacities" in *The Christian Year*: "To one who is familiar with Keble's diction . . . there is no difficulty in understanding how the ambiguity of expression might occur."[28] It is a cry taken up by Brian Martin against the syntax of "Fourteenth Sunday after Trinity": "[T]he poem as whole is uncertain, and leads into areas of *The Christian Year* where syntax makes for a lack of clear expression, and therefore a lack of understanding. It is difficult to sort out exactly what the following images represent, for instance, in the second stanza."[29] He thereupon proceeds to quote the offending images, which I shall offer in their full stanzaic context:

> Yet 'twas not wonder, but His love
> Our wavering spirits would reprove,
> That heaven-ward seem so free to move
>   When earth can yield no more:
> Then from afar on God we cry,
> But should the mist of woe roll by,
> Not showers across an April sky
>   Drift, when the storm is o'er,

> Faster than those false drops and few
> Fleet from the heart a worthless dew.
> What sadder scene can angels view
>   Than self-deceiving tears,
> Pour'd idly over some dark page
> Of earlier life, though pride or rage
> The record of to-day engage,
>   A woe for future years?[30]

Far from prejudicing the quality of the poem, this syntactic virtuosity seems (in my eyes at least) to enhance it. The idea itself is ordinary—even banal—but Keble's *hyperbaton* dramatizes the flighty, unstable nature of the vows taken on sickbeds. The flurried dissolution of syntactic elements and the feverish enjambment of stanza with stanza likewise image unraveling cloud rack. April storms, as witness the famous second stanza of Keats's "Ode on Melancholy," are notorious for their sudden arrivals and departures, but whereas Keats shows how they nurture a landscape,[31] Keble suppresses even that positive construction, and, cutting directly to the tears that the storms image, stresses their infertility, their tendency to *stunt* rather than to enhance the growth of faith: "a worthless dew."

If we set "Fifteenth Sunday after Trinity" against Wordsworth's "Look at the fate of summer flowers," we can also gauge Keble's ability to freshen up a faded theme or worn-out topic. Wordsworth's reading of those summer flowers is dead central (though none the worse for being that); Keble's is oblique. Compare the respective opening stanzas of the poems:

> Look at the fate of summer flowers
> Which blow at daybreak, droop ere evensong;
> And, grieved for their brief date, confess that ours,
> Measured by what we are and ought to be,
> Measured by all that, trembling, we foresee,
>   Is not so long![32]

and

> Sweet nurslings of the vernal skies,
>   Bath'd in soft airs, and fed with dew,
> What more than magic in you lies,
>   To fill the heart's fond view?
> In childhood's sports, companions gay,

In sorrow, on Life's downward way.
How soothing! in our last decay
Memorials prompt and true.[33]

Wordsworth opts for a solemn memento mori; Keble is tender and reverential, seeding his verse with appositive phrases that derive (via Herbert) from the litany. Stanza 2 supplies the key to this untraditional treatment of transience—flowers have escaped the fall, the vestiges of paradise lost. Like Wordsworth's Lucy, they *dwell* in rooted stability alongside paths and homes, paths and homes, which, far from conveying direction and contentment, are given a negative charge:

Ye dwell beside our paths and homes,
Our paths of sin, our homes of sorrow,
And guilty man, where'er he roams,
Your innocent mirth may borrow.

Here as nowhere else the naïveté of Keble's emblematic mode declares itself. It is a truth universally acknowledged (in 1826 as in 1995) that birds flee human beings out of fear of harm. With an almost Franciscan innocence, Keble assumes that they fly away in horror of our sinfulness. We might well balk at this, but when all is said and done, it is a statement no *more* problematic than Keats's about the nightingale's song, where the poet overlays a biological fact—territoriality—with rich mythic carapace. If we resist Keble, it is because he employs a simple declarative mode, whereas Keats repeatedly underlines the speculative and imaginative aspects of his enterprise. The finale of "Fifteenth Sunday after Trinity" also brings Keats to mind, while at the same time underscoring the huge differences between the two poets. Like the "Ode on a Grecian Urn," Keble's lyric resolves into an aphorism spoken by the subject. But how cheerful and unoracular Keble's flowers seem alongside that sibylline vase. Both flowers and urn represent serene indifferentism, but Keble's belief in Providence gives his blooms an altogether friendlier, more tender ethos. The flowers ventriloquize the famous verse from the Sermon on the Mount but at the same time give it an additional charge. Whereas the Bible again and again stresses the short-livedness of flowers, Keble, without denying that simple truth, chooses to Christianize the idea of *carpe florem* and turn its hedonism into a posture of calm submission: "Live for today."

The opening stanza of "Sixteenth Sunday after Trinity" paraphrases its epigraph from Eph. 3:13. Keble does not, however, develop the original context of the verse. Instead he utters it *in propria
persona*, substituting his readers for the Christians in Ephesus. And
even that appropriation undergoes no further development, for in
stanza 2 the personal "I" yields to impersonal gnomic statements
and later figures as an equally impersonal "we"—that collective
pronoun so typical of sermons:

> Wish not, dear friends, my pain away—
> Wish me a wise and thankful heart,
> With GOD, in all my griefs, to stay,
> Nor from his lov'd correction start.[34]

There is considerable wisdom in Keble's method here, for the topic
is a difficult one, and the resistance we all feel to the idea of suffering is countered by our sense of its having been the lot of a great
apostle and also of the poet who is leading us toward its contemplation. Stoic ataraxia centered on the inner resources of the sufferer,
whose "highest calling and election," in the words of George Eliot,
was "to do without opium, and live through all our pain with conscious clear-eyed courage."[35] For Keble on the other hand, individual
suffering is lightened by the consciousness that God subjected himself to the Crucifixion. There is a particularly arresting sequence of
lines in which the cross blocks off all avenues of escape and con-
fronts every nuance of human distress: "Lovest thou praise? the Cross
is shame: / Or ease? the Cross is bitter grief." That is the germ of a
hymn that John Mason Neale would compose later in the century—
"Art thou weary, art thou languid"[36]—a hymn that also presents an
Eliotic, "clear-eyed" interrogation of human suffering.
    "Seventeenth Sunday after Trinity" superimposes the glories of
Zion on the physical glories of the Anglican Church—its cathedrals
and colleges—and then cuts to their respective profanations at the
time of the exile and in 1822. For several stanzas Keble versifies the
sacrilege recorded in the visions of Ezekiel (like him a priest to the
temple); then, himself slipping on Ezekiel's title ("son of man"), he
finds its allegorical analogue in contemporary England. Typology
ensures that parallels can be drawn as much from the apostasies of
Israel as from its salvation history: "Yet turn thee, son of man—for
worse than these / Thou must behold: thy loathing were but lost /
On dead men's crimes, and Jews' idolatries."[37] Indeed, in Keble's

mind, Christian apostasy is more culpable than its Judaic equivalent, since it entails a falling away from a final truth, not its
foreshadowment. That is why he quotes Plato's parable of the cave
in the next stanza: "To worship pleasure's shadow on the wall." The
lyric ends by internalizing the temple cultus, rather as Herbert spiri-
tualizes the concrete data in "The Church-floore" to read off their
allegorical values.[38] The temptation facing Christians is not the dramatic kind of idolatry depicted in Ezekiel, but other, more insidious
displacements of God—materialism and creature comforts. To pray
the Lord's Prayer properly, we ought not to seek our remission of
earthly evil but rather of the supernatural evil that threatens to assail us: "Nor by 'our daily bread' mean common food, / Nor say,
'From this world's evil set us free'."

"Eighteenth Sunday after Trinity" swings, like its predecessor,
on a typological hinge, finding its pattern of fulfillment in mental
rather than in physical events. It begins with a prophetic affirmation, as though, like Adam's dream, we were waking and finding it
to be true—the desert through which the Israelites wandered now
manifests itself as the sterility of England in 1823:

> In the waste howling wilderness
>   The Church is wandering still,
> Because we would not onward press,
>   When close to Sion's hill.[39]

In a poem that reads like a prolix expansion of Herbert's "Bunch of
Grapes,"[40] Keble presents some standard typological couplings, e.g.,
the Communion and the manna (for which he borrows a phrase
from the anthem *Panis angelicus*):

> Yet Heaven is raining angels' bread
>   To be our daily food,
> And fresh, as when it first was shed,
>   Springs forth the SAVIOUR's blood.

The springing of that blood telescopes into itself an earlier allusion
to Moses' striking of the rock: "The living waters brightly shine."
But that is only the affirmative "arm" of the antithesis; the negative
is the formalism rife within the Church. A provisional resolution
comes through in the concluding hymn of penance—a format possibly borrowed from Marvell's "Bermudas."[41] However else it might

differ from "Eighteenth Sunday after Trinity," Marvell's poem also ends in a congregational hymn, and also aligns the sojourn in the Wilderness with the plight of contemporary Christians. I cannot understand why hymnographers and compilers have never detached the final hymn of "Eighteenth Sunday after Trinity" and taken it into one of the Anglican hymnals. Its clear doctrinal formulations and its suppression of personal imagery make it ideal for congregational use.

"Nineteenth Sunday after Trinity," while extracting standard lessons from Old Testament narratives, actually rings a change on Keble's usual procedure. We have seen how he often versifies the utterance of an historical character and then applies it to the contemporary situation of his readers; here he does the reverse, introducing Nebuchadnezzar's utterance as the cry of contemporary persecutors, so that we shift from the gnomic present of "cries" back toward the specific aorist of "cried." For Keble the relevance of the Bible (especially of the Old Testament, which for Broad Church Christians was waxing dimmer and dimmer) is thus affirmed, whether as a means of explaining a present spiritual malaise or of finding current factors in a past narrative of redemption. Anachronistic details also point to this sense of an enduring spiritual purpose that abolishes traditional categories and modes in an inclusive continuum. This is Keble's way of weaving fairy-lore into Christian discourse, and, like his beloved Spenser, giving it a soteriological color: "Thou, Saviour, art his Charmèd Bower, / His Magic Ring, his Rock, his Tower." That couplet marries the prayerful iterations of a litany with romance material in a charming, childlike way. But "Nineteenth Sunday after Trinity" comes close to subverting the sort of heroics with which it begins, and alerts us to the witness provided by three country people—"witness," after all, is the literal etymon of "martyr." Keble then projects them back onto the youths in the furnace to reveal the purpose they share across the centuries.

In "Twentieth Sunday after Trinity" Keble goes back on an assertion made in "First Sunday after Epiphany," viz., that the sublime is not the only (or even the chief) avenue to God. Here he rather thinks it might be:

> The wheeling kite's wild solitary cry,
>   And scarcely heard so high,
> The dashing waters when the air is still,
>   From many a torrent rill

> That winds unseen beneath the shaggy fell,
>   Track'd by the blue mist well:
> Such sounds as make deep silence in the heart
>   For Thought to do her part.[42]

This strikes me as distinguished poetry, the more so for going against the grain of Keble's cosy sensibility—grandeur and spareness are more the notes of Newman's verse. The stanza pattern is particularly felicitous, for its choppy alternation of five- and three-stress lines gives it a sort of panting eagerness. Forgetting his renunciation of the "cloister'd cell" in "Morning," Keble centers the romantic landscape on the figure of the *isolato* ("romantic note and clear, / Meet for a hermit's ear") and doubles that solitude in the image of the lonely kite. Of course, he is also looking back at Gray and remembering the cumulative surge at the start of "The Progress of Poesy":

> A thousand rills their mazy progress take:
> The laughing flowers, that round them blow,
> Drink life and fragrance as they flow.
> Now the rich stream of music winds along,
> Deep, majestic, smooth, and strong,
> Through verdant vales and Ceres's golden reign:
> Now rolling down the steep amain,
> Headlong, impetuous, see it pour:
> The rocks and nodding groves rebellow to the roar.[43]

Juxtaposing that with Keble's stanza about the torrent rills, we can see how much he owes to Gray and also the extent to which he has inched ahead of him. He has taken that smooth Claudian landscape, roughened its textures, and subtracted the comforts of nurture, retaining only its watery noise and its sense of a pattern disclosed by distance. It is a moot point, though, as to whether "Track'd by the blue mist well" is marred by inertia or enhanced by energetic *hypallage*. "Well" might simply be a flat, inactive adverb; or, more interestingly, Keble could have used a substantive instead of the gerund "welling," and so imparted a nounish density to otherwise insubstantial vapors.

At this point, however, the poem seems to break in half. Keble has taken Mic. 6:2 as his starting point, where mountains function simply as appropriate sites for Yahweh's arraignment of Israel. In his own arraignment, however, he fails to refer to the vivid setting of the start, and the "wither'd bents" and "wheeling kite" fall out of sight. What the thunder said accordingly turns out to be a tame, generalized sermon. This itself is awkward, for it deals with a typological collective—the Israelites in the Wilderness—only to revoke that sense of community and focus on the rebellious individual. Keble does, however, try to make amends for the clumsiness in his final stanza, for there he takes up the landscape again, though only in the general terms of parable. He is more interested in the fact that it has been viewed by an individual whose vantage has caused it to concenter on himself or herself. This use of a theological Claude glass recalls a claim in Rom. 8:28: "And we know that all things work together for the good to them that love God, to them who are the called according to *his* purpose."

Although Keble appended a poem by G. J. Cornish to "Twenty-first Sunday after Trinity," he could as easily have cited Wordsworth's "Animal Tranquillity and Decay,"[44] since all three poems share an ethos of unprotesting submission. Keble begins in a late summer landscape for which a robin has become the spokesperson. The romantics had readily correlated larks and cuckoos with the spring, but only Keats anticipated Keble in taking the robin's song as the "sound track" of Autumn. Both might also have been influenced by the lyrics at the end of *Love's Labour's Lost*, which connect season and birdsong and then attach a human response. We can indeed catch a faint echo of Shakespeare ("Cuckoo, cuckoo; O word of fear, / Unpleasing to the married ear")[45] at the start of Stanza 4: "O cheerful tender strain!"[46] The verblessness of this stanza also provides a telling image of quietude and resignation, qualities sustained by the nonfactive verbs in those that follow. These seem in turn to have been shaped by the *hic est* formula at the end of Herbert's "Elixir": "That is the heart for thoughtful seer"; "That is the heart for watchman true." The watchman comes from Isa. 21:11, but Keble has modified the promise of a local dawn and forced him to concentrate instead on the New Jerusalem. Like Plato's reluctant cave-dweller, he moves from mere approximations to an ideal reality:

> Forc'd from his shadowy paradise,
> His thoughts to Heaven the steadier rise
> There seek his answer when the world reproves:
> Contented in his darkling round,
> If only he be faithful found,
> When from the east th' eternal morning moves.

That unusual adverb "darkling" is only one of several elements in the poem that connect it with "The Darkling Thrush." However, whereas Hardy sees his bird as a challenge to human gloom, Keble's robin, far from defying the dusk, helps prepare the soul for its departure.

We need to remember Wordsworth's *Intimations Ode* when we read "Twenty-second Sunday after Trinity." This starts with a mountain boy who, recalling the happy shepherd of Wordsworth's poem, probably lives in Cumberland. Like that boy, and like Gray's "little victims" in the "Eton College Ode," he begins life as the happy "prisoner" of his ignorance:

> O blest restraint! more blessèd range!
>   Too soon the happy child
> His nook of homely thought will change
>   For life's seducing wild:[47]

While this last stanza paraphrases Gray's blissful ignorance as a *felix culpa*, it reverses Wordsworth's sense of paradise lost by substituting freedom for "Shades of the prison-house."[48] The boy's is a choice of Hercules disposed on a vertical rather than on a lateral axis, for the landscape, read in the manner advised by "Septuagesima Sunday," embodies the polar opposites of heaven and hell. (It is hard not to assimilate the "darksome mere below" to the *profundus lacus* of the Requiem Offertory:)

> Two ways alone his roving eye
>   For aye may onward go,
> Or in the azure deep on high,
>   Or darksome mere below.

That the landscape invites this sort of construction can further be gathered from Keble's use of "deep," his favorite image for the immeasurability of divine love. And Gray's use of a similar phrase in "The Progress of Poesy" no doubt exerted its influence in turn: "Sailing with supreme dominion / Through the azure deep of air."[49]

However, having characterized the mountain-dweller, and having invested him with a local habitation and something approximating a name, Keble lets him fade away in a participle. "Unheard" enables him to eliminate the agent and to move into the first-person plurals of the next stanza. From there it is easy to shift to a generic second-person address of the "ransom'd sinner" who recalls the boy in the up-down range of his vision ("Whatever owns, in depth or height, / Creation's wondrous bond"). Despite this faint effort at recapitulation, Keble has chosen such a circuitous route to arrive at his epigraph ("Lord, how oft shall my brother sin against me, and I forgive him") that one suspects the mountaineer was recycled from a different poem. Perhaps the topic of forgiveness was one that Keble found difficult to handle in the abstract, since he himself was capable of extraordinarily uncharitable gestures. It is very hard not to say "Heal thyself, physician" when such unctuous lines as these:

> Yes, ransom'd sinner! wouldst thou know
>   How often to forgive,
> How dearly to embrace thy foe,
>   Look where thou hop'st to live;—

are placed alongside the following anecdote. An associate of Thomas Arnold's, seeing his friend Keble "on the other side of the High Street[,] . . . crossed the road to shake him by the hand." The man reports, "[H]e held his hand out of my reach, and, glaring at me, said solemnly: 'Grenfell! you have sacrificed at the altar of Jupiter, and I renounce your friendship from this day.'"[50] Such behavior seems to reflect the narrow experience of the mountain boy without its associated holiness.

"Twenty-third Sunday after Trinity" has been universally admired. We have seen in an earlier chapter how Saintsbury compared it with Gray's *Elegy*,[51] though the similarity does not extend beyond the quietude and serenity common to both poems:

> Red o'er the forest peers the setting sun,
>   The line of yellow light dies fast away
> That crown'd the eastern copse: and chill and dun
>   Falls on the moor the brief November day.
>
> Now the tir'd hunter winds a parting note,
>   And Echo bids good-night from every glade;
> Yet wait awhile, and see the calm leaves float
>   Each to his rest beneath their parent shade.
>
> How like decaying life they seem to glide!
>   And yet no second spring have they in store,
> But where they fall, forgotten to abide
>   Is all their portion, and they ask no more.[52]

It seems to me that Goethe's voice is as audible in these lines as Gray's, for the two *Wanderers Nachtlieder* offer a comparable coupling of evening and peace, and the phrasing of the second, which associates nightfall and the greater night of death, picks up Keble's "wait awhile." Visual items in the poems also resonate, for both include treetops in their catalog of quiet things:

> Über allen Gipfeln
> Ist Ruh.
> In allen Wipfeln
> Spürest du
> Kaum einen Hauch;
> Die Vögelein schweigen im Walde.
> Warte nur, balde
> Ruhest du auch.[53]

It is also just conceivable that Keble's hunter (a rather jarring element) might have been suggested by Goethe's companion piece *Das Jägers Nachtlied*. So much for the echoes of the stanzas in hand, echoes which ought not blind us to the many felicities unique to Keble. There is, first of all, the interesting way in which zones of warm color are neutralized by the "dun" onset of night, an observation that, because it is clearly based on experience and not on poetic generalities, gives it right of admission to Geoffrey Tillotson's catalog of nineteenth-century skies:

> The nineteenth-century poets have a strong sense of the individual quality of each moment of experience. . . . And so they write of skies, for instance, in the following ways:
>
> > . . . the western sky
> > And its peculiar tint of yellow-green.
>
> The orange sky of evening died away.
>
> Deep in the orange light of widening morn.[54]

Another distinctively nineteenth-century feature can be found in the anxious, vigilant way in which the poet actually observes the dying of the eastern light—a moment that might well have lodged in Arnold's mind when he came to write "Dover Beach" ("on the French coast, the light / Gleams, and is gone"[55]). To admit Keble's

skyscape to Tillotson's roll call is for the moment to separate him
from his predecessors in the Age of Sensibility, though the allusion
to Gray's "Eton College Ode" in stanza 3 ("To breathe a second
spring")[56] serves to remind us how firmly he remains anchored to
that tradition even as he makes his short, tremulous excursions into
contemporary modes of seeing. Gray reclaimed the metaphysical
conceit when, following Dante, he made the curfew toll the knell of
parting day, and Keble seems to have smuggled in a similar
adventurousness when, under cover of the conventional phrase
"nightfall" he has the *day* fall and die on the moor: "and chill and
dun / Falls on the moor the brief November day." The enclosure
and separation of the "rude forefathers" in the *Elegy* have likewise
suggested such phrases as "each to his rest" and "beneath their parent shade" in stanza 2, but Keble strikes out on his own in the
catachresis that links singular and plural pronouns in "Each to his
rest beneath their parent shade." This poignantly blends the individual with the collective. The poet makes no effort to console the
leaves for their deprivation, whereas in his "Ode to the West Wind"
Shelley promises a triumphant resurrection to the seeds—"Each like
a corpse within its grave until / Thine azure sister of the Spring
shall blow / / Her clarion o'er the dreaming earth":[57]

> Unconscious they in waste oblivion lie,
>   In all the world of busy life around
> No thought of them; in all the bounteous sky,
>   No drop, for them, of kindly influence found.

While this recalls the list of deprivations in *Elegy Written in a Country Churchyard* ("For them no more the blazing hearth shall burn, /
Or busy housewife ply her evening care"),[58] it advances none of
Gray's countervailing compensations. Instead Keble uses those
leaves to rebuke people who, blessed with the prospect of a second
life, nonetheless remain discontented with their lot. They ought in
his view to be grateful that the Christian heaven projects a transfiguration of this life, not its mere extension. Shifting from the quietude and declension of the start, Keble now proceeds to render life
as a series of frustrations. He takes physical speed as an image of
human desire and measures the streamlined cutters of 1825 against
the arrowy movement of fish—measures them, and finds them want-
ing. Given the gross impediment of flesh, only death itself will release the soul into that thrilling vortex of motion, an idea that Keble

seems to have culled from 1 Cor. 3:15 ("If any man's work shall be burned, he shall suffer loss: but he himself shall be saved; yet so as by fire").

An almost unbridgeable chasm separates the communalism and shared purpose in Donne's *Devotions upon Emergent Occasions* ("No man is an island, entire of itself; every man is a piece of the continent, a part of the main")[59] from the self-entrapment of Arnold's "To Marguerite, in Returning a Volume of the Letters of Ortis": "Dotting the shoreless, watery wild / We mortal millions live *alone.*"[60] Keble's "Twenty-fourth Sunday after Trinity" does, however, provide a thin line of connection between them, for like Arnold, it acknowledges the essential solitariness of human experience. It reveals nothing, however, of Arnold's regretful, questioning postures (which have much more in common with the "Kuza-Nama" episode in the *Rubaiyat of Omar Khayyam*). Compare the *epizeuxis* of resentful incredulity in the Marguerite poem—"A God, a God their severance rul'd"[61]—with the note of quiet surrender on which Keble opens his poem: "Why should we faint, and fear to live alone, / Since all alone, so Heaven has will'd, we die."[62] The very fact of subjectivity is, in Keble's view, a barrier to shared experience. In *Tintern Abbey*, Wordsworth had affirmed an epistemological union between himself and Dorothy after acknowledging the confluence of self with sense experience,[63] but we find no comparable empathy in Keble, where like the village forefathers in Gray's *Elegy*, human beings are enclosed in separative capsules. And whereas in "The Progress of Poesy" Gray had spoken of "orient hues, unborrowed of the sun,"[64] Keble subverts that transcendence, claiming that all experience will take its color from the perceiving self: "Our eyes see all around in gloom or glow / Hues of their own, fresh borrow'd from the heart."

At this point "Twenty-fourth Sunday after Trinity" develops into a theodicy. Keble's first argument for justifying the ways of God to "man" is a version of the "Pulley" principle. Here, as elsewhere in *The Christian Year*, the unsatisfactoriness of life ensures that we find satisfaction in the Author of creatures rather than the creatures themselves. Then, as theodicies often do, the poem offers a speculative alternative to the world as we know it and shows how fitting its apparent deficiencies actually are. This we might call the Leibnitz principle, or, in Pope's phrasing, the idea that "Whatever IS, is RIGHT":[65]

> Or what if Heaven for once its searching light
>   Lent to some partial eye, disclosing all
> The rude bad thoughts, that in our bosom's night
>   Wander at large, nor heed Love's gentle thrall?
>
> Who would not shun the dreary uncouth place?
>   As if, fond leaning where her infant slept,
> A mother's arm a serpent should embrace:
>   So might we friendless live, and die unwept.[66]

Tennyson's fear that friends in the afterlife have access to the thoughts of their survivors might have been triggered by these stanzas:

> Shall he for whose applause I strove,
>   I had such reverence for his blame,
>   See with clear eye some hidden shame
> And I be lessened in his love.[67]

His solution to his dilemma is to imagine that the dead, as it were by contagion with transcendent Divinity, "watch, like God, the rolling hours / With larger other eyes than ours, / To make allowance for us all."[68]

According to Keble, there is also a positive side to our separation (by death or by physical circumstance) from those we love. The denial of happiness invites us to exercise the theological virtue of hope, to whose place in the scheme of things he once again gives a providential sanction. Hope figures large in the definition of faith adduced by the author of Hebrews—"faith is the substance of things hoped for, the evidence of things unseen" (11:1)—and it is this hope that carries us through our sorrows. In an inset palinode, Keble gives up unreal fantasies that image perfection in this world, but he takes care to exempt hope from the judgment:

> Farewell, for her, th' ideal scenes so fair—
>   Yet not farewell her hope, since Thou hast deign'd,
> Creator of all hearts! to own and share
>   The woe of what Thou mad'st, and we have stain'd.

The Incarnation gave God firsthand knowledge of human misery, since he volunteered to share it and so reversed the customary human yearning for heaven. In earlier stanzas Keble had claimed that omniscience would be intolerable to humankind, for it would access all the concealed data of sin. God, on the other hand, "Knows all, yet loves us better than He knows." That, perhaps, is an instance of holy wit, for it implies that love mercifully clouds the otherwise keen vision of omniscience.

"Twenty-fifth Sunday after Trinity" amplifies the adage "Red sky at night is the shepherd's delight, / Red sky in the morning is the shepherd's warning." Keble, however, has supplanted the color of the sunset with a rainbow, and thus summoned up memories of a Wordsworth poem:

> My heart leaps up when I behold
> A rainbow in the sky:
> So was it when my life began;
> So is it now I am a man;
> So be it when I shall grow old,
> Or let me die![69]

Whereas Wordsworth uses the rainbow as a common denominator between childhood and adult experience, Keble use the emblem as a differentiating factor. Beginning with the shepherd of the proverb, he allows his canny peasant the judgment to qualify any Wordsworthian leapings:

> Pride of the dewy morning!
> The swain's experienc'd eye
> From thee takes timely warning,
> Nor trusts the gorgeous sky.
> For well he knows, such dawnings gay,
> Bring noons of storm and shower,
> And travellers linger on the way
> Beside the sheltering bower.[70]

All of which serves as the vehicle for an extended metaphor, the tenor of which Keble expounds in the next stanza. He effects the transition with a clerical pun, allowing shepherd to blend with pastor. From his own experience in rural parishes, Keble can claim that morning rainbows, or, in de-allegorized language, "the eye of keenest blaze" and "quick-swelling breast," often produce disappointments, whereas "the voices low and gentle" and "timid glances shy" are more likely to issue in final perseverance, the evening rainbow of fulfillment. Perhaps because "quick-swelling breasts" aspire for things beyond the bounds of parochial life, they migrate toward the urban centers, and that, in Keble's eyes, comes close to mortal sin! To twentieth-century ears, at least, the poem seems to strike a false note by exalting mere docility.

After the long stint of nonspecific lectionary poems for the long, nonspecific season of Trinity, "Sunday Next before Advent" has a welcome sense of occasion. It offers a solemn survey of the Christian year, and so poises itself to complete the cycle. Keble begins in apparent hopelessness, and, as in "Second Sunday in Lent," imagines an infidel sailor *in extremis*:

> Will God indeed with fragments bear,
>> Snatch'd late from the decaying year?
> Or can the Saviour's blood endear
>> The dregs of a polluted life?
> When down th' o'erwhelming current toss'd
> Just ere he sink for ever lost,
> The sailor's untried arms are cross'd
> In agonizing prayer, will Ocean cease her strife?
>
> Sighs that exhaust but not relieve,
> Heart-rending sighs, O spare to heave
> A bosom freshly taught to grieve
>> For lavish'd hours and love mis-spent!
> Now through her round of holy thought
> The Church our annual steps has brought.
> But we no holy fire have caught—
> Back on the gaudy world our wilful eyes were bent.[71]

The abrupt movement from the turmoil of the ocean drama to the survey of the Christian year in "Now through her round" gives the impression that questions formulated so frantically at the start cannot be answered, or, like all rhetorical questions, contain an answer in their unanswerability. Nonetheless, after an intermission of several stanzas, Keble does in fact turn back to the opening position of his poem and complete its unfinished arch: "But love too late can never glow: / The scatter'd fragments Love can glean, / Refine the dregs and leave us clean." The interlusive stanzas, a sorry record of human failing and unresponsiveness, imply the necessity of grace. Without its supplement, the poverty of our devotional life would be irredeemable. In his catalog of the major feasts and sacraments of the Church, Keble calls to mind the procedure of Wordsworth's great

sonnet "The world is too much with us," in which, after listing the
perennial beauties of nature, the poet denounces our insensitivity
to them. "For this, for everything, we are out of tune" inverts the
customary word order, and, placing the prepositional phrase in the
forepart of the sentence, enacts the laggardness and indifference of
the reaction that comes behind:

> This sea that bears her bosom to the moon;
> The winds that will be howling at all hours,
> And are up-gathered now like sleeping flowers;
> For this, for everything, we are out of tune;
> It moves us not.[72]

And this is Keble's analogous way of proceeding:

> No, not for each and all of these,
> Have our frail spirits found their ease.
> The gale that stirs th' autumnal trees
>   Seems tun'd as truly to our hearts
> As when, twelve weary months ago,
> 'Twas moaning bleak, so high and low,
>   You would have thought Remorse and Woe
> Had taught the innocent air their sadly thrilling parts.

In his speculation about the causes of this apathy and falling off
Keble suggests that it might proceed from our sense of incapacity,
the belief that *imitatio Christi* lies beyond our human reach. But he
points at once to the communion of saints to refute such feeble ex-
cuses: "But see, around His dazzling shrine / Earth's gems the fire
of Heaven have caught." The rest of *The Christian Year* centers on
those very gems, which of course the reader is expected to have
calated on the correct days set out in the *Prayer Book* calendar, but
which the sequential format of this survey requires us to treat as a
separate section.

Since the Anglican Church of Keble's day did not permit the
veneration of the saints (that mild form of worship that Catholics
call *dulia*), his poems about saints' days are only commemorative in
nature. However, being High Church in allegiance, he was also ready
to treat saintly lives as paradigms for our own, especially in circumstances to which the template of Christ's own life cannot be fitted.
In *Lyra Innocentium* he urges little children, "Do as they do."[73] "Do
as they do," because it requires at least a basic knowledge of

hagiology, might for Evangelicals imply the idolatrous deflection of sight from God to creature, but it would not have raised eyebrows within the mainstream of the Church of England. Later, however, when under Newman's influence Keble had moved closer to the Roman position, he went so far as to say that the saints of Scripture "were (be it spoken with all reverence) types of the ALMIGHTY; their conduct in many respects analogous to His economies; and if we use ourselves to speak or think of them hastily or irreverently, the transition will be found less violent than some imagine, to irreverent ways of thinking and speaking about Him."[74]

"St. Andrew's Day" does not, however, present the saint as "a type of the ALMIGHTY" but rather as the ideal pattern of brotherhood. It begins on a mentorial note, as though Keble were posing a Socratic question, and, sifting and editing the responses that might have been given, guiding us to the truth as he conceives it:

> When brothers part for manhood's race,
>   What gift may most endearing prove
> To keep fond memory in her place,
>   And certify a brother's love?[75]

Not surprisingly, a disjunctive breaks in on these worldly idylls: the memory of shared experience is, for Keble, too weak and ephemeral a basis for a lasting bond: "But yet our craving spirits feel." The mentor then turns magus, and once again baptizes the romance formulae of charms and spells that the Age of Sensibility had brought into vogue. Spells, like their modern descendant, the recipe, are often manuals of instruction, as witness these lines from *The Eve of St. Agnes:* "As, supperless to bed they must retire, / And couch supine their beauties, lilly white."[76] But even though Keble relies on the language of medieval superstition ("love-charm"; "potent with the spell of Heaven"), he uses it to articulate the orthodox doctrine of *imitatio Christi.* The Church figures as a domestic dwelling and the Savior as an intimate friend:

> First seek thy Saviour out, and dwell
>   Beneath the shadow of His roof,
> Till thou have scann'd His features well,
>   And known Him for the Christ by proof:
>
> Such proof as they are sure to find
>   Who spend with Him their happy days,

> Clean hands, and a self-ruling mind
> Ever in tune for love and praise.

There are characteristic Keble-isms in these stanzas—the anadiplosis that uses "proof" to weave an irresistible line of logic; and the way in which spiritual disposition is itemized as a list of physical metonyms ("Clean hands, and a self-ruling mind"), an effect already encountered in "Septuagesima Sunday" ("Pure eyes and Christian hearts").[77]

The lyric for the feast of St. Thomas follows a different strategy, for here Keble paraphrases a Gospel narrative of the Resurrection in terms more suited to a medieval morality play. Again and again historical figures, St. Thomas amongst them, evaporate into abstract qualities which Keble's footnotes then reconvert back to their concrete equivalents:

> Reason and Faith at once set out
>   To search the SAVIOUR's tomb;
> Faith faster runs, but waits without,
>   As fearing to presume,
> Till Reason enter in,[78]

If at first glance this seems a little strained, we must remember that it simply extends the symbolic historiography of St. John's Gospel, as when, for example, Pilate, arraigning Christ as Johannine Truth, asks, "What is truth?" (John 19:38). Even so, Keble's allegory, dictated by the preexisting format of the narrative, undergoes a some procrustean adjustments here and there. One might argue that presumption is the very element in which Faith has its being, and that Reason is more likely to hang back in its reluctance to accept the miraculous. After all, we are told that St. John *followed* St. Peter in accepting the Resurrection: "Then went in also that other disciple, which came first to the sepulchre, and he saw, and believed" (John 20: 8). The virtue of this sort of allegorization, however, lies in its timelessness. Just as for Aristotle "poetry . . . is a more philosophical and a higher thing than history: for poetry tends to express the universal, history the particular,"[79] so for Keble, as for patristic exegetes before him, abstract truths (*credenda*) are concealed within the integument of narrative (*acta*). Hence he takes the highly specific "came" of John 20:24 ("But Thomas, one of the twelve, called Didymus, was not with them when Jesus came") and widens it in

the first verse to encompass the thirty-odd years of the Incarnation—
"We were not by when Jesus came"—and from that launching pad
of generalization begins his allegorical gloss. He takes each and every participant in the events following the Resurrection as a prototype of contemporary Christian postures, whether it be the
Magdalene in her faithfulness or the disciples on the Emmaus road.
Since the Emmaus meal took place at evening ("Abide with us: for it
is toward evening, and the day is far spent"—Luke 24:29), he is able
to modulate from external to internal darkness, darkness gradually
dispersed by a Resurrection dawn. No leaping from the tomb in this
slow, self-augmenting *éclaircissement*:

> Thus, ever brighter and more bright,
> > On those he came to save,
> The Lord of new-created light
> > Dawn'd gradual from the grave;
> Till pass'd th' enquiring day-light hour,
> And with clos'd door in silent bower
> The Church in anxious musing sate,
> As one who waits redemption still had long to wait.

Keble has flanked "brighter" with a doublet ("more bright") so as to
stabilize and reify that brightness by paring away its extra syllable,
and has furthermore shored up his allegory by imposing the dignified title "Church" upon disciples otherwise frightened and discom-
posed. Since almost all the protagonists have, as it were, found their
typological "abrogation" in contemporary modes of belief and devotion, there remains one more role in search of a meaning, that of
the Christian doubter, "Scarce daring, through the twilight pale, /
To think he sees the Lord." And that "twilight pale," coming as it
does upon "th' enquiring day-light hour," is banished by the clarity
of "every line."

"The Conversion of St. Paul" begins with a characteristic *compositio loci*:

> The mid-day sun, with fiercest glare,
> Broods o'er the hazy, twinkling air;
> > Along the level sand
> The palm-tree's shade unwavering lies,
> Just as thy towers, Damascus, rise
> > To greet yon wearied band.

> The leader of that martial crew
> Seems bent some mighty deed to do,
>   So steadily he speeds,
> With lips firm clos'd, and fixèd eye,
> Like warrior when the fight is nigh,
>   Nor talk nor landscape heeds.[80]

Withholding the identity of a protagonist is a standard narrative device in the nineteenth century. Of the countless instances in Dickens, we could cite that chapter midway through *Little Dorrit* that introduces several familiar characters without at first naming them, though their various leitmotifs give us clues.[81] Dickens uses this device to connect new selves with old not by authorial fiat but by inference. In much the same way, Keble gives us time and place (midday; the towers of Damascus), but literally estranges us from St. Paul by suppressing his name and using that deictic of separation: "The leader of *that* martial crew." Keeping up the fiction of our estrangement, he describes the light that accompanied the conversion as though it were a phenomenon observed by a co-traveler: "What sudden blaze is round him pour'd[?]" This follows the Ignatian method to the letter, but, as so often in Keble, the stage is set only to be dismantled at a stroke, like the masque in *The Tempest*. He deploys one of his allegorical abstractions to break from the narrative in Acts into the eternal present of moral discourse. St. Paul has been displaced by a morality play personification, while the local judgment on the Damascus road dilates into the *dies irae*: "'Who art Thou, Lord?' he falters forth— / So shall Sin ask of heaven and earth / At the last awful day." And so we find ourselves plumped down in the middle of Matt. 25:44, and searching our consciences for that more subtle allotrope of Saul's persecutions, our neglect of the poor and the dispossessed in whom Christ remains perpetually embodied. The solution to such failures will lie in Christocentric habits of thinking—which cues a return to St. Paul, that most Christocentric of teachers, an apostle who has carried the blaze of his conversion into every aspect of his life. At this point the poem dramatizes its own imagery by ending the march of its syntax and allowing grammatical elements to mill about like fragmentary sounds:

> And as each mild and winning note
> (Like pulses that round harp-strings float
>   When the full strain is o'er)

> Left lingering on his inward ear
> Music, that taught, as death drew near,
>   Love's lesson more and more:

Such marvelously expressive writing as this earned *The Christian Year*'s its many reproaches of obscurity.

If "The Conversion of St. Paul" marries discrete texts for their mutual illumination, so too does "The Purification," where a beatitude from the Sermon on the Mount coalesces with the story in Luke. The result seems to have been too rambling in the eyes of hymnologists, and so the beatitude component (or rather two stanzas of it) has been excised and set up as a hymn in its own right, propped up by an additional two that *Hymns Ancient and Modern* ascribes to "others." But that is to compromise the poem's originality. When Christ pronounced the beatitude in question, his selection of a future verb clearly indicated a subsequent (heavenly) reward for earthly purity—the enjoyment of God's presence. Keble, on the other hand, takes that purity as a precondition for apprehending God incarnate, and sees it most richly embodied in St. Mary, St. Joseph, Simeon, and Anna. Augmented by the angels, these saints form a royal procession, the regality of which will declare itself only to those with the right disposition:

> Yet are there more with Him
> Than all that are with you—
> The armies of the highest Heaven,
> All righteous, good, and true.[82]

Whereas such earthly-minded spectators as kings and rulers see only a humble domestic party, the pure in heart see the procession of God incarnate, and that apparent negation ("No pomp of earthly guards") is revoked in the disclosure of the angelic train. If a false is canceled by a true messianic ideal in this domestic tableau, Keble concludes that wrong ideas still obtain and that pride prevents us from seeing God. For that, we must conform our vision to St. Joseph's and St. Mary's, a vision of perfect trustfulness and humility: "Him child-like sires, meek maidens find, / Where pride can nought discern." Only pedants might cavil at the fact that Keble has played fast and loose with the original phrasing of the beatitudes, where the meek are promised not that they shall see God but that they shall inherit the earth.

Since St. Matthias is an altogether faceless saint (next to no information exists beyond a sentence recording his succession to in the apostolate), Keble does not attempt to focus on the man in his patronal poem but rather to define his ideals of priesthood. The format he chooses owes something to the *Beatus vir* formula, familiar above all from the Psalms—the Eighty-Fourth, for example: "Blessed *is* the man whose strength *is* in thee; in whose heart are the ways of *them*." Here and elsewhere, various conditions of blessedness hang on the antecedent noun, a feature typical of poems that set out to inscribe an ideal. (Henry Wotton's lyric "On the Character of a Happy Life" comes to mind: "How happy is he born and taught / That serveth not another's will.")[83] Then again, Keble seems to have drawn on the sense of liturgical antiphony in such psalms as the Twenty-Fourth:

> 3 Who shall ascend into the hill of the LORD? or who shall stand in his holy place?
> 4 He that hath clean hands, and a pure heart; who hath not lifted up his soul unto vanity, nor sworn deceitfully.

The same antiphonal rhythm occurs in "St. Matthias": "Who is God's chosen priest? / He, who on Christ stands waiting day and night."[84] And so the magisterial definition of the office proceeds stanza by stanza, until the speaker, overwhelmed by his own ideals, despairs of realizing them. Because this definition of the priesthood is so exalted (pitched above the earlier asides about rural pastors), Keble comes to share the sense of unworthiness that Herbert dramatizes in "Aaron."[85] However, the middle stanzas set forth Christ's various promises concerning the Church, and fortified by these, he eventually plucks up courage to embrace his vocation.

The poem entitled "The Annunciation of the Blessed Virgin Mary" has, like that about the Purification, been pruned for church use. But, once again, the congregational concern for succinctness and clarity has maimed an otherwise imaginative and searching meditation. Only the Marian part of Keble's lyric has reached the pages of the *English Hymnal* (as "Ave Maria! blessèd Maid!"), but its greater part centers rather on the sonship of Christ. The Incarnation entailed the *kenosis* (or emptying) of Christ's godhead, and it is this which renders him accessible to sinners:

> Oh! Thou who deign'st to sympathize
> With all our frail and fleshly ties,

> Maker yet Brother dear,
> Forgive the too presumptuous thought,
> If, calming wayward grief, I sought
>   To gaze on Thee too near.
>
> Yet sure 'twas not presumption, Lord,
> 'Twas thine own comfortable word
>   That made the lesson known:
> Of all the dearest bonds we prove,
> Thou countest sons' and mothers' love
>   Most sacred, most Thine own.[86]

Keble correlates the idea of the unworthy priest with the idea of a transcendent Divinity; that which is limited must feel its limitation in the face of the illimitable. Even Keats approaches his pagan mysteries with a sense of trepidation: "O Goddess! hear these tuneless numbers, wrung / By sweet enforcement and remembrance dear, / And pardon that thy secrets should be sung";[87] and Collins expresses his unworthiness as the officiant of his pagan evensong: "If aught of oaten stop or pastoral song / May hope, chaste Eve, to soothe thy modest ear."[88] The Incarnation on the other hand, turning on a partial and provisional disempowerment of God, gives Keble confidence to approach the mighty Maker as a "Brother dear." But since this is a poem about the Annunciation, Keble has also to focus the privilege of the woman chosen as *Theotokos*. Not surprisingly, therefore, when he adapts a famous clause in the *Te Deum* to this end, he omits altogether the harshness of "thou didst not abhor" (*Tu, ad liberandum suscepturus hominem, non horuisti Virginis uterum*):[89]

> When wandering here a little span,
> Thou took'st on Thee to rescue man,
> Thou hadst no earthly sire:

By logical deduction, we can assume that the brotherhood of Christ, lacking as it does an earthly sire, entitles Keble to claim the heavenly motherhood of St. Mary—all this very daring for an Anglican poem in 1823. The very use of the Latin words for the angelic salutation later in the poem must have made hackles rise all over England, though it is conceivable that the thousands of Evangelicals who bought and read *The Christian Year* gave wide berth to the later poems of the collection as offering homage to "deified sinners." (For the more extreme among them, the very use of saints' days instead of calendar dates embodied a kind of idolatry.) Keble, on the other hand, had a real devotion to the Virgin Mary, and even recommended the recitation of the *Ave Maria* in *Lyra Innocentium*, where he further developed his belief that Christians are her adoptive children. It is perhaps the mark of Anglican Mariology that, unlike its ultramontane equivalent in the Roman Catholic Church, the figure of the Virgin is always depicted with the Christ child in her hands, not in deific isolation. This maternal note certainly predominates in Keble's fervent poem, the stanzas of which read like a pastiche of medieval lyric:

> Ave Maria! blessèd Maid!
> Lily of Eden's fragrant shade,
>   Who can express the love
> That nurtur'd thee so pure and sweet.
> Making thy heart a shelter meet
>   For Jesus' holy Dove?
>
> Ave Maria! Mother blest,
> To whom, caressing and caress'd,
>   Clings the Eternal Child;
> Favour'd beyond Archangels' dream,
> When first on thee with tenderest gleam,
>   Thy new-born Saviour smil'd:—

The chiastic inversion of "blessèd Maid" and "Mother blest" recalls the paradoxes of thirteenth- and fourteenth-century lyrists, and so too the allusion to "lily of Eden," which implicitly turns "Eva" into "Ave" in the manner of a medieval hymn:

> All this world was forlore
> Eva peccatrice,
> Till our Lord was ibore,
> De te genetrice.
> With "Ave" it went away[90]

Perhaps Froude had alerted Keble to the riches of medieval hymnology.

We have seen how *The Christian Year* repeatedly stresses the frailty of human happiness and how its theodicies make use of the "Pulley" principle. Much the same idea informs the design of "St. Mark's Day," which takes the quarrel of holy men (St. Paul and St. Mark) as grounds for its own pessimism:

> Oh! who shall dare in this frail scene
> On holiest happiest thoughts to lean,
>   On Friendship, Kindred, or on Love?
> Since not Apostles' hands can clasp
> Each other in so firm a grasp,
>   But they shall change and variance prove.[91]

However, as in "The Pulley," Providence does give humankind enough inklings of divinity to make it thirst for heaven. Keble presents a general proposition ("The Saviour gives a gracious boon / When reconcilèd Christians meet") before narrowing the focus back to the reconciliation of the apostles.

A distrust of earthly happiness also pervades "St. Philip and St. James." This recapitulates the structural arc of "Epiphany" by claiming that, in contrast to childhood and old age, midlife tends to be marked by indifference and even infidelity:

> Dear is the morning gale of spring,
>   And dear th' autumnal eve;
> But few delights can summer bring,
>   A Poet's crown to weave.[92]

Keble gives a clue to his own misprision here, however, for his thoughts focus on self-advancement. Indeed, the "Poet's crown" (even the capitalization creates an image of self-important grandeur) recalls two Metaphysical poems: Herbert's "Collar," where a disconsolate and self-centered speaker complains "Have I no bayes to crown it? / No flowers, no garlands gay?"[93] and Marvell's "Coronet": "Thinking, (so I my self deceive) / So rich a Chaplet thence to weave / As never yet the king of Glory wore."[94] Keble's self-concern is slightly more innocent than Marvell's, however, for it relates to his retirement from a world hostile to Christian values. Nonetheless, he is forced to judge himself for being blind to the comparable suffering of Christ's Incarnation—God's firsthand encounter with human pain. This experiential emphasis issues naturally enough in self-reproach. Human sorrow will always pale in comparison with the divine:

> O shame upon thee, listless heart,
>   So sad a sigh to heave,
> As if thy SAVIOUR had no part
>   In thoughts, that make thee grieve.

And just as the Incarnation provided a prelude to the great work of redemption, so too ought sublunary suffering be borne with the knowledge of its eventual relief. That is an obvious enough resolution to the poem, but Keble introduces an additional nuance, based upon his epigraph from St. James. If redemption renders tolerable the load of human misery, then human joy ought likewise to be tempered with a sense of its frailty. The result is an Aristotelian mean between extremes, and it places the soul in the temperate middle ground of the Church:

> Thus souls, by nature pitch'd too high,
>   By sufferings plung'd too low,
> Meet in the Church's middle sky,
>   Half way 'twixt joy and woe.

Among the "treasur'd hopes and raptures high" (one assumes) is the "Poet's crown" and all the egotism that goes with it. That makes "St. Philip and St. James" a sort of "Jordan" poem.

The real name of St. Barnabas was Joses, but he earned his nickname (son of consolation) by the compassion that Keble celebrates in this patronal poem. As so often, however, the saint's identity is blurred and generalized to encompass the human type he exemplifies. This minister to human sorrow is so self-effacing, so imbued with proto-Tractarian reserve, that he is an indetectable as angels:

> The truest wisdom there, and noblest art,
>   Is his, who skills of comfort best;
> Whom by the softest step and gentlest tone
>   Enfeebled spirits own,
> And love to raise the languid eye,
> When, like an angel's wing, they feel him fleeting by:—
>
> *Feel* only—for in silence gently gliding
>   Fain would he shun both ear and sight,[95]

If, as Keble claims in his somber opening stanza, the whole world is sick, then it follows that the Church will function as an asylum and a hospital. Hence the comfort of enclosure and embowerment in the section that invites all refugees to the bosom of the Church. Such invitations often entail a sense of pilgrimage, as witness Donne's "Twicknam Garden," where the speaker also promises reassurance and refreshment: "Hither with crystal vials, lovers come, / And take my tears, which are love's wine."[96] An additional allusive color from Gray's "Eton College Ode" suggests that like the schoolboys of Eton, those within the embrace of the Church enjoy a paradisal exemption from at least some woe. "Sweet thoughts are theirs" recollects the phrasing of "Gay hope is theirs."[97] Of course Keble, even while he might privately advocate a limited cultus of St. Mary, could not recommend, and probably would not have wanted to recommend, a general invocation of St. Barnabas. He does offer a sort of Anglican compromise towards the end of his poem, though, suggesting that the saints retain a sympathetic consciousness of human misery:

> Ye banquet there above,
> Yet in your sympathetic heart
> We and our earthly griefs may ask and hope a part.

Keble claims that the saints in heaven would not, in the privilege of their comfort, forget the turmoil of their lives on earth. And in that memory would lie an impetus toward voluntary, unsolicited intercession:

> Comfort's true sons! amid the thoughts of down
>   That strew your pillow of repose,
> Sure, 'tis one joy to muse, how ye unknown
>   By sweet remembrance soothe our woes,
> And how the spark ye lit, of heavenly cheer
>   Lives in our embers here,

In his *Elegy*, Gray had pointed out how "in our ashes live their wonted fires,"[98] and in Keble's own adaptation of Gray in turn, a spark of apostolic fervor persists in the dying fires of the modern church, entitling it to call upon the saints that have gone before.

In "St. John Baptist's Day" Keble retracts the idea of saints as sympathetic spectators of earthly life, suggesting rather that they are shielded from its distress. This, as "Twenty-Fourth Sunday after Trinity" makes plain, can be endured only by a Being whose omniscience is supported by omnipotence:

> Now resting from your jealous care
> For sinners, such as Eden cannot know,
>   Ye pour for us your mingled prayer,
> No anxious fear to damp Affections's glow,
>   Love draws a cloud

From you to shroud
Rebellion's mystery here below.[99]

That plural address, while it implicitly embraces the communion of the saints, actually specifies only two figures—Elijah and St. John the Baptist, New Testament saint and typological antecedent. The ecclesiastical calendar sometimes pairs saints, as in the conjunction of St. Philip and St. James, or it singles out whole groups (Holy Innocents) and echelons (St. Michael and All Angels). Keble's procedure here seems to have no precedent. In the first stanza, Elijah and the Baptist dawn upon dark apostasy in a manner that recalls the march of Hyperion in "The Progress of Poesy":

Night and all her sickly dews,
Her spectres wan and birds of boding cry,
He gives to range the dreary sky:
Till down the eastern cliffs afar
Hyperion's march they spy and glittering shafts of war.[100]

And here is Keble's version:

Twice in her season of decay
The fallen Church hath felt Elijah's eye
Dart from the wild its piercing ray:
Not keener burns, in the chill morning sky,
The herald star,
Whose torch afar
Shadows and boding night-birds fly.

In Keble's eyes, the contemporary church calls for new rigor and purity (exemplified above all by Elijah's contest with Baalism and St. John's ascetic lifestyle) This double-exposure of prophet on saint accordingly offers a pattern for the priesthood in 1826. The remodeled clergy must purge and reorient their ailing Mother, and so inherit the starry fires associated with prophet and saint alike: "And ready prove / In fires of love, / At sight of Thee for aye to burn."

In "St. Peter's Day" Keble offers a transcript of the dreams that might have visited the saint before his escape from prison. It begins with an invocation of Christ, uttered, it would seem, in the present; but the second stanza suggests that Keble has projected himself back into the past, and that the invocation was answered then, not now:

> Thou thrice denied, yet thrice belov'd,
> 　Watch by Thine own forgiven friend;
> In sharpest perils faithful prov'd,
> 　Let his soul love Thee to the end.
>
> The prayer is heard—else why so deep
> 　His slumber on the eve of death?
> And wherefore smiles he in his sleep
> 　As one who drew celestial breath?[101]

The situation is a moving one, for the poet has taken up watch beside the vulnerable sleeping figure of the saint, rather like Coleridge beside his son in "Frost at Midnight"[102] or, more than a century later, Auden beside his lover in "Lay your sleeping head, my love."[103] The dreams attributed to St. Peter are reminiscent on the one hand, and prophetic, on the other, the denial of Christ giving cause for expiation ("One look lives in him, and endears / Crosses and wrongs where'er he rove") and martyrdom ("Then laid on him th' inverted tree"). The crucifixion on an upended cross shows that Keble was happy to use apocryphal materials when they suited his purpose. Once Keble has traced the course of St. Peter's escape, which he treats as a temporary stay of execution, he cuts to the future climax of the martyrdom and, displacing the angel with the figure of Christ himself, effortlessly releases the saint from his cross as dream intersects with reality: "Then from his cross to spring forgiven, / And follow JESUS out of sight."

"St. James's Day" owes something to Herbert's "Love (III)," not only because it centers on the trope of the messianic banquet but also because it presents an intimate colloquy between soul and Savior. Somewhat unfairly (for the sake of structural economy), Keble attributes the ambitious enquiry of St. James's mother to the saint himself. Since the poem begins with his admission into heaven, that enquiry is relayed in a flashback:

> "Seek ye to sit enthron'd by Me?
> 　"Alas! ye know not what ye ask,
> "The first in shame and agony,
> 　"The lowest in the meanest task—["][104]

But that flashback is left flashing, as it were, and instead of following the narrative further, Keble eagerly assimilates the situation to his own life, learning (as in "St. Philip and St. James") to moderate his spiritual ecstasy with memories of the suffering that must accompany it:

> If ever on the mount with Thee
> I seem to soar in vision bright,
> With thoughts of coming agony,
> Stay Thou my too presumptuous flight:
> Gently along the vale of tears
> Lead me from Tabor's sunbright steep,
> Let me not grudge a few short years
> With Thee tow'rd Heaven to walk and weep:

Two allusions to Gray shape this careful mediation of extremes (St. James, be it noted, was chosen to witness both the Transfiguration and the Agony in the Garden). First there is a reminiscence of Milton's fate, who "rode sublime / Upon the seraph-wings of Ecstasy, / The secrets of the abyss to spy"[105] and who was thus—or so Gray's conceit maintains—blinded by the vision. And then there is the "vale of tears," which combines the valley of the shadow of death in Ps. 23, with the "cool sequestered vale of life" in Gray's *Elegy*.[106]

In "St. James's Day" we saw Keble projecting himself into the life of the saint and reliving its key episodes through the Ignatian method. In "St. Bartholomew," on the other hand, he conducts his meditation in the spectatorial third person. Its opening stanza furnishes proof—if proof were needed—of Keble's intense conservatism. Not only is he bent on retaining the formulae and speech habits of the eighteenth-century poets upon whom he cut his teeth, but he also retains outmoded materials on the grounds (one presumes) of their superior "poeticality":

> Hold up thy mirror to the sun,
> And thou shalt need an eagle's gaze,
> So perfectly the polish'd stone
> Gives back the glory of his rays:[107]

It is odd to find bestiary lore applied in 1821: the world had long discarded belief in the eagle's self-renewal, and yet Keble feels no embarrassment about recycling it here. It is not a conscious medievalism (such as Keats or Scott might have employed), for there is no frame to give it the status of pastiche. So too the reference to the "polish'd stone." In Keble's day, mirrors were almost universally made by attaching tinfoil to glass, but here he borrows an archaizing periphrasis from *King Lear*: "Lend me a looking-glass; / If that her breath will mist or stain the stone, / Why, then she lives."[108] The point of Keble's parable (directing the mirror at the sun and earth in turn) is to show the way in which Scripture combines the divine and the quotidian. This is not the glass through which we see darkly in 1 Cor. 13:12, but rather the medium of radiant disclosure: "The veil is rais'd; who runs may read, / By its own light the truth is seen." The stanza simply asserts its transition, however, and there is next to nothing in the rest of the poem to connect it to its elaborate prelude about Scripture.

Since Keble recoiled from cities, we must salute the fair-mindedness of "St. Matthew," which tries to find hints of heaven where even Shelley perceived elements of Hell ("Hell is a city much like London— / A populous and a smoky city.")[109] He begins by invoking "hermits blest" and "holy maids," an address which, centuries after the dissolution of the monasteries in England, is bound to raise a smile. Presumably he means the country people, even though their lusty appetites were attested by the many pregnant brides at Hursley: "Ye hermits blest, ye holy maids, / The nearest Heaven on earth, / Who walk with God in shadowy glades."[110] Since St. Matthew began life as a tax collector, far removed from hermits blest and holy maids, Keble bravely infers that grace is no more a respecter of places than it is of persons. However, even as he imagines the vocation of Levi, he cannot blot out a glimpse of Galilee ("But not in vain, beside yon breezy lake, / Bade the meek Publican his gainful seat forsake"). To help him in his revaluation of urban sinfulness, Keble turns to Wordsworth's sonnet "Composed upon Westminster Bridge, September 3, 1802":

> This City now doth, like a garment, wear
> The beauty of the morning; silent, bare,
> Ships, towers, domes, theatres, and temples lie
> Open unto the fields, and to the sky;
> All bright and glittering in the smokeless air.
> Never did sun more beautifully steep
> In his first splendour, valley, rock, or hill;[111]

Keble had confidence enough in Wordsworth's judgment to accept the epiphany at second hand, for one rather doubts if he ever experienced it himself:

> These gracious lines shed Gospel light
>> On Mammon's gloomiest cells,
> As on some city's cheerless night
>> The tide of sun-rise swells,
> Till tower, and dome, and bridge-way proud
> Are mantled with a golden cloud,
> And to wise hearts this certain hope is given;
> "No mist that man may raise, shall hide the eye of Heaven."

There is, however, one stroke of imagination that is wholly original to Keble. He has displaced real gold (hidden in a Spenserian cave of Mammon) with the intangible gold of sunlight on cloud, a cloud that in turn recollects the cloud of witnesses in Heb. 12:1.

"St. Michael and All Angels," falling as it does in the second half of the year, provides Keble with an occasion to write a sweeping conspectual poem like "Sunday Next Before Advent." It gathers up various angelic references in the Gospel narratives, from the Nativity through the Temptation and the Resurrection to the Ascension, and ends by looking forward to the *dies irae*. There are moments, however, when this workmanlike précis takes fire. Keble celebrates the Nativity with a conceit of cosmic unsettlement—ideas familiar from such seventeenth-century poems as Herbert's "Whitsunday," where a miraculous event is signalized by a disruption of stable elements. But where Herbert strikes a note of comic whimsy ("The starres were coming down to know / If they might mend their wages, and serve here"),[112] Keble chooses rather to be magisterial: "As if the stars should leave / Their stations in the far ethereal wild, / And round the sun a radiant circle weave."[113] No less vivid is his version of the *pleroma*, which dissolves the figure of Christ into sheer luminousness, his robe streaming like the tail of a comet: "Brighter and brighter streams His glory-robe, / And He is lost in light."

"St. Luke" functions as a pendant for "St. Mark's Day," for whereas the latter traced an earnest of heaven in the reconciliation of St. Mark and St. Paul, the latter describes St. Paul's desertion by Demas. The poem makes use of Hogarthian tableaux to which Keble directs the reader with strong moralizing gestures:

> Look in, and see Christ's chosen saint
>> In triumph wear his Christ-like chain;
> No fear lest he should swerve or faint;
>> "His life is Christ, his death is gain."

.   .   .   .

Pass a few years—look in once more—
 The saint is in his bonds again;
Save that his hopes more boldly soar,
 He and his lot unchang'd remain.

But only Luke is with him now:—
 Alas! that e'en the martyr's cell,
Heaven's very gate, should scope allow
 For the false world's seducing spell.[114]

Keble's distress at this infidelity registers in a touching, childlike coda where his clinging to God figures in a chiasmus so secure that everything seems simply to bounce off its field of containing tension ("Thy true, fond nurselings closer cling, / Cling closer to their Lord and thee").

"St. Simon and St. Jude" seems to wheel chaotically from topic to topic, but as so often in *The Christian Year*, careful reading will disclose a line of thought, which in this instance makes a detour through a footnote. Keble has taken his epigraph from the Epistle of St. Jude ("That ye should earnestly contend for the faith which was once delivered to the saints") but feels compelled to supply additional nuances to the blunt "contend": "ἐπαγωνίζεσθαι: 'be very anxious for it:' 'feel for it as for a friend in jeopardy'." There lies the key to the poem, which revolves the topics of empathy and consolation. We begin with the Crucifixion, being invited, like St. John, to take a mother into our care—not St. Mary, as it happens, but the Church for which, as in Newman's *Essay on the Development of Christian Doctrine*, she is here the type:

Seest thou, how tearful and alone,
 And drooping like a wounded dove,
The Cross in sight, but Jesus gone,
 The widow'd Church is fain to rove?

Who is at hand that loves the Lord?
 Make haste, and take her home, and bring
Thine household choir, in true accord
 Their soothing hymns for her to sing.[115]

As the Evangelist consoled the grieving mother, so (by implication) must we console our fellow Christians in their travail. With the image of the mother and surrogate son in place, Keble can use the paired saints of his title to focus the doubling of the apostolic commission in Mark 6:7. That in turn prompts a discourse on ways in which doublings can lead to mediation—we remember Keble's crucial sense of the Church as a "middle sky" ("St. Philip and St. James")—and the "Aristotelian" spirituality of the *via media*. Thus by a sort of inter-infection, youth acquires the serenity of age, and age the fervor of youth, and a double first from Oriel can give it all up for a rural curacy:

> He loves when age and youth are met,
>   Fervent old age and youth serene,
> Their high and low in concord set
>   For sacred song, Joy's golden mean.
>
> He loves when some clear soaring mind
>   Is drawn by mutual piety
> To simple souls and unrefin'd
>   Who in life's shadiest covert lie.

If that last stanza clearly reflects the life choice of the author, it also recalls the grave, sympathetic tone of the *Elegy Written in a Country Churchyard*—a reminiscence which gives the stanza the right generality. Its use of shade as an emblem of retirement furthermore shows the temperamental link between Gray and Keble. In the "Ode on the Spring" the poet searches for a "broader, browner shade,"[116] while after the distressing events of 1845, when Newman's secession had rocked the Church of England, Keble conceived Anglicanism in similar terms. Outside its "shade" lies the glare of public disgrace and controversy: "For sure thine holy Mother's shade / Rests upon thine ancient home."[117] The end of the poem presents the poet as pastor/ shepherd, watching his flock by night. The landscape, never clearly specified, has turned mountainous, presumably to register the difficulty of the pilgrimage to a Truth set (in Donne's words) on a "huge hill, / Cragged and steep,"[118] and also no doubt to hint at an imminent theophany. The fellow shepherd whose voice he hears is St. Jude, calling across the centuries, and returning the poem to its epigraph: "How timely then a comrade's song / Comes floating on the mountain air, / And bids thee yet be bold and strong— / Fancy may die, but Faith is there."

In "All Saints' Day" Keble abandons that dissociation of faith and fancy, conceived as an opposition of permanence and transience,

in "All Saints' Day." Here "purged eyes" turn out to be eyes clarified by an imaginative penetration beneath the dross of experience:

> Sure if our eyes were purg'd to trace
> God's unseen armies hovering round
> We should behold by angels' grace
> The four strong winds of Heaven fast bound,[119]

Keble even goes so far as to revoke Newtonian physics, suggesting
that his grand cityscape (flooded by the dawn in "St. Matthew," here
set against an apocalyptic sunset) owes its stability to the intercession of all saints: "But sure from many a hidden dell, / From many
a rural nook unthought of there, / Rises for that proud world the
saints' prevailing prayer." London, Keble implies, is another Sodom,
its destruction held off only for the sake of a few good people.

"All Saints' Day" is followed by "Holy Communion," which
introduces the final phase of *The Christian Year*. This celebrates the
weekly and monthly events that flesh out the annual contour, and
so recalls the two lyrics ("Morning" and "Evening") with which
Keble prefaced his design. Like "All Saints Day," the poem displaces
empirical data with their imaginative alternative, and re-cements
the bond between faith and fancy that had been severed in the final
stanza of "St. Simon and St. Jude":

> The eye of Faith, that waxes bright
> Each moment by Thine altar's light,
> Sees them e'en now: they still abide
> In mystery kneeling at our side;[120]

"They" are Saints Paul and John, whose "comfortable words" (along
with those of Christ) have been incorporated into the poem. We have
seen elsewhere in *The Christian Year* how, when it suits his purpose,
Keble can take segments of Scripture and, with only minimal adjustments, slot them into the meter of his poems. Here, however, he
has strayed so far from his original texts that he has had to footnote
them. Christ's address to all "that travail and are heavy laden" becomes "Come unto me, thou trembling heart" while St. John's claim
that "we have an Advocate with the Father" has been given a con-
versational vigor that anticipates Browning: "'What? fall'n again?
yet cheerful rise['']." To find the reason for these adaptations, we
must turn to the opening invocation of the poem which sets up a

tension between power and compassion: "O God of Mercy, God of Might." It is might that causes the heart to tremble and mercy that converts divine advocacy into a cheerful invitation to rise. The same paradoxical forces cause the communicant to waver later on in the poem. We know from Crabbe that some rural parishioners avoided Communion for fear of eating and drinking damnation unto themselves, and it is this misgiving, at a time when daily masses were unknown in the Church of England, that Keble addresses here. What I find striking, however, is the way in which the poet has come within a hair's breadth of embracing the Tridentine version of the Sacrament. Whereas the *Prayer Book* wordily insists that Christ made "a full, perfect and sufficient sacrifice, oblation, and satisfaction," Keble seems to endorse the idea of its reenactment: "Fresh from th' atoning sacrifice / The world's Creator bleeding lies." However, in the 1850s, when Bishop Forbes was censured for his views on the real presence, Keble wrote a pamphlet in which, as summarized by Lock, "he proves that the Fathers have always held that Christ is the real Priest, and that the offering in the Eucharist is really identical with, not the Sacrifice on the Cross, but rather with the present offering of Himself by Christ in heaven; the same Person offers the same Body and Blood, but for different purposes—'on the Cross for expiation of sin, with vicarious suffering, pain, bloodshedding, and death; in heaven for pleading and application of those atoning pains'."[121] But without these nice discriminations, the image of a fresh, bleeding sacrifice in "Holy Communion" seems to offer a statement almost as radical (given the date of its composition) as the emendation of "Not" to "As" sanctioned by the dying Keble in "Gunpowder Treason." As Georgina Battiscombe has pointed out, the "stanza is one of several contrasting the doctrines of the Church of England with those of the Church of Rome, but in its altered form it differs in no way from accepted Roman Catholic teaching."[122] The coda of "Holy Communion" falls back on a more sober Protestant position, however, because it replaces carnal reality with a metonym: "Offering by turns on JESUS' part / The Cross to every hand and heart." That, and the Platonic dispensing with shadows in the final stanza, helps distinguish the Anglican doctrine of the real presence (unspecific though it be) from transubstantiation.

"Holy Baptism" is the poem over which Wordsworth shook his head regretfully—not at its content, which is Wordsworthian in the extreme, but at its neoclassical diction. One imagines that he winced above all at the phrases "lucid flood" and "tender gem," which reactivate the Latin etyma *lucidus* ("transparent") and *gemma* ("bud") under the English surface of the words. But what Wordsworth saw as vicious latinizing, we can gratefully accept as enrichment, for *lucidus* can also mean "filled with light," and so establish a continuity between the "lucid flood" of the baptismal font and the oceanic light of God's presence, that idée fixe of *The Christian Year*. In *Lyra Innocentium* Keble, the idea similarly fixed in his mind, would liken baptism to a sacramental immersion in "Love's boundless sea,"[123] while in "Judas's Infancy" he speaks of "baptismal wave and flame."[124] *Gemma* also releases other meanings into the poem, for in addition to its organic sense, it can signify a gemstone. "Tender gem" therefore fuses the mineral brilliance of the stars and the softness of flowers, from which it is later distinguished:

> O tender gem, and full of heaven!
> Not in the twilight stars on high,
> Not in moist flowers at even
> See we our God so nigh.

A gem "full of Heaven" obviously contains the blossom of sanctity, and it seems likely that Keble remembered Herbert's "Sunday" when he wrote this line, for the "tender gem" develops the idea of the Sabbath's being the "fruit of this, the next worlds bud."[125] Then again, *gemma* can mean a signet ring, an idea picked up in the stanza that Keble addresses to parents: "But happiest ye, who seal'd and blest / Back to your arms your treasure take." There is a venerable line of succession behind this "sealing" that extends through St. Paul to Abraham. In Rom. 4:11 we read that "he [Abraham] received the sign of circumcision, a seal of the righteousness of the faith which *he had yet* being uncircumcised." The Greek word here is σφραγίς, originally meaning "a seal," but eventually applied, by a metonymic shift, to baptism. If Wordsworth caviled at the diction of "Holy Baptism," he could not have faulted Keble's treatment of the child, as much indebted to the *Intimations Ode* as to "The Progress of Poesy." It is easy to trace the line of succession through three consecutive excerpts from Gray ("the dauntless child / Stretched forth his little arms and smiled")[126] through Wordsworth ("Mighty Prophet! Seer blest!")[127] to Keble ("His innocent gestures wear / A meaning half divine").

"Catechism" continues the same reverential treatment of the child—a sort of dress rehearsal for *Lyra Innocentium*. Here, however, the "tender gems" have burst into "spring-flowers in their best array,"[128] and set in cryptomilitary order (like the blooms in *Upon Appleton House*),[129] as if anticipating the militarism of "Confirmation," the poem it precedes: "These bright and order'd files." Here too Keble carries over the seal image of "Holy Baptism" ("Bear, to the end, Thy Spirit's seal").[130]

"Confirmation" also demonstrates Keble's heavy debt to Old Testament materials, a debt deplored his *Times* obituary.[131] Instead of reworking the stylized armor in Eph. 6:11, he chooses rather to draw on the bloody genocidal battles of Joshua: "The shadow of th' Almighty's cloud / Calm on the tents of Israel lay."[132] In an odd structural twist, however, Keble's attention shifts from the confirmation candidates to the congregation and preaches on a favorite topic—the mediation of extremes:

> Draw, Holy Ghost, Thy seven-fold veil
> Between us and the fires of youth;
> Breathe, Holy Ghost, Thy freshening gale,
> Our fever'd brow in age to soothe.

In the "middle skies" of the Church, fervor must be moderated, lassitude invigorated. The "seven-fold veil" refers, of course, to the seven gifts of the Holy Spirit extrapolated from the Epistles of St. Paul; Keble was not to know what horrific developments his image would undergo at the hands of Oscar Wilde and Hugo von Hofmannsthal!

In "Matrimony," also, we find a careful mapping of middle ground between eros and agape. Indeed, it would be truer to speak of the subordination of erotic to agapaic love, for the balance of power tilts firmly toward the latter: the carnal is admitted only as the basis of procreation: "All blessings of the breast and womb / Of Heaven and earth beneath."[133] This rather staid epithalamion even goes so far as to anathematize other more impassioned examples of the form. The following palinode directs itself *inter alia* at Catullus:

> Ill fare the lay, though soft as dew
>   And free as air it fall,
> That, with Thine altar full in view,
>   Thy votaries would enthrall
> To a foul dream, of heathen night,
> Lifting her torch in Love's despite,

> And scaring with base wild-fire light
> The sacred nuptial hall.

Since even the puritanical Spenser felt no comparable urge in his two wedding songs to exorcise the fires of Hymen, it would seem that Keble has turned to less obvious models. The baleful imprecation ("Ill fare the lay") originates in a poem of mourning, not of celebration—Goldsmith's *Deserted Village* ("Ill fares the land, to hastening ills a prey, / Where wealth accumulates and men decay").[134] More strangely still, Keble picks up the renunciatory phrasing of Gray's "Sonnet [on the Death of Mr Richard West]" ("These ears, alas! for other notes repine, / A different object do these eyes require"[135] in "Far other strains, far other fires, / Our marriage grace"). Marriage, in a word, has been desexualized. For Keble, as for the Fathers before him, the Song of Songs had nothing to do with the flesh.

"Visitation and Communion of the Sick" also begins with a renunciation, this time of "Youth and Joy,"[136] which, we are told, have "eye-glances" too "bright, / Too restless for a sick man's sight." Keble seems to have had *Il Penseroso* in mind here—"Hence vain deluding joys / The brood of folly without father bred"[137]—but we ought not to forget the exorcism at the start of Gray's "Ode for Music": "'Hence, avaunt, ('tis holy ground) / 'Comus and his midnight-crew['],"[138] which he would later replicate in "Prayer at Home and at Church"—"Avaunt, ill thoughts and thoughts of folly! / Where christen'd infants sport, that floor is holy."[139] Despite the many precedents for the start, the rest of the poem proves to be more original. It comprises a set of narrative tableaux, rather like the "ruined cottage" part of *The Excursion*, where the narrator comes back to the same space at carefully marked intervals and monitors the story implicit in change: "I journeyed back this way;"[140] "I returned, / And took my rounds along this road again";[141] "when, / In bleak December, I retraced this way."[142] Whereas all the other narratives in *The Christian Year* are biblical paraphrases, Keble here follows the example of Crabbe and Wordsworth and draws on personal experience to render general truths:

> I came again: the place was bright
> "With something of celestial light"—
> A simple Altar by the bed
> For high Communion meetly spread,

> Chalice, and plate, and snowy vest.—
> We ate and drank: then calmly blest,
> All mourners, one with dying breath,
> We sate and talk'd of Jesus' death.
>
> Once more I came: the silent room
> Was veil'd in sadly-soothing gloom,

In *Lyra Innocentium* Keble would subsequently use the same device in "Bereavement."[143]

"Burial of the Dead," falls back on the poet's more usual versifying and moralizing of a biblical incident. To the extent therefore that it relays the story of the widow's son in Luke 7:13-14, it differs from the other poems associated with church ritual:

> Yet is the voice of comfort heard,
>   For Christ hath touch'd the bier—
> The bearers wait with wondering eye,
> The swelling bosom dare not sigh,
>   But all is still 'twixt hope and fear.
>
> E'en such an awful soothing calm
>   We sometimes see alight
> On Christian mourners, while they wait
> In silence, by some church-yard gate,
>   Their summons to the holy rite.[144]

There is the familiar *sicut/ita* design that relates this poem to earlier items in *The Christian Year*. Rather less predictable, however, is the long seasonal proem, in which Keble seems to evoke the autumnal dirge in Shakespeare's sonnet 73:

> That time of year thou mayst in me behold,
> When yellow leaves, or none, or few do hang
> Upon those boughs which shake against the cold,
> Bare ruined choirs where late the sweet birds sang.[145]

In *his* autumn scene, Keble seems even to have recalled the image of a ruined monastery that some commentators have read into the first quatrain of sonnet 73:

> Where bright leaves, reddening ere they fall,
>   Wave gaily o'er the waters brown.

> And let some graceful arch be there
> With wreathéd mullions proud,
> And burnish'd ivy for its screen,

Many defensive and controversial poems begin with a *quis dicit?* formula, whether it be visibly present in the indignant start of "Jordan (I)"—"Who sayes that fictions onely and false hair"[146]—or, folded up within the lines that initiate Shakespeare's "My mistress' eyes are nothing like the sun"[147] and Wordsworth's "Scorn not the Sonnet."[148] Keble, in his effort to give autumn a better press than Shakespeare had done, falls back on a curious romance formula, familiar from Apuleius's story of Psyche and possibly inspired also by Ezekiel's transportation to Zion: "Waft him . . . and gently lay him down." The idyll is characterized also by another fanciful indulgence—the decor-by-*fiat* in the poetry of Hunt and Keats. Here is a comparable episode from *I Stood Tip-Toe*: "And let a lush laburnum oversweep them, / And let long grass grow round the roots to keep them / Moist, cool and green."[149] Just as the autumn can prove a season not of loss but of graceful acceptance (as the ruin accepts its own reoccupation by nature), so, Keble argues, can human grief be tempered by resignation. The death of someone close to us should not prompt wintry thoughts but rather an expectation of the spring—"Hope of new spring and endless home." Because Keble has omitted an article from the phrase "endless home," he has given "home" the status of an adverb, so that heaven registers as a sense of eternal containment rather than as a locality.

There is a distinct weakening in *The Christian Year* from this point onward, as though Keble had written the material to complete the cycle, not relieve the overflowing heart in which his *Praelectiones* would later trace the mainspring of poetry. Since these items were added only in 1828, they have that forced and dutiful air of those poems cobbled up ad hoc by the laureates of past centuries. That is not to deny that the characteristic Kebelian note is struck from time to time, but only to say that it is seldom sustained enough to render its context very memorable. That marginal ceremony called the "Churching of Women" shows Keble so desperate in his bid to flesh out the situation that he has to invoke the fancy that in an earlier and sterner poem had been displaced by faith. Orthodox Catholics differentiate the various offices of angels, but not their temperaments. A dearth of material prompts Keble to this odd supposition, however, when he invokes "One known from all the seraph band / By softer voice, by smile and wing / More exquisitely bland."[150] But when he speaks of the "all-gracious Dove's" brooding in the "tender bosom" of his subject we at once recognize a ventriloquial echo of Herbert: "Listen sweet Dove unto my song, / And spread thy golden wings in me; / Hatching my tender heart so long."[151]

We have already noted how discomfitingly comfortable Keble seemed to be with Old Testament vindictiveness. His later rejection of the liberalizing *Essays and Reviews* would likewise testify to a conservatism capable of enunciating "The Gibeonites" in *Lyra Innocentium* ("Be sure thou crush him: deal him blow on blow: / Set thy stern foot upon his neck, and hide / His corse, unpitying, in the dark cave's side").[152] "Commination" likewise celebrates the vicious office once inserted into Morning Prayer. The poet who twenty or so years later would write a poem regretting the "disuse of excommunication"[153] was clearly made of stern stuff. Although the rubric for "Commination" directs the priest to recite from the pulpit, Keble is eager to recover the bleak sublimities of Mount Ebal, displacing English surplice with priestly ephod:

> Why swell'st thou not, like breeze from mountain cave,
> High o'er the echoing nave,
> The white-rob'd priest, as otherwhile, to guide,
> Up to the Altar's northern side?—[154]

The following poem, "Forms of Prayer to be Used at Sea," proves much more sympathetic to modern ears, for it is a moving hymn to divine omniscience. Despite its awkward moments (Hurrell Froude objected to the internal contradiction of "piping" and "rustling" in line 4) it confers epistemological reality—like Berkeley's God—on materials otherwise out of sight

> The shower of moonlight falls as still and clear
> Upon the desert main
> As where sweet flowers some pastoral garden cheer
> With fragrance after rain:[155]

If this recalls the deprivation stanza of Gray's *Elegy*,[156] so too do the lines that marry Ariel's dirge[157] with the turfy graves of his churchyard:

> The eye that watches o'er wild Ocean's dead
> Each in his coral cave,

> Fondly as if the green turf wrapt his head
> Fast by his father's grave.—

Ocean burial might sometimes present to mourners a desolate sense of placelessness, of a body weltering in the parching wind. Keble revokes that in the silence and security of coral caves, comfortingly removed from the surface turmoil of the sea.

"Gunpowder Treason," the "feast" on which Manning waved Protestant flags after Newman's resignation from St. Mary's, evokes so such vehemence from Keble here. Rather he remembers the tone of Herbert's "The British Church,"[158] where the Anglicanism figures as a *via media* (though not in Newman's sense) between the ornateness of Rome and the austerity of Geneva. Herbert's lyric has no doctrinal basis, but Keble surveys some theological differences between Rome and Canterbury. What makes the poem unusual is not so much its uncontroversial quietude, as its sirenical quality. The English Church sings a beguiling invitation to rest and comfort in the best tradition of the Lorelei. This is how she dispenses with the doctrine of purgatory:

> If thou hast lov'd in hours of gloom,
>   To dream the dead are near,
> And people all the lonely room
>   With guardian spirits dear,
>
> Dream on the soothing dream at will:
>   The lurid mist is o'er,
> That shew'd the righteous suffering still
>   Upon th' eternal shore.[159]

This makes a useful pendant to *Villette*, where a Roman tract, equally stocked "soothing dreams," makes no impression on the staunch Kebelian Lucy:

> It was milk for babes—the mild effluence of a mother's love towards her tenderest and her youngest, intended wholly and solely for those whose head is to be reached through the heart. . . .
>   I remember one capital inducement to apostasy was held out in the fact that the Catholic who had lost dear friends by death could enjoy the unspeakable solace of praying them out of purgatory. The writer did not touch on the firmer peace of those whose belief dispenses with purgatory altogether.[160]

A "mild effluence" also characterizes Keble's invocation of Charles I as a martyr, a martyr to the untenable belief in the divine right of kings. Its unctuous, reverential tone is a little hard to swallow when we set it against Marvell's plausible (because judicious) account of the same event in his *Horatian Ode*.[161] The monarch whom H. G. Wells described as "one of the meanest and most treacherous occupants the English throne has ever known"[162] Keble presents as a man who loved "to trace her [the Anglican Church's] daily lore"[163]—so lovingly, be it remembered, that he cast a *sortes vergilianae* before the Battle of Naseby. And when we turn from this dubiously pious poem to "The Restoration of the Royal Family," we are jolted still further by the false position into which the poet's royalist sympathies have led him. Since all royalists are required to distinguish office from personality, Keble is not alone in hailing the return of Charles II in almost messianic terms:

> Such were the lights and such the strains,
> When proudly stream'd o'er Ocean plains
> Our own returning Cross;[164]

Nicholas Jose has cataloged similar excesses in Restoration literature: "Charles was born, or restored, as a redeemer. Such was the language and vision of imperial panegyric, elaborate, metaphorical and metaphysical"[165]—a language and vision as unreal as Keble's own when it comes to acknowledging the irregular life of the "redeemer" in question. But can he have felt very comfortable in writing a poem about the accession with George IV on the throne? Probably not, however firmly he might have tried to differentiate regal office and dissolute person. Because he cannot hymn a fat Adonis of fifty, however, "The Accession" actually rises to greater heights than its congeners, for it presents ideals rather than doubtful historical judgments. Particularly striking is the way in which it gives a lapidary strength and energy to its pronouncements by drumming them in by chiastic repeats and anadiplosis:

> Let storm and darkness do their worst;
> For the lost dream the heart may ache,
> The heart may ache, but may not burst:[166]

And again: "Such is the thought of Love and Might, / True Might and ever-present Love"; "Heaven's light is pour'd on high and low;

/ To high and low Heaven's Angel spake." This is Keble at his most Drydenic.

"Ordination" has little of the clarion confidence and issues strong verbal patterning of "The Accession." It is Keble at his most reserved and tentative, recalling once again his misgivings about the demands of an office so demanding. By placing the prayerful silence of Israel alongside the awful silence that precedes the breaking of the seventh seal in Revelation, he builds a temporal arch of reference. Ordinands must look to the type-laden past and to the judgmental, apocalyptic future for their bearings and temper the comfort of their office with a sense of "holy Fear."

Having thus taken stock of *The Christian Year*, we can acknowledge that it is best savored as a cumulative experience, an unspooling of gentle, unstrenuous verse, marked by the author's continuity of purpose and consistent vision. There is, as we have seen, nothing flashy, nothing boldly innovative, nothing that might draw attention to the "meaner shrine" of the poet and so deflect the reader's attention from God himself. Keble felt uncomfortable with the self-dramatization and flaunting ingenuity of conceits, and even felt compelled to apologize for his beloved Herbert's "failing" in this regard. But after we have made the necessary subtractions and adjustments, after we have made due allowance for the doctrine of reserve implicit in his compositional procedure, we cannot help acknowledging that *The Christian Year* does embody an original voice and that its poetry is full of quiet surprises. Biblical events are given quirkish turns and integrated into the experience of nineteenth-century Christians, daring elisions of item with item all but hide behind the even tread of the verse, and allusions develop new resonance in the poetic acoustic into which they have been transposed. A certain patience is needed to perceive these things, just as little brown birds (warblers and the like) will disclose themselves only to watchers who are prepared to sit it out. Those little brown birds, when eventually they *do* show themselves, might well disappoint a temperament habituated to species more gorgeous and arresting, but there can be no denying their charm, nor the fact that their charm is partly connected with their shyness.

4

Newman's Contribution to
Lyra Apostolica: I

IN contrast to *The Christian Year*, which intended "to promote a *sober* standard of feeling in matters of practical religion and to illustrate the *soothing* tendency of the Prayer-book,"[1] *Lyra Apostolica* proved altogether more combative in conception and design. Ian Ker has set out the circumstances of its birth in his biography of Cardinal Newman:

> Towards the end of November 1832, Newman wrote to H. J. Rose to say that he and Froude were planning . . . "to systematize a poetry department" for the *British Magazine*, the review recently started by Rose "to make a front against the coming danger." Their "object" would be "to bring out certain truths and facts, moral, ecclesiastical, and religious, simply and forcibly, with greater freedom, and clearness than in the *Christian Year*." They could not promise "greater poetry" than Keble's best-selling collection. But they would undertake to produce for each number four short poems, each bringing out forcibly *one* idea.[2]

Nothing could have been farther from the inceptors' minds than a desire to soothe, and their stress on "clearness" and need for "bringing out forcibly *one* idea" points to the posterlike simplicity and vigor of their purpose. The Catholicism latent in *The Christian Year* was to be formulated in strong, unequivocal terms, and the gage tossed down before Erastians and "Liberals" in the Establishment. Needless to say, whereas the gentle obliquities of *The Christian Year* cut across sectarian divisions, *Lyra Apostolica* drove in as many wedges as it could find. The banner cry of the Movement, "Choose your side," would admit of no partial or Laodicean commitment to the cause. We can monitor the difference between Keble's and Newman's enterprise by juxtaposing two Presbyterian reactions. Shairp's admiration for *The Christian Year* has already been cited,[3] and here is Alexander Whyte's vehement rejection of *Lyra Apostolica*: "Surely never was written book worse named than this proud, scornful, ill-natured, and most anti-apostolical ebullition."[4] He goes on to remark that its prefatory motto "is out of the *Iliad,* and, most certainly, the fierce little volume is written much more in the spirit of the *Iliad* than in the spirit of the New Testament."[5]

Rather as Christ's apostolic commission centered only bare essentials ("Provide neither gold, nor silver, nor brass for your purses, Nor scrip for *your* journey, neither two coats, nor yet staves"—Matt. 10:9–10), so a sort of bleak minimalism pervades Newman's early verse. The gentle, decorative amplitude that Keble had taken forward from the Age of Sensibility finds no place in these austere, uncompromising utterances. But even though commentators have associated them with stone, they have none of the elaborateness ordinarily conveyed by the epithet "lapidary." Here the physical constraints on inscription have led rather to strict economy. Perhaps the distance between Newman's idiom and Keble's can be traced to the latter's mental cast, which was more adaptable and progressive than his mentor's. Like Keble, Newman once held eighteenth-century diction in high esteem, and, as Maisie Ward points out, remarked that Pope's Homer "is the finest body of verse, certainly in this, perhaps in any language; it is so harmonious, sweet and elegant throughout."[6] Unlike Keble, however, he moved on to forge a mode of expression so spare as to seem in advance of its time. What William Barry has said of his prose style could be applied with very little adaptation to the early verse as well:

> Thus he is the opposite of Carlyle, whose vocabulary we learn as though a foreign tongue, which in fact it is, made harder still by what Johnson would term the "anfractuosities"—a prophet's dialect, not the medium by which men in the street talk to one another. Newman's, on the contrary, is common English made perfect.[7]

Which is not to say that the limpidity and chasteness of Newman's early verse disqualifies it from its prophetical office—indeed, most of his contributions to *Lyra Apostolica* are as oracular as any exhortation by Carlyle—but it does stress the directness and clarity for which most oracles do not strive. The economy and pungency of his poems sometimes bring even Housman to mind.

Economy, of course, is often the handmaiden of reserve, and reserve itself the mother of oracularity—all of which explains the sorts of metaphor invoked by Meriol Trevor (and Emily Bowles before her) to register her reaction to *Lyra Apostolica*:

> The sermons, as literary creations, are like an avenue of wonderful trees; the poems stark as bits of stone in a field. Yet they have a directness and simplicity which has its own attraction.
>
> There was more in many young ladies than a liking for prettiness, and one, Emily Bowles, recorded that when she read Newman's verses in the *Lyra* they seemed like "startling oracles or newly discovered inscriptions in a strange character," quite different from the "running water" of Keble's gentle hymns. There was certainly a fierce ring to some of the lines, and a prophetic strain in their attack on the contemporary scene. The chief heroes were the patriarchs of Israel and St. Paul. But some were intensely personal, and concerned with guilt, penitence and absolution.[8]

This endorses, almost to the very phrasing, a judgment made by J. M. Cameron:

> Keble's verses are thin and sweet, faint echoes of the great period of Anglican religious verse in the seventeenth century: Newman's are almost disagreeably arresting. They breathe the determination of a reformer of the Church; but the fierceness towards the internal and external enemies of the Church is tempered by anguish for sin and an intermittent sense of desolation.[9]

In what Trevor terms a concern with "guilt, penitence and absolution" and Cameron "anguish for sin" we can detect the obsessive mortification associated with the Oxford Movement, which *Punch* would satirize in 1851. In this cartoon a soulful, emaciated Newman presents his "discipline" to an outraged (and portly) Mr. Punch.[10]

Even though an almost violent urgency characterizes many of his verses, Newman's first contribution to *Lyra Apostolica* is surprisingly tender. Entitled "Home," it purports to present the Anglican Church not in its contemporary state but rather in its Catholic potentiality. The key word here is "vision," which creates the epistemological wavering in the poem. Romantic poets had used "vision" to suggest an earthly reality touched by the numinous (as in the "Ode to a Nightingale"—"Was it a vision, or a waking dream");[11]

but in conventional religious usage, a vision is wholly divine. In Newman's poem, both senses are present and compete against each other:

> Where'er I roam in this fair English land,
> The vision of a temple meets my eyes:
> Modest without; within, all glorious rise
> Its love-enclustered columns, and expand
> Their slender arms. Like olive-plants they stand
> Each answering each, in home's soft sympathies,
> Sisters and brothers. At the Altar sighs
> Parental fondness, and with anxious hand
> Tenders its offering of young vows and prayers.[12]

Although the likelihood of influence is slim indeed, it is hard not to think of Blake's "London" when one reads the opening lines of this poem. There, too, firsthand knowledge results from an active survey ("I wander thro each charter'd street")[13] and there, too, something visionary and supernatural supervenes upon that empiricism. For while at first blush Newman would seem to be describing any parish church in any village of England ("Modest without"), the very use of "temple" cuts from historical to typological time, and the interiors (while obviously taking the bundled shafts of the decorated style as their starting point) are soon animized and allegorized in a way that recalls Herbert's "Church-floore":

> Mark you the floore? that square & speckled stone,
> Which looks so firm and strong,
> Is *Patience*:[14]

Here a floor, concretely specified, is at once dissolved into its allegorical equivalent—a movement reproduced in Newman's shift through simile from "love-enclustered columns" to "olive-plants" and thence to the metaphoric equation of "Sisters and brothers." The living temple (or body of Christ) is presided over by a presence called "Parental fondness"—a tactful way of hinting "Father," the Catholic honorific reserved for priests.

A similar ontological slipperiness occurs in the rest of the poem:

> The same and not the same, go where I will,
> The vision beams! ten thousand shrines, all one.
> Dear fertile soil! what foreign culture bears

> Such fruit? And I through distant climes may run
> My weary round, yet miss thy likeness still.

"The same and not the same" obviously reproduces a line from *A Midsummer Night's Dream*—"And I have found Demetrius like a jewel, / Mine own and not mine own"[15]—which implies a magical discontinuity between the old and the new. So likewise Newman, whose vision of a harmonious, sacerdotal church is undercut by its actual state, however consistently the vision may "beam" beyond it. The ten thousand shrines, recalling the host of Revelation, point once again to the poem's ideality and make it difficult for the reader to find purchase on the hard facts of Newman's experience. His motive, however, is clear. He wishes to establish his credentials as a faithful adherent of the English Church, but also as a visionary who believes it ought to reclaim its Catholic heritage. So when he gives an exilic twist to the final lines (recalling the dispirited, weary tone of Goldsmith's *Traveller*), he implies that no Continental church can boast the apostolic purity of Anglicanism. Having established his "home church" as a community of "Sisters and brothers," he implies that his disaffected, unrooted wanderings will confirm the intimacy and sense of belonging to which that church it entitles him. The georgic images of "fertile soil" and "culture" similarly impart a note of sanctity to the English Church and recall the messianic planting in Isa. 61:3: "that they might be called the trees of righteousness, the planting of the LORD, that he might be glorified."

The following lyrics, though untitled, all center on home allegiance and exile. Even so, "Ere yet I left home's youthful shrine" does not reflect Newman's personal experience, but rather takes the romantic topos of the world-weary traveler (hardly applicable to someone visiting the Mediterranean for the first time) to monitor the contest between the world and the spirit:

> Ere yet I left home's youthful shrine,
>   My heart and hope were stored
> Where first I caught the rays divine,
>   And drank the Eternal Word.
>
> I went afar; the world unrolled
>   Her many-pictured page;
> I stored the marvels which she told,
>   And trusted to her gage.[16]

Home has undergone an allotropic transformation in this lyric, for it no longer implies the *British* Church but rather the Church in the abstract. This the speaker accepts trustingly in childhood but betrays in adult years. By drinking (rather than eating) the Word made flesh, Newman creates the image of a suckling babe, one that furthermore clutches (as babies do) at the sunbeams irradiating its life. (In his first draft, he had used a verb less concretely infantile—"Where first I hailed the rays divine.")[17] Either consciously or unconsciously, Newman has recollected a line from Gray's *Elegy* ("But Knowledge to their eyes her ample page / Rich with the spoils of time did ne'er unroll")[18] and fused it with another from "The Progress of Poesy" ("Bright-eyed Fancy hovering o'er / Scatters from her pictured urn / Thoughts that breathe and words that burn"),[19] so as to oppose the world as a composite image of knowledge and fancy against the faith of childhood. The weaned child strays, and a temptress displaces the nurse. Childlike drinking now changes to the eager, gluttonous ingestion of "quaff'd," and the adult is robbed of his earlier innocence:

> Her pleasures quaff'd, I sought awhile
> The scenes I priz'd before:
> But parent's praise and sisters' smile
> Stirred my cold heart no more.

An autobiographical element lodges in the abstract allegory of the poem, for the singular parent would almost certainly refer to the widowed Mrs. Newman, and the plural sisters to Mary, Jemima, and Harriett—he was already alienated from Charles and was fast losing patience with Francis. What makes this poem so unusual is its withheld resolution. The speaker remains in his alienated state, typologically harnessed to Adam exiled from paradise. There never was a religious poem more discomfiting, more intent on exalting godliness above comfort: it leaves its subject standing in the cold. The world, as in Marvell's "Garden"[20] is associated with heat and exposure—"sear," "fierce"—redemptive retirement imaged by "Eden's sacred shade." There too we hear an echo of Keble, who describes St. Mary as "Lily of Eden's fragrant shade."[21]

Unlike its predecessor "My home is now a thousand mile away" alludes directly to England, the home from which Newman has been separated as a result of his Mediterranean journey. Like Goldsmith once again, and like Browning after him, he retains a memory of those homely spaces and imprints them on his actual surroundings. However, the nostalgia is no sooner stated than it is placed *sub specie aeternitatis*. Here no wistful catalog of English sights and sounds impinges on an alien Continental landscape, but rather a reminder that all earthly existence involves an exile from heaven and that Earth itself will one day seem like England as the soul speeds towards its judgment. Meriol Trevor has pointed out the curious fact that even at the planning stage Newman tended to associate mortal thoughts with the Froude expedition: "[T]he inspiration of them was this voyage into the unknown, image of the last voyage of death."[22] Hence the "turning" in the curious ablative absolute ("turning me") suggests the turning of Orpheus toward his beloved Eurydice, an attachment that entails forfeiture. It also suggests a renunciation of the experience in hand, as in the repeated turnings of Goldsmith's *Traveller* ("My soul, turn from them; turn we to survey").[23] That turning, moreover, contrasts with the unturnability of "Death's unaverted day" and the irresistible magnetic rise of the soul towards its destiny, so reminiscent of Goethe's great poem on Ganymede:[24]

> And so upon Death's unaverted day,
>   As I speed upward, I shall on me bear
>   And in no breathless whirl, the things that were,

Without turning, that burden of "things that were" will confront the speaker in a vision of judgment, and his soul will be forced to sentence itself even before the *Judex* himself: "So to gaze on till the red dooming hour. / Lord! in that strait, the Judge! remember me!" How magnificently pregnant that adjective is, recalling as it does the red of guilt (*Culpa rubet vultus meus,* in the *Dies Irae,* and the blood of Macbeth that will "the multitudinous seas incarnadine, / Making the green one red").[25] Since it also suggests the red of a sunset that marks the onset of the night, it suggests a cry *in angustiis* like that of Gerontius several decades later: "O Jesu, help! pray for me, Mary, pray!"[26] Much the same shift from biography into an apocalyptic future occurs in "How can I keep my Christmas feast," which Newman wrote in December 1832. By casting doubt on the Catholic priesthood as a vector of grace, he projects a "Protestant" disaffection amid the festivities that surround him. This recalls Gray's "Sonnet [on the Death of Mr Richard West],"[27] in which the mourner finds he cannot participate in the fecund rhythms of great creating nature:

> How can I keep my Christmas feast
>   In its due festive show,
> Reft of the sight of the High Priest
>   From whom its glories flow?
>
> I hear the tuneful bells around,
>   The blessed towers I see;
> A stranger on a foreign ground,
>   They peal a fast for me.[28]

One might expect a loving exaltation of the English Church to follow such a prelude, but Newman turns swiftly—even shockingly—to the *dies irae* once again and projects the discomposure of a proud, imperial people when they too will be arraigned as he is now arraigning Continental decadence:

> O Britons! now so brave and high,
>   How will ye weep the day
> When Christ in judgment passes by,
>   And calls the Bride away!
>
> Your Christmas then will lose its mirth,
>   Your Easter lose its bloom:—
> Abroad, a scene of strife and dearth;
>   Within, a cheerless home!

In his original draft, Newman focused on English people rather than Britons ("O Englishmen, truth-scorners brave"[29]), and targeted their ecclesiology rather than their imperial aspirations. But even though the *sic transit* for which he finally opted gives the poem a wider application, the message remains much the same. Whatever nostalgia Newman may feel for his "home" church, its pride and secularism stand in desperate need of reform. Such apocalyptic endings, though unusual, are not without precedent in poems about imperfect institutions. One is reminded of the expunction of Timon's vulgar home in Pope's *Epistle to Burlington*:

> Another age shall see the golden Ear
> Imbrown the Slope, and nod on the Parterre,
> Deep harvests bury all his pride has plann'd,
> And laughing Ceres re-assume the land.[30]

There is also just a hint of Gray's "Ode on the Spring"[31] in Newman's startling turnabout, where the moralizers (sturdy, anti-Catholic Britons) are moralized in turn, just as the insects in the earlier poem turn on the speaker and administer a Parthian sting.

"Banished the House of sacred rest," another exilic poem, was written on 9 January 1833. In it Newman argues that although the Roman Catholic Church fosters a mindless devotion in the "thoughtless throng,"[32] it nonetheless retains the "apostolic" formularies of the creeds. (The Tractarians scorned Roman *additions* to the deposit of faith but applauded its preservation of primitive materials.) For this reason, he enjoys a transient sense of participating in the communion of saints who, he graciously concedes, are present at Catholic devotions. However, the tone takes on a humbler color in the final two stanzas. Here Newman admits the benefit of a simple Catholic homily that he might have scorned if it had issued from the pulpit of St. Mary's. The spiritual deprivations of the exile have chastened him and taught him to salute the notes of apostolicity wherever they might occur. In a curious way the poem gives an intimation of the path that would eventually lead Newman to see his *Anglicanism* as a banishment from the "House of sacred rest," and to glory in the fact that Catholicism, less intellectually strenuous in the nineteenth century than his native church, made itself accessible to simple or uneducated congregants. This is how he describes Catholic populism in *Loss and Gain*: "What particularly struck him was, that whereas in the Church of England the clergyman or the organ was everything and the people nothing, except so far as the clerk was their representative, here it was reversed."[33] This testifies to the "abiding grace" for which Newman had prayed in "Banished the House of sacred rest."

Newman no doubt composed "Shame" to challenge the complacency of the Anglican establishment, the very establishment that would later be outraged by the mortifications of Froude's *Remains*. It makes interesting use of the romantic topos of the *isolato* and half recalls a passage from Shelley's *Adonais*. Compare "He answered not, but with a sudden hand / Made bare his branded and ensanguined brow, / Which was like Cain's or Christ's"[34] with:

> I bear upon my brown the sign
> Of sorrow and of pain:
> Alas! no hopeful cross is mine,
> It is the mark of Cain.[35]

The same sense of dramatic self-prostration informs "Bondage,"[36] which also turns on the *non sum dignus* theme and renders its self-doubts in passionate, near-Tridentine language. Anglicanism has always tended to discourage such dramatics, as those of us old enough to recall the *Prayer Book* service will know. How many times have sleek, worldly congregations claimed that the burden of their sins was "intolerable" to them—in even, unflurried tones. Poems like "Bondage" point to a new urgency and disquiet in the would-be reformers of the English Church. It is of a piece with Newman's characteristic way of throwing himself into a kneeling position.

"Terror," because it dramatizes the catharsis of auricular confession, is the first specifically Tractarian poem in our survey. Meriol Trevor has found a strain of unreality in this lyric, claiming that the priest "appears in gothic guise, like a character out of a romance, to pronounce (in capital letters) ABSOLVO TE. The priest was not as real to Newman as Moses and Jeremiah and the rest, whose trials made him understand his own; he was an anonymous medieval character in 'austere garb'."[37] Surely, though, the Catholic theory of the priesthood turns on the "anonymous" office, and not on the personality that clothes it. Newman is less interested in character than in function, the more so because he renders the priest as an impersonal channel of grace. One can imagine the somewhat shocking effect the poem must have had in 1833, since its opening vocative would have been taken as an address to God and the poem itself as a colloquy poem, a successor in a tradition that stretches to the seventeenth century. Here is Herbert's "Dialogue": "Sweetest Saviour, if my soul / Were but worth the having."[38] Imagine reading the poem with Herbertian expectations and being drawn up short by a sort of *contre-rejet* in the final line of stanza 1, where "Saint" humanizes the father, and turns God into a priest:

> Father, list a sinner's call!
> Fain would I hide from man my fall—
>   But I must speak, or faint—
> I cannot wear guilt's silent thrall:
>   Cleanse me, kind Saint![39]

That the mode of Anglican spirituality before the Oxford Movement was bland rather than intense can be gathered even from *The Christian Year*, which pacifies strong emotions through the *vis medica* of poetry. Such great hymns as the *Dies Irae*, on the other hand, proved that Catholicism had an altogether more developed tradition of emotive meditation. A sensibility accustomed to such anguished, broken utterances as those of the requiem mass *(Tremens factus sum ego et timeo)* would have had no problems with a poem entitled "Terror." But imagine the shock to a decorous Anglican soul brought up on the tranquility of the "comfortable words"! The dramatic punctuation of dashes, like swooning aposiopesis, must likewise have seemed very discomfiting. Newman was sounding a new note, one that resonated with Crashaw rather than with Herbert and Vaughan. Equally innovative was the way in which the verse ingested its own stage directions, anticipating comparable moments in Browning's monologues: "This wouldst thou? It shall be! / Kneel down, and take the word divine, / ABSOLVO TE."

"Restlessness," like "Terror," takes an established seventeenth-century topic as its starting point, viz., the inadequacy of human praise, tardy or tainted by self-interest. We think once again of Herbert, and most especially of "Easter":

> I got me flowers to straw thy way;
> I got me boughs off many a tree:
> But thou wast up by break of day,
> And brought'st thy sweets along with thee.[40]

Nor should we forget Marvell's "Coronet":

> Alas I find the Serpent old
> That, twining in his speckled breast,
> About the flow'rs disguis'd does fold,
> With wreaths of Fame and Interest.[41]

Both poems share with "Restlessness" a sense of self-dissatisfaction and disquiet—resigned in Herbert, fretful and despairing in Marvell. But whereas Marvell writes in an unresolved present, Herbert chooses the preterite of resolution, a choice that also stabilizes and directs Newman's lyric:

> Once, as I brooded o'er my guilty state,
> A fever seized me, duties to devise
> To buy me interest in my Saviour's eyes:
> Not that His love I would extenuate,
> But scourge and penance and perverse self-hate,
> Or gift of cost, served by an artifice

> To quell my restless thoughts and envious sighs
> And doubts, which fain heaven's peace would antedate.
> Thus as I tossed, He said:—"Even holiest deeds
> Shroud not the soul from God, nor soothe his needs;
> Deny thee thine own fears, and wait the end;"
> Stern lesson! let me con it day by day,
> And learn to kneel before the Omniscient Ray,
> Nor shrink, while Truth's avenging shafts descend![42]

Since the poem is cast in sonnetary form, we need also to invoke Milton's "Sonnet XIX," where anxieties about serving God are also resolved in acquiescent trust. A primary difference lies in the fact the latter comprises a dialogue between the poet and patience personified. While Milton's disregard for works can be explained in terms of his Protestant theology ("God doth not need / Either man's work or his own gifts"),[43] Newman's would be rather more difficult to square with his newfound Catholic allegiance if it were not for the fact that he carried over little pockets of theology from his Evangelical days. (Even in the Catholic *Meditations and Devotions* we find the following utterance: "If I have the right to pray and the gift of impetration, may I not thereby secure that perseverance to the end, which I cannot merit, and which is the sign and assurance of my predestination?")[44] We see this concern in the stern, rather comfortless tercet that ends the sonnet, for while its rhythm of restlessness and submission owes a debt to Herbert's "Collar,"[45] it does not end with the trustful surrender of that poem. Instead we are offered a bleak, stoical submissiveness based on Newman's exaltation of holiness above comfort. This renunciation of spiritual fuss would almost certainly have been inspired by Keble, about whose mode of spiritual direction Walter Lock has this to say:

> At the same time he would avoid the technical terms of "direction" and "auricular confession," "because they are associated in almost all minds with something more absolute, peremptory, and indispensable than we should practically mean by them." He is especially anxious to avoid minute and incessant direction, as the desire of it seemed to him to be a form of self-will.[46]

"A form of self-will"—that is precisely how Newman conceives his anxieties in "Restlessness."

"The Pains of Memory," a sonnet manqué, also helps measure the temperamental divide between Keble's *Christian Year* and

Newman's contributions to *Lyra Apostolica*. Keble has a genuine attachment to natural beauty, even though he chooses to refract it through the stylized lens of poetic diction. Although he makes brave efforts to remind himself of its transience and subordinate role in the scheme of things, he nonetheless allows the attachment to shine through, as when he claims (on what theological grounds it is impossible to say) that flowers have been exempted from the Fall. Newman, on the other hand, when he chooses to document natural beauty, lapses into an uncharacteristic preciosity, as though it were an impertinence to the two great absolutes into which he had sublimated his life:

> I received it [the doctrine of final perseverance] at once, and believed that the inward conversion of which I was conscious, (and of which I still am more certain than that I have hands and feet,) would last into the next life, and that I was elected to eternal glory. . . . I believe it had some influence on my opinions, in the direction of those childish imaginations which I have already mentioned, viz. in isolating me from the objects which surrounded me, in confirming me in my mistrust of the reality of material phenomena, and making me rest in the thought of two and two only absolute and luminously self-evident beings, myself and my Creator. . . .[47]

It is a peculiar kind of sensibility that exalts an abstract doctrine above the ontological reality of hands and feet, and affirms its alienation from the material phenomena in which, by contrast, Hopkins saw a type of the Incarnation. Not surprisingly, when it attempts to address those phenomena it can lead to a corresponding unreality of expression. Here, by way of example, is an outpouring from *Loss and Gain*. It is just possible that the author is laughing at the character in question, but such questions of tone are hard to resolve: "[T]he planes are so touching just now, with their small multitudinous green hands half-opened; and there are two or three such fine dark willows stretching over the Cherwell; I think some dryad inhabits them."[48] The epithets here are general to the point of facelessness ("beautiful"; "fine"), and when the writer attempts to individuate, his language aches with the strain ("small, multitudinous green hands half-opened"), anticipating the "Aesthete idiom" of Oscar Wilde. Later in the same chapter, Newman says that "as we gain views—we advance towards philosophy and truth, but we recede from poetry."[49] *De se fabula*, if by "poetry" Newman means Charles's speech about dryads and willow trees—so different from the cold, impressive denudation of his own verse.

When therefore "The Pains of Memory" informs us of the illusory and corruptible nature of natural things, we do not feel the tension of Keble's verse, where theological orthodoxy runs counter to a strong regional sense:

> What time my heart unfolded its fresh leaves,
>   In spring-time gay, and scatter'd flowers around,
>   A whisper warned of earth's unhealthy ground,
> And all that there faith's light and pureness grieves;
>   Sun's ray and canker-worm,
>   And sudden-whelming storm:—
> But, ah! my self-will smiled, nor recked the gracious wound.
>
> So now defilement dims life's morning springs;
>   I cannot hear an early-cherished strain,
>   But first a joy, and then it brings a pain—
> Fear, and self-hate, and vain remorseful stings:
>   Tears lull my grief to rest,
>   Not without hope, this breast
> May one day lose its load, and youth yet bloom again.[50]

Since Newman's poetic idiom is altogether more austere than Keble's (and altogether more restrained than Charles Reding's prose effusions), it is odd to find him using the *quo tempore* device, that clichéd item of poetic diction. He seems however to have had other motives than "poeticizing" ones in mind. "What time" has a strongly interrogative flavor in English. Even when, as here, it specifies a point in the past, it produces a slight clash with the syntax into which it has been embedded. Add to this the syntactic ambiguity of "and scatter'd flowers around" (did the heart scatter the flowers, or is it a sort of ablative absolute establishing a flowery matrix for bitterness to come?); the fragmentary annotations of the two trimeters; the anacoluthon that cuts from them to the regretful memory of smiling self-will—add all these together, and we have a sense of disorientation and disorder, reducing the past to a chaos in which memory can find no pattern. The pulling and pushing of the syntax against the containment of the stanza and the disruptive exclamation ("But, ah! my self-will smiled") anticipate aspects of Hopkins's verse. Hopkins would certainly have read Newman, and he seems to have learned from him. Could it be that this line is the precedent for the rapt, interjected expletive in "God's Grandeur": "Because the Holy Ghost over the bent / World broods with warm breast and ah! bright wings."[51] And while the voice of Hopkins echoes proleptically at the end of the "octave" of this quasi-sonnet, there is a real echo of Shakespeare's sonnet 33 ("Full many a glorious morning have I seen")[52] at the point where Newman's sense of loveliness is soured by mutability. But whereas Shakespeare's disenchantment serves only to increase his generosity, Newman cannot rise even to the affirmation of a future forgiveness. Like Tennyson, who in "Crossing the Bar"[53] turns Job's *Scio enim* into a tentative hope, he will likewise only *hope* for absolution.

On the evidence of "Dreams," it would appear that the austerity of Tractarian discipline extended also to the unconscious life. Newman seems to have recalled a story about St. Benedict's habit (apocryphal, one hopes) of plunging into briars whenever he dreamt improper dreams. That, at any rate, might account for the thorn image in stanza 2, which serves to check the hubris of a votary otherwise bent on scaling the ladder of perfection. A more obvious source, of course, would be St. Paul's confession of the thorn in his flesh:

> Nay, hush thee, angry heart!
> An Angel's grief ill fits a penitent;
> Welcome the thorn—it is divinely sent,
>   And with its wholesome smart
> Shall pierce thee in thy virtue's home serene,
> And warn thee what thou art, and whence thy help has been.[54]

While on the linguistic surface of the poem, Newman seems to be using "serene" in the atmospheric sense made famous by Keats's sonnet "On First Looking into Chapman's Homer,"[55] it is just as likely to be an epithet qualifying the substantive "home"—in which case the serenity signifies security, that complacent Evangelical conviction of having been "saved." Keble represents the general Tractarian stance in this regard:

> So even with regard to our feelings towards God; we have no right to demand of God or to be uncomfortable if we do not feel sensible comfort or the certain assurance of salvation. "To say that such assurance is a sure and necessary sign of God's favour must be a mistake, if it were only that it contradicts our Lord's agony and the feeling that He had upon the Cross, not to speak of many saintly examples in

Scripture." . . . For such assurance tends so readily to a low standard of life, and to that which seemed to him the most fatal thing to spiritual life, the feeling of self-complacency.[56]

Dreams, because they index the incorrigible motion of original sin within the soul, thus become the humbling instrument of Providence.

The title of "Confession" is deliberately ambiguous. Approaching the poem for the first time, the reader might think that confession has been personified and is speaking in the first person:

> My smile is bright, my glance is free,
>   My voice is calm and clear;
> Dear friend, I seem a type to thee
>   Of holy love and fear.[57]

As we read on, however, we are forced to place a different construction on the title:

> But I am scanned by eyes unseen,
>   And these no saint surround;
> They mete what is by what has been,
>   And joy the lost is found.

In the light of this statement, "Confession" must be redefined as a self-revealing utterance, not the Catholic sacrament. Our initial misconstruction nonetheless offers itself as a solution to the spiritual disorder in which the speaker claims to find himself. The admiring gaze of the dear friend is stanza 1 yields to the horrified glance of a guardian angel, a strong contrast that confirms a Tractarian distinction between the world (indulgent and lax) and the spirit (exacting and remorseless).

"Awe" restates the sense of personal sin adumbrated in "Confession." Tractarian prejudice towards Dissent centered, among other things, on the way in which it handled sacred topics with an easy familiarity. Reserve, indeed, was their formulated response to this perceived "degradation" of the divine. So whereas in Charles Wesley's great hymn Jesus is the "lover of [the] soul" to whose bosom the sinner can fly,[58] Newman's Jesus is like a fierce Byzantine *pantakrator*, where mercy is all but swallowed up in terrific grandeur:

> I bow at Jesus' Name, for 'tis the Sign
> Of awful mercy towards a guilty line.—

> Of shameful ancestry, in birth defiled,
>   And upwards from a child
> Full of unlovely thoughts and rebel aims,[59]

The reader might smile momentarily at the fact that the second line is "guilty" of an unaccommodated stress in the medial anapest ("-cy towards"), but that shaft of Metaphysical wit is soon lost in gloom—Tractarian gloom. We know that contemporary critics were astonished that the journal section of Froude's *Remains* failed to mention the name of Christ, and while Newman here has the grace to name him, he does so in terms so remote and unloving that one wonders once again whether to blame the Calvinism of his youth. This is how Edmund Wilson has defined the posture taken up by "Awe": "To read Calvin's *Institutes* today is to be struck by the brutal audacity of his efforts to eliminate this spirit [the spirit of Jesus] from the Gospels. Christ's gospel of forgiveness quite disappears, as does his offering to all human sinners the possibility of eventual repentance—since faith must precede repentance and only those elected are given faith."[60] That would certainly account for the magisterial remoteness of the Christ in "Awe." However, it is coupled with an obsessive empathy with the Passion (something more typical of such Catholic devotions as the stations of the cross than of Calvinism). This Passion, perpetually relived, perpetually poisons the well of life like the Mosaic plague of blood:

> And so, albeit His woe is our release,
> Thought of that woe aye dims our earthly peace;
> The Life is hidden in a Fount of Blood!—

What a curious, bloody paraphrase of the famous line in Col. 3:3 ("Our life is hid with Christ in God") where the hiding guarantees security, not occlusion. And whereas in Herbert and in other Caroline writers the hands of Christ are extended toward believers in loving attentiveness ("Who takes thee by the hand, that thou likewise / With him mayst rise"),[61] in Newman they ward them off with a *Noli me tangere*: "For the many laden with the spot / And earthly taint of sin, 'tis written, 'Touch Me not.'" Such bleak, uncompromising lyrics seem the very reverse of poetry as John Keble had defined it: "But is it not the very office of poetry to develope and display the particulars of such complex ideas? in such a way, for example, as the idea of God's omnipresence is developed in the 139th Psalm? and thus detaining the mind for a while."[62] Nothing in "Awe" and its congeners can be said to "detain" the mind with patient explication. The oracle pronounces—often in the most discomfiting way— and leaves the mind to puzzle over the wound thus administered.

There is a further purpose behind the doom-laden pronouncements of "Awe" and of "The Cross of Christ"—that of establishing characteristically Tractarian rituals. While the opening of the first ("I bow at Jesus' Name") might have seemed an innocently metaphoric statement to readers unaccustomed to bowing at the name of Jesus, there could be no doubting the ritualist implications of "The Cross of Christ":

> Whene'er across this sinful flesh of mine
>   I draw the Holy Sign,
> All good thoughts stir within me and collect
>   Their slumbering strength divine:
> Till there springs up that hope of God's elect,
>   My faith shall ne'er be wrecked.[63]

The "Whene'er" at the start of this stanza gives a frequentative color to the action, recalling the repeated contemplations of Watts's hymn "When I survey the wondrous cross."[64] The difference is that for Newman, the focus has shifted inward, charting the way in which his soul, its energies concentered on that cross, enjoys the promise of "final perseverance" (a doctrine that Newman claims to have abandoned at the age of twenty-one, but which nonetheless seems to have kept a purchase on his mind). We have noted how throughout *The Christian Year* Keble allows little dabs of fancy (spells and fairies) to supplement his Judeo-Christian materials. Here Newman does something similar, except that his mythology derives not from English folklore and medieval romance, but from a corpus of Catholic folklore—the banishment of demons by holy water and the odor of sanctity. Even so, his statements remain very guarded:

> And who shall say, but hateful spirits around,
>   For their brief hour unbound,
> Shudder to see, and wail their overthrow?
>   While on far heathen ground
> Some lonely Saint hails the fresh odour, though
>   Its source we cannot know.

—but in less than a decade Newman would install a holy water stoup at Littlemore, an alarming development in the eyes of the Bisleyite Tractarians!

"David and Jonathan," far from celebrating the love of friends, actually denigrates human friendship as something tainted by the mutable world. The lyric starts with a salute, but the tone of the breathless vocative phrases is hard to establish:

> O heart of fire! misjudged by wilful man,
>   Thou flower of Jesse's race!
> What woe was thine, when thou and Jonathan
>   Last greeted face to face!
> He doomed to die, thou on us to impress
> The portent of a blood-stained holiness.[65]

How are we to construe "misjudged"? Is Newman saying that David has been the victim of unfair assessments, or is he rather saying—and this seems to me to be the chief implication—that humankind has, in its own willfulness, glamorized an essentially sinful figure. It is certainly true that the popular conception of David underplays his adultery and "murder" of Uriah and stresses instead his ardor and heroism—seldom, if ever, is he taken as a "portent" (or, to use one of Newman's favorite words, a "type") of "blood-stained holiness." Yet the whole concern of the poem is to reduce Jonathan to a sort of Banquo's ghost, arraigning the proud king in the midst of his earthly triumphs, much as Roman custom required a slave to occupy the chariots of conquering heroes as a *signum humilitatis*:

> Yet it was well:—for so, mid cares of rule
>   And crime's encircling tide,
> A spell was o'er thee, zealous one, to cool
>   Earth-joy and kingly pride;
> With battle scene and pageant, prompt to blend
> The pale calm spectre of a blameless friend.

The anti-establishment impulse behind *Lyra Apostolica* no doubt dictated this virtual equation of sinfulness with life in the world. For Newman, holiness will be secured only by death itself—that most final statement of *contemptus mundi*. It was easy to canonize and iconize the memory of the deceased when their continuing human imperfections were not there to challenge and disrupt the process—as witness his sanctification of his sister Mary, to whom (alive) his attitude had been rather patronizing. Sublunary friendship being *ipso facto* doomed, David and Jonathan would in time have quarreled as violently as St. Paul and St. Mark: "Paul's strife unblest its serious lesson gives, / He bides with us who dies, but he is lost who lives." That is how Newman revised a first draft that, because it did not pass so harsh a judgment on St. Paul ("Strife-wounded Paul his wholesome witness gives"),[66] might therefore have seemed partially to have exempted him from the poem's blanket judgment.

"I have been honoured and obeyed" takes up the *renuntium mundi* implicit in "David and Jonathan" and couches it in the first person. The speaker, indeed, presents himself as having the choice of Hercules, with vice and virtue recast as worldly acclaim and marginality. As so often in poems using personal experience to validate a position, Newman chooses the perfect tense, much as Keats had done in his sonnet "On First Looking into Chapman's Homer."[67] It is the natural tense of testimony:

> I have been honoured and obeyed,
>   I have met with scorn and slight;
> And my heart loves earth's sober shade
>   More than her laughing light.
>
> For what is rule but a sad weight
>   Of duty and a snare?
> What meanness, but with happier fate
>   The Saviour's Cross to share?[68]

This is David reconstituted in the image of Newman, giving up power for "shade," the image of unwitnessed, unacclaimed retirement. The second stanza justifies a choice that might otherwise seem inscrutable to worldly eyes, by redefining the terms *sub specie aeternitatis* rather than *mundi* (just as in *Twelfth Night*, from a totally different perspective, Feste "redefines" love in carnal terms: "What is love? 'Tis not hereafter, / Present mirth hath present laughter").[69] Of course, a poem like this opens itself to charges of "Jordan" paradoxicality—how can a choice be hidden when it is declared for all to read? Is it not a little like disfiguring one's face to prove that one is fasting?

If "David and Jonathan" reinvented the "sweet singer of Israel" as a guilt-haunted sinner, so "Moses" gives an equally offbeat account of the prophet:

> Moses, the patriot fierce, became
>   The meekest man on earth,
> To show us how love's quickening flame
>   Can give our souls new birth.
>
> Moses, the man of meekest heart,
>   Lost Canaan by self-will,
> To show where grace has done its part,
>   How sin defiles us still[70]

The effect of this poem is curiously static, like the frames from a Hogarthian suite, the very gaps between which are pregnant with meaning. Gone are the heroism and dynamism of the Exodus narrative, and in their place are two contrasting icons to which a schooldame Providence gestures with pointer in hand. Newman has revived the emblematic method of the *Biblia Pauperum*—a method of tags and simplifying woodcuts—but the message remains peculiarly Tractarian, with *contemptus mundi* realized in a life of physical deprivation. No doubt he scrapped the first draft of the penultimate line ("Grant me to lose with Moses here")[71] to avoid giving comfort to enemies of the Oxford Movement!

That same stern voice intones the opening line of "Mortal! if e'er thy spirits faint":

> Mortal! if e'er thy spirits faint,
>   By grief or pain opprest,
> Seek not vain hope, or sour complaint,
>   To cheer or ease thy breast;
>
> But view thy bitterest pangs as sent
>   A shadow of that doom,
> Which is thy soul's just punishment
>   In its own guilt's true home.
>
> Be thine own judge: hate thy proud heart;
>   And while the sad drops flow,
> E'en let thy will attend the smart,
>   And sanctify thy woe.[72]

Whatever happened, one is inclined to ask, to the Comfortable Words that the *Prayer Book* sets out before the prayer of Consecration? Or had Newman begun even in 1833 to shiver (as in 1862 he claimed he did) at the thought of the Anglican service? No refreshment for those that travail and are heavy-laden, only a penal construction of suffering that Dickens would attack so memorably in *Little Dorrit*. Once again it seems that the austerity of the poem derives from a Tractarian desire to neutralize false emphases on comfort and security in establishment Anglicanism—the kind satirized by Pope in the *Epistle to Burlington*: "To rest, the Cushion and soft Dean invite, / Who never mentions Hell to ears polite."[73] Deplorable though this sort of enervation might be, J. M. Neale, a Tractarian himself, has proved that redress is possible without joining St. Antony in the desert. "Art thou weary, art thou languid" is a poem quite as unsentimental as Newman's and yet infinitely closer to the spirit of Christ: "'Come unto me,' saith One,'and coming / Be at rest'."[74] At least there is no doubt that the tears in that hymn are salt tears, but when Newman talks about "sad drops," it is hard not to envisage runnels of blood from the wounds inflicted—with grim satisfaction—by his "discipline."

In "David Numbering the People" Newman looks at the three choices of suffering presented to David by the prophet Gad in 2 Sam. 24—famine, pestilence and rout in battle—and then says an apotropaic prayer for release. What he seeks, however, is not release from suffering but rather from the necessity of choice. Even while advocating a sort of numb, fatalistic submission, he flinches from his topic in a sort of despairing aposiopesis. After that, his composure returns and he reorients himself by separating world and spirit. I take it that "Satan and man and tools of wrath" is a vocative addressed to a "Benthamite" world that (most would say correctly) perceives suffering as an evil and finds no fascination in the scourge:

> If else . . . then guide in David's path,
> Who chose the holier pain;
> Satan and man and tools of wrath,
> An Angel's scourge is gain.[75]

The same divinized Choice of Hercules supplies the underlying structure of "Abraham." The octave of this sonnet hails the patriarch as though he were a Bunyanesque fellow traveler with the Tractarians, and stalls while Newman heaps up appositive phrases to force the reverential contemplation of faith itself. In the first draft Abraham had been only "a true type"; here the superlative has the effect of turning him into a Platonic ideal:

> The better portion didst thou choose, Great Heart,
>   Thy God's first choice, and pledge of Gentile-grace!
> Faith's truest type, he with unruffled face
>   Bore the world's smile, and bade her slaves depart.[76]

Renouncing the world here involves a sort of moral levitation, as though, untrammeled by its values, Abraham floated upward into the presence of God. Newman has furthermore borrowed the *Beatus ille* formula from the Psalms but has redefined the Psalmist's beatitude in the strict terms of the contemplative life: "O happy in their soul's high solitude, / Who commune thus with God and not with earth!" Later on, the heavy downward tug of "wealth-enslaved" makes the worldlings' life seem immobile and heavy, as opposed to the freedom with which contemplatives move upward, lightened by their apostolic "stripping." *Verus incessu patuit sanctus.*

Newman's popular reputation as a poet rests primarily on the one item in *Lyra Apostolica* that has crossed virtually every denominational barrier and entered virtually every hymn book. Ian Ker has given the following account of its genesis and of its subsequent popularity:

> On 16 June [1833], while still at sea, Newman wrote "The Pillar and the Cloud," better known by its opening words, "Lead, Kindly Light." It is not surprising that the poem has become one of the most famous hymns in the language, for its mood of thanksgiving and trust is easily applicable either to the individual believer's present predicament or to his or her more general pilgrimage of faith through life.[77]

Meriol Trevor has also remarked that it was the "image of finding one's way in the dark that appealed to the Victorians, lost in a spiritual wilderness in the midst of a powerful development of material resources."[78] The poem is a late successor to a long line of nocturnals, a genre that Donne adapted from the Catholic night offices in "A Nocturnal upon S. Lucy's Day, Being the Shortest Day."[79] The pillar is not mentioned within the body of the poem, but it nonetheless provides a dependable beacon in the heart of darkness. This is made the more discomfiting by the fact that Newman stresses the solitude of his journey, in contrast to the communality of the Israelites'. In its typological context, the darkness of the Mosaic wilderness was simply that—darkness—whereas here it registers as an enemy about to close for combat:

> Lead, kindly Light, amid the encircling gloom,
>   Lead Thou me on!
> The night is dark, and I am far from home—
>   Lead Thou me on!
> Keep Thou my feet; I do not ask to see
> The distant scene,—one step enough for me.[80]

An arresting aspect of the stanza design is the way in which the dimeter, already compressed and pregnant, is further weighted by two spondees. These accordingly club out the prayer with a redoubled energy after the expansion and rhythmic variety of the lines that flank them. Even the syntax, stripped by apostolic necessity to a hard, almost inelegant *residuum*, sheds its verb and its connector in "one step enough for me." The total surrender implied by the forfeit sense of destination sounds yet another note of austerity. In Newman's typological source, the hardship of the journey was sugared—or should that be honeyed?—by its goal in Canaan. Here, by contrast, the poet accepts the darkness almost as a mystic might follow the *via negativa*. His only request is underpinned by Ps. 91:11–12—"For he shall give his angels charge over thee, to keep thee in all thy ways. They shall bear thee up in *their* hands, lest thou dash thy foot against a stone." This turns the enterprise into an act of pure faith rather than a potentially "interested" service and therefore recalls the baroque hymn *O Deus, ego amo te*, which Edward Caswall (a colleague at the Birmingham Oratory) subsequently translated: "Not from the hope of gaining aught, / Not seeking a reward."[81] That the journey is to some extent a penitential pilgrimage is supposed by the next stanza. It is also worth remarking that "far from home" has a curious ambivalence in the larger context of *Lyra Apostolica*. In "Mortal, if e'er thy spirits faint" we find the traditional domestication of home subverted into something penal—"In its own guilt's true home," while "Dreams" renders home as the space of stuffiness and complacency, "Shall pierce thee in thy virtue's home serene." In that sense, therefore, "Lead, kindly Light" is a transitional poem, recalling (without enunciating) the suffering Newman underwent in Sicily and the exorcism of his pride. Later, he came to think his decision to return to that country without the Froudes had been a willful one.

Stanza 2 puts both the trustfulness of the speaker and the dismal setting into perspective:

> I was not ever thus, nor prayed that Thou
>> Shouldst lead me on.
> I loved to choose and see my path; but now,
>> Lead Thou me on!
> I loved the garish day, and, spite of fears,
>> Pride ruled my will: remember not past years.

Such stock-taking is common in poetry that has turned inward, and among many examples that could cited is Horace's first ode in *Carmina* IV, with its famous *non sum qualis eram*.[82] But whereas Horace looks back on past passions with a mildly regretful resignation, Newman makes a sacramental confession. Because his will has been dissociated from God's, the incremental refrain becomes less purposive, its spondee lightened into an iamb by the subjunctive of "Shouldst lead me on." Furthermore, the past indicative verbs, unlike the imperatives of stanza 1, do not assume the presence of the other; they convey a sense of profound loneliness, of a solipsism so complete as to exclude even God. The light, too, because of its harsh exposure, seems as distressful as the "encircling gloom" through which it has formerly glimmered. Newman is here almost certainly alluding to Keble's "Advent Sunday," where the sufficiency of human reason also registers as a midday glare: "an age of light, / Light without love, glares on the aching sight."[83] There is something bleakly moving in the transition from that godless self-absorption to the broken entreaty at the end of stanza 2, with its reminiscence of Psalm 25:7: "Remember not the sins of my youth, nor my transgressions: according to thy mercy remember thou me for thy goodness' sake, O LORD."

Whereas stanza 2 devoted itself to a penitential survey of the past, the last verse addresses the future:

> So long Thy power hath blest me, sure it still
>> Will lead me on,
> O'er moor and fen, o'er crag and torrent, till
>> The night is gone;
> And with the morn those Angel faces smile
> Which I have loved long since, and lost awhile.

In *Paradise Lost*, Satan undertakes a quest of damnation "O'er bog or steep, through strait, rough, dense, or rare,"[84] a line that Newman seems to have recalled and subverted in his passage over comparable terrain. Dawn is personified as smiling (as in Gray's "Sonnet [on the Death of Mr Richard West]"—"In vain to me the smiling mornings shine"[85]—but that decorative personification is absorbed in the actual smiling faces of angels, the psychopomps of his journey. As a result of his trust, God has given them charge of his feet. The loneliness of the poem (the "two luminously self-evident beings" of stanza 1, the profound self-encased loneliness of stanza 2) is thus dissipated in the communion and fulfillment of the coda.

"The Pillar and the Cloud" is a sort of *hodoiporikon* or journey poem; "When I sink down in gloom and fear" is an utterance that seems to have escaped from its interstices—a slumped, travel-weary cry:

> When I sink down in gloom or fear,
>   Hope blighted or delayed,
> Thy whisper, Lord, my heart shall cheer,
>   "'Tis I: be not afraid!" [86]

Even so, the poet screws his courage to the sticking place ("Nor will I quit Thy way, though foes / Some onward pass defend"), recalling Valiant's resolute hymn in *The Pilgrim's Progress*: "One here will constant be, / Come Wind, come Weather."[87] Both poems vigorously prosecute their purposes, and both render their courses as journeys fraught with danger. One is also reminded of Blake's poem in the preface to *Milton*, where the declaration is similarly strong and the energy irremissive: "I will not cease from Mental Fight, / Nor shall my Sword sleep in my hand."[88] This ruggedness extends even into the way that Newman has imaged his companions in the quest. It is hard to imagine Keble, Williams, and Froude speaking with "rough voices," though the epithet manages to convey the vigor and soldierliness of those involved in the quest. If Bunyan has supplied Newman with the journey topos, then it is Ralegh and Herbert who have given him the idea of repeating a line from stanza to stanza to convey the tenacious, dogged adhesion to a central truth. Both poets have taken the lyrical function of the refrain, which steadies and demarcates the design of the poem in which it occurs, and given it a thematic purpose, as witness Ralegh's bitter envoi, "The Lie":

> Say to the court, it glows
> And shines like rotten wood;
> Say to the church, it shows

> What's good, and doth no good.
> If church and court reply,
> Then give them both the lie.[89]

Such sober iterativeness seems in turn to have influenced Herbert's "Quip," as in the following stanza:

> Then Money came, and chinking still,
> What tune is this, poore man? said he:
> I heard in Musick you had skill.
> *But thou shalt answer, Lord, for me.*[90]

And again in "The Forerunners": "Yet have they left me, *Thou art still my God.*"[91] This divine monomania functions furthermore in Newman's poem as an image of God's omnipresence, forever able to address the needs of the speaker, no matter what the circumstances in which he may find himself.

The doctrine of omnipresence also supplies the thematic core of "O say not thou art left of God," which begins with a moving, impetuous intensity that Newman might have learnt from a chorus in *Hellas*: "O cease! must hate and death return."[92] The expletive and the earnest command together suggest the interjection of a poet unable any longer to endure the false construction his interlocutor has placed upon events; it imparts a tone of urgent prophecy to his utterance:

> O say not thou art left of God,
> Because His tokens in the sky
> Thou canst not read; this earth He trod
> To teach thee He was ever nigh.[93]

Once again Newman seems to be thinking of the Blake's prefatory poem in *Milton*, where the physical proximity of Christ (guaranteed by the Incarnation) issues in an effort to reconstruct and redeem the otherwise incoherent and dispiriting data of experience: "And did those feet in ancient time / Walk upon England's mountains green?"[94] Newman, however, makes a dramatic transition from the past tense of distant history to a tense that we could call the omniscient present, reincarnating God in the syntax of the poem: "He sees, beneath the fig-tree green / Nathaniel con His sacred lore." What is more, the poet has domesticated the almost inconceivable doctrine of omnipresence by placing it within the context of an ordinary household—"Shouldst thou the closet seek, unseen He enters through the unopened door"—much in manner of Herbert's "Miserie": "No man shall beat into his head, / That thou within his curtains drawn canst see."[95] That domesticity is mingled, moreover, with details from the Gospels in such a way as to suggest the continuity of the miraculous past with a present whose miraculous nature the Tractarians were trying to reaffirm, combating the rationalist temper of contemporary Anglicanism. Newman turns Christ's entering through an unopened door (a detail in the Resurrection narratives) into an immediate fact. This elision of past and present also figures in the second stanza, where Emmaus is both the actual town in Palestine and also—through the figure of antonomasia—*any* place in which Christ will reveal himself. A much more temperate and humane image of the Savior results from this. It is as if the Christology of Herbert had rubbed off with the earlier reference to his verse. The tender intimacy of "He takes thy hand" is, after all, anticipated by such lyrics as "Easter": "Who takes thee by the hand."[96] The final stanza extends these blends of past and present, taking in more becalmments than Newman's actual delay on the voyage home from Sicily:

> Or, on a voyage, when calms prevail,
>   And prison thee upon the sea,
> He walks the wave, He wings the sail,
>   The shore is gained, and thou art free.[97]

The definite article of "The shore," coming as it does after abstract commonplace of "a voyage," tends to give it a framing specificity, and so to imply the sea of Revelation.

Newman also explores the thematics of tense in "James and John," which opens in the historic present—the tense in which the brothers formulate their hopes without consulting God: "Brothers in heart, they hope to gain / An undivided joy." But the great unstated epigraph of *Lyra Apostolica* is Piccarda's utterance in *Paradiso*—"and His will is our peace"[98]—and the actual events redesign the ideals that people have set themselves. The modulation into the past at this point is so sharp that it functions almost like a *Verfremdungseffekt*, especially since the phrase "the Lord heard" is often used in Scripture to preface the granting of petitionary prayer:

> Christ heard; and willed that James should fall
>   First prey of Satan's rage;
> John linger out his fellows all,
>   And die in bloodless age.

But the tense helps to mark the stanza as a parenthesis, for the final verse (in the present indicative) is morphologically closer to the historic present of the first two, so that, as it were, they join hands over the gulf. What therefore seems a reversal of illusory hope proves only to be a passing circumstance. The brothers do indeed obtain "an undivided joy" *sub specie aeternitatis.*

We have seen in *The Christian Year* how Keble addresses an apparent limitation in human knowledge and experience only to point out how, in the wisdom of Providence, that limitation guards us from suffering. Hence the palinode in "Twenty-Fourth Sunday after Trinity":

> Farewell, for her, th' ideal scenes so fair—
>   Yet not farewell her hope, since Thou hast deign'd,
> Creator of all hearts! to own and share
>   The woe of what Thou mad'st, and we have stain'd.[99]

Newman's frame of mind in "Did we but see" is so close to Keble's that he must have had that poem in mind:

> Did we but see
> When life first opened, how our journey lay
> Between the earliest and its closing day;
>   Or view ourselves, as we one time shall be,
> Who strive for the high prize, such sight would break
> The youthful spirit, though bold for Jesus' sake.[100]

God's omniscience is underpinned by his omnipotence; for humankind's aspiring to knowledge without the attendant power would, as Newman suggests, issue in despair. The general first stanza thus substantiates itself in the confessional second, where the poet admits to having thought more of his temporal reward than of the service required to secure it:

> But thou, dear Lord!
> Whilst I traced out bright scenes which were to come,

> Isaac's pure blessings, and a verdant home,
>   Didst spare me,

The inspiration here is probably Herbert's "Affliction (I)": "When first thou didst entice to thee my heart, / I thought the service brave: / So many joyes I writ down for my part."[101] Because this is so self-willed, God enters by warping the imagery and redirecting the poet's attention. An identical rhythm of disappointment and chastening informs Newman's poem, where the transitive use of "Willing" (i.e., God's exercise of his will for the fulfillment of his designs) also implies a displacement of human by divine will: *en la sua volontade è [sua] pace.* A hiatus between the speaker's aspiration and his present state implies a suffering so intense that it has had to be offstaged. The data of his appearance, his pallor and his girdle of self-mortifying chastity provide the only indices of an earlier struggle.

"Guardian Angels" also involves a biographical retrospect, except that here the poet scans his life for signs of God's intervention. We know that Newman had held an intense belief in angels from childhood: in the *Apologia* he tells us, "I thought life might be a dream, or I an Angel, and all this world a deception, my fellow-angels by a playful device concealing themselves from me, and deceiving me with the semblance of a material world."[102] Here, however, he pays homage to the skeptical temper of his times by interrogating his material. Even though he has the Pauline assurance that "all things work together for good to them that love God, to them that are the called according to *his* purpose" (Rom. 8:28), he still wants to *track* the cooperation of those things and the agencies by which it is effected: "Are these the tracks of some unearthly Friend, / His footprints, and his vesture-skirts of light."[103] The octave of this sonnet records the speaker's uncertainty not only in its interrogative structure but also by setting down such speculative and unprovable data as "the might of ill I see not." In the same way, the repeated "ors" suggest the tentative fitting of hypotheses to the facts of a case, rather as one might provisionally place the segments of a jigsaw puzzle against the gaps into which they might go. The sestet fails, however, to supply the certainty with which sonnets more usually follow a questioning octave. A cry of *non sum dignus* gives up the right to know: "But when on common men such shadows fall, / These dare not make their own the gifts they find." Newman at one stage contemplated "plead" as an alternative to "eye," but clearly preferred the fearful deference of gazing to the presumption of speaking. Once again this allows us to gauge the distance between *The Christian Year* and *Lyra Apostolica,* for whereas Keble allows Christ to impart himself to the lowly heart, Newman will acknowledge only half-glimpses and fleeting intimations to sinful humankind. The more intense the belief in human degeneracy, the more remote and inaccessible—as in Calvinism—the figure of Christ becomes. It is not surprising that from time to time, as in the persecution of Hampden or in the reaction to *Essays and Reviews,* the Tractarians could forge alliances with the Evangelical party—for all their differences, they shared a great deal of ground.

"Warnings," because it is subtitled as being *For Music,* advances itself as a song lyric different from the brief, meditative poems that flank it. That difference registers chiefly in the stylized stanza form, two dimeter couplets contained within an outer dimeter frame. The effect is odd but arresting, portents are glimpsed, as in Beethoven's Fifth Symphony, through the skittishness of a scherzo.

> When Heaven sends sorrow
> Warnings go first,
> Lest it should burst
> With stunning might
> On souls too bright
> To fear the morrow.[104]

Whether those warnings will bear inspection or not we shall never know, because Newman preempts all enquiry and falls back on the antirationalism that the Oxford Movement made its own: "Can science bear us / To the hid springs / Of human things?" But whereas Keble would have uttered a resounding no to such a question, Newman's more flexible, more searching mind pretends to leave the issue unresolved.

"Discipline" belongs to a line of stock-taking, reminiscential poems exemplified, inter alia, by Shakespeare's sonnets 29 and 30— "When in disgrace with Fortune and men's eyes" and "When to the sessions of sweet silent thought."[105] In Newman's case, however, there is a heuristic purpose as well, an effort to trace those warnings so indecisively treated in "Guardian Angels" and "Warnings":

> When I look back upon my former race,
> Seasons I see, at which the Inward Ray
> More brightly burned, or guided some new way;[106]

Newman conveys the motion of the mind as it surveys and marshals the biographical matter and then detects the pattern beneath its contingency—"And next I mark." That resolution, however, is tentative and provisional. Far from clarifying the way in which Providence works, it simply recognizes the signs that accompany its intervention. For Newman's sonnet is a *hodoiporikon:* the journey, not yet complete, has still to be shaped by the final destination. One might have imagined that the interpretative triumph of the octave would have brought with it a certain peace of mind, but for many Tractarians, as for the witches in *Macbeth,* "security / Is mortals' chiefest enemy."[107] Whereas the AV conveys God's providential support as something underpinning human frailty ("The eternal God *is thy* refuge, and underneath *are* the everlasting arms"—Deut. 33:27), Newman has the hand raised as if to strike, arbitrary and punitive like Nancy's in *To the Lighthouse,* "which brought darkness and desolation, like God Himself, to millions of ignorant and innocent creatures."[108] A semantic conflict in the language parallels the mental conflict of the victim. In "Deep breathless stirrings shoot across my breast," the spatial discrepancy between "deep" and "across" (implying passage over a surface) is recapitulated in the clash of "breathless" against "stirrings," themselves contradicted by the energy of "shoot." What better way than this to register the stricken torment of a soul awaiting a blow?

In a collection concerned to sharpen and "deliberalize" the theology of the Church of England, "Whene'er I seek the Holy Altar's rail" provides an odd demonstration of the speaker's negative capability. The doctrine of the real presence had not yet become a burning issue—Keble's problems with the bishop of Winchester were decades away—and, as on most points of dogma, the Anglican Church offered comprehension instead of clarity. Whereas Roman Catholicism made confident pronouncements about the carnal presence, the Church of England tended to sound the note that Newman sounds here. A line from G. H. Bourne's "Lord, enthroned in heavenly splendour" ("Thou art here, we ask not how")[109] reveals much the same mental posture, opting for the vagueness that must follow when the reason surrenders and accepts the ineffable: "It is no time to task my reason frail, / To try Christ's words, and search how they may be."[110] When Cardinal Manning enticed Robert Wilberforce to follow him into the Roman Catholic Church, he had to field many questions from his wavering friend. One of them concerned the Catholic doctrine of the Mass, which, to Wilberforce's (then) Anglican eyes, seemed problematic. His correspondent dismissed his hesitations with a flick of the hand: "But a change does take place in a sphere into which no natural criteria such as sense can penetrate. . . . Beyond this affirmation the Church affirms nothing."[111]

So, it would seem, Catholics as well as Anglicans "ask not how"— only they stop asking at a later stage of the event. Try as he might, however, Newman finds it hard to leave things as indeterminately Anglican as that, and in his second stanza provides some subtle co-ordinates for the plotting of his doctrinal position. The intimate deictic "these" tends to place him in spatial proximity to the Catholics who believe the carnal presence, even while he disavows their doctrine—"I will not say with these, that bread and wine / Have vanish'd at the consecration prayer"—and the emphatic adverbial preface to the "commemorative" school of Protestants has the effect of pushing him still closer to the Roman side of the *via media* he would later claim to be treading—"Far less with those deny that aught divine / And of immortal seed is hidden there."

In "The Fathers are in dust" Newman reverses the orthodox sequence of deduction, creating premises in defiance of reason and common sense to explain the conclusion that he has taken as his starting point. Following Keble's habit of extracting personifications from biblical personages, Newman presents Christ as Truth incarnate (a substitution that also derives from the enquiry of Pilate in the Gospel of St. John):

> "The Fathers are in dust, yet live to God:"
>   So says the Truth; as if the motionless clay
> Still held the seeds of life beneath the sod,
>   Smouldering and struggling till the judgment-day.[112]

Newman seems to have remembered two lines from Gray's *Elegy* in the composition of this stanza—"Where heaves the turf in many a mouldering heap,"[113] and "Ev'n in our ashes live their wonted fires"[114]—where the imagination also imposes a continued vitality on inert materials. Yet the second stanza exalts "as if" above "is" to demonstrate the energy of a faith that sees beyond Ezekiel's "dry bones" to an apparently impossible resurrection. Here the subjunctive and indicative positions are reversed—the sophist *may* urge, but the faithful speaker asserts, that "they *are* heavenly shrines." From this point of vantage, indeed, the prospect of resurrection confers glory on the otherwise contemptible body, and Newman embraces St. Paul's belief in its being the temple of the Holy Ghost (1 Cor. 3:16) not so much because he takes it on trust, but because he has deduced it from the synoptic texts on which he has based his poem. It seems not to have worried him that Christ's argument is couched in terms virtually identical to those put forward by his adversaries. G. B. Caird, a modern commentator on St. Luke's Gospel, has remarked that in "form the argument is typically rabbinic, relying as it does on the precise wording of the sacred text, and, as Luke tells us, the scribes were impressed by it." He goes on to add that it is "capable of being expressed in a form more congenial to the modern mind."[115] Although Keble would never have felt the need to recuperate the argument and suit it to the "modern mind" (believing such minds to be godless and self-willed), Newman, fitted with a broader and more malleable mentality than his mentor, allows us in to empathize if only for a moment with the mental disposition of modernism—and then seals up the casket of faith to save it from that "taint." The final line recalls the great affirmation of Job, which also moves through a disjunctive from a statement of mortality to a statement of faith.

"There is not on the earth" is an apostolic counsel of perfection, stressing an ideal of sanctity much more rigorous than that advanced in the pulpits of the Established Church. Newman sounds a Tractarian note when he gives first place to fasting in his list of spiritual desiderata: "by fastings gained, / And trials well sustained."[116] Self-salvation, the great enterprise of Evangelicalism, is pygmified in this stanza by its context of towering apostolic minds. These practice an altruism more comprehensive, and, in contrast to the earthbound concerns of ordinary Christians, move on a sublime vertical axis between heaven and earth.

"Joseph" belongs to a set of patriarchal sonnets composed within days of each other in January 1833. Like "Abraham," it gives a personal turn to the impersonal mechanism of typology. Whereas Isaac, the filial sacrifice, is more usually presented as the patriarchal type of Christ, Newman takes Joseph as Christ's exemplar: "O purest semblance of the Eternal Son!"[117] One might at first glance be tempted to read "purest" as a reference to Joseph's rejection of Potiphar's wife, but it is clear that Newman intends the meaning "most exact" or "least qualified." "Semblance," of course, is a synonym for "type," but Newman gives it a quirkish Aristotelian turn in the sestet, suggesting that the relation between type and antitype is better viewed as that between accidents and substance:

> Lest it might seem, what time the Substance came,
> Truth lacked a sceptre, when It but laid by
> Its beaming front, and bore a willing shame.

Joseph is the accidental husk for the essential substance of Christ, the greater reality apprehended through the accidents that point to its existence.

"The Haven" (December 1832) clearly derives from Newman's Mediterranean journey with the Froudes and uses the disruption of travel to offset the blessedness of rest—an old enough figure for salvation, as witness St. Anatolius' Ζοφερας τρικιμιας ("Fierce was the wild billow, / Dark was the night")[118] and Charles Wesley's "Jesu, lover of my soul" ("While the gathering waters roll, / While the tempest still is high").[119] What differentiates Newman's poem from lyrics such as these is the relish with which he registers the storm:

> Whence is this awe, by stillness spread
>   O'er the world-fretted soul?
> Wave reared on wave its boastful head,
> While my keen bark, by breezes sped,
> Dash'd fiercely through the ocean bed,
>   And chaf'd towards its goal.[120]

The combative exhilaration of the speaker who pits his "keen bark" (eager as well as piercing) against the "boastful wave" and the impatience that chafes "toward its goal"—these suggest his failure to attune self-will to the will of God. But in the quietude of his arrival he is given an intimation—Elijah-like because of its mediation by the "still small voice"—of peace to come. Newman's vocative ("Sinner") aligns the tempest not so much with world as with the soul disturbed by the world, and so repents of the self-centered energy to which he had earlier succumbed. His original epithet for the waves was "godless,"[121] which proves the extent to which he conceived them as projections of the willful self.

"The Desert" is an odd poem for Newman to have written, for a decade later the table talk at Littlemore would center appreciatively on the palm-leaf diet of St. Macarius. Here, however, he queries that futile asceticism so brilliantly exposed by Tennyson in *St. Simeon Stylites*: "Let this avail, just, dreadful, mighty God, / This not be all in vain, that thrice ten years, / Thrice multiplied by superhuman pangs."[122] It is those "superhuman pangs"—those efforts of self-deification—

which give the game away. Newman seems to have anticipated Tennyson's critique, for he begins with the desert and mountain retreats of Elijah and Moses, reading them as instances of withdrawal sanctioned by God and therefore "grace-endued":

> Two sinners have been grace-endued,
>   Unwearied to sustain
> For forty days a solitude
>   On mount and desert plain.[123]

Just as in "The Haven" Newman implied that divine service can be distorted into self-service, so here he brings a similar charge—loveless misanthropy—against the saints who have taken *contemptus mundi* to fanatical extremes:

> But feverish thoughts the breasts have swayed,
>   And gloom or pride is shown,
> If e'er we seek the garden's shade
>   Or walk the world, alone.

We have seen that the renunciation of Roman Catholic doctrine in "Whene'er I seek the Holy Altar's rail" ends with a set of theological coordinates revealing the speaker's closeness to a position ostensibly denied. We know in fact that Newman loved the "garden's shade"—the Kebelian (and before that, Marvellian) image of retirement. Ward records that his "walks were often solitary. The Provost meeting him one day gave a kindly bow and said, 'Numquam minus solus quam cum solus.'"[124] It is not surprising, therefore, given the ascetical cast of Tractarianism, that "The Desert" should betray a gleam of admiration for these fanatics. It declares itself in the way Newman sets "Christian" maceration against heathen "rage" and metes out blame with the greatest reluctance. *Lyra Apostolica*, as its Homeric epigraph made clear, was a declaration of war upon an establishment that Keble and Rose had conceived, almost in so many words, as the vector of "heathen rage." So even while the poem nods toward the Arnoldian rationalism that saw fasting and scourging as the obsolete baggage of Christianity, Newman half-articulates the Tractarians' belief that self-mortification actually provided a form of witness.

Richard Wilbur has pointed out how some of his poems "pay homage to the word 'or',"[125] meaning that a poet will at times try out attitudes or positions foreign to his or her dominant modes of thought. Similar vacillations and semiretractions can be glimpsed from poem to poem in the Newman sector of *Lyra Apostolica*. In "Death" he makes an entirely human (even sentimental) plea to die in England, not abroad:

> But let my failing limbs beneath
> My mother's smile recline;
> My name in sickness and in death
> Heard in her sacred shrine.[126]

This poem belongs to a well-defined subgenre that we could call the testamentary lyric. It is characterized by a calm anticipation of the speaker's death and careful, clear-eyed funeral arrangements. There is one in *Twelfth Night* ("Come away, come away death, / And in sad cypress let me be laid")[127] and there are also burial directives written into several of Donne's poems—"The Funeral," for instance: "Whate'er she meant by it, bury it with me."[128] That the tradition persisted into the twentieth century is furthermore proved by Brooke's "Soldier."[128] The sentiments of Newman's "Death," then, are standard—even predictable. What makes the poem unusual, however, is the discord between such local (and be it said, irrational attachments) and the apostolic mandate which ignores earthly discomfort in pursuit of the Kingdom. Newman's personification of England belongs to a tradition of pagan goddesses, however much he might try to Christianize the image with a hint of the *Mater Dolorosa*—"But let my failing limbs beneath / My mother's smile recline." Confessions like these help humanize the austerity of *Lyra Apostolica* and show the persistence of vigorous human impulses that even the most self-denying creed cannot wholly censor. Just as in the *Dies Irae* the anguished speaker tries to avert damnation by cataloging the sufferings of Christ *(Tantus labor non sit casus)* so "Death" ends in a curious separation of the Father and the Son. The Father is addressed in the second person as a Being indifferent to the claims of family and locality, administering succor to all alike:

> Thou, Lord! where'er we lie, canst aid;
> But He, who taught His own
> To live as one, will not upbraid
> The dread to die alone.

Christ, on the other hand, oddly placed alongside that vocative in the remote third person, will, by virtue of the Incarnation, understand the (illogical) human feeling from which the prayer has sprung.

"They do but grope in learning's pedant round" articulates the antirational bias of Tractarianism, which came to birth in response to a perfectly rational decision vis-à-vis the church in Ireland. Keble's cry of "Apostasy" in 1833 implied, however, that any human adjustments to the divine constitution of the Church amounted to a betrayal of the faith. Such hatred of Liberalism—the winnowing of faith by reason—issued in the intransigent fideism that made Keble reluctant to judge the immoral sections of the Old Testament. What God has ordained, human reason dare not question. And if, like Newman, you had a lively mind, then you had better write sonnets to chasten it and cut it down to size:

> They do but grope in learning's pedant round,
> Who on the fantasies of sense bestow
> An idol substance, bidding us bow low
> Before those shades of being which are found
> Stirring or still on man's brief trial ground;[130]

Newman claims that sense data, far from accessing the real, can offer only a fantastic approximation to the truth. His source is easily found—the cave parable in *The Republic*[131]—and, like Plato, he reduces sense data to intangible "shades," "shapes and moods," and stresses their dubiousness by having them "come and go." While his epigraph from Ps. 39 implies that humankind lives in a shadow that blocks off "reality," he goes a step further in Plato's direction when he suggests that reality is itself a shadow and that science, so proud of its unsuperstitious devotion to the truth, is a mere idolatry of phantasms. (This sort of anti-intellectualism originated with Keble, of course, who, a few years later would devote the *Eighty-Ninth Tract* to the hopeless enterprise of reclaiming the obsolete thought of the Fathers.) If empirical experience is, in this view, an ontological mirage, then reality must subsist in the mind, the mind that connects the creature *capax rationis* to the Creator. Newman's idea of an irresistible, concentering force that absorbs everything into its mentality seems to owe something to Wordsworth: "A motion and a spirit, that impels / All thinking things, all objects of all thought."[132] But in *Tintern Abbey* this informing mentality has a vector in tangible items:

> . . . Therefore am I still
> A lover of the meadows and the woods,
> And mountains; of all that we behold
> From this green earth; of the mighty world
> Of eye and ear,—both what they half create,
> And what perceive;[133]

For Newman, on the other hand, there are no empirical checks on the mind that intersects with God. His distance from the romantic ethos can be gauged the way he has mentalized and spiritualized the concrete elements of nature. Not for him Apollo's great cry in *Hyperion:* "Knowledge enormous makes a God of me."[134] For Tractarians, such a cry would have embodied the very essence of modernism. But because Newman saw himself spearheading a revival, recuperating lost truths, the tone of his sestet is no less magisterial and imposing than that of Apollo's self-deification. In keeping with tracts that urged priests to magnify their office and choose their side, Newman's sestet presents the theocentric vision of humankind as an idea temporarily in abeyance but soon to be restored. His manner has a grave, hieratic urgency well suited to the occasion.

Although the Old Testament figure of Melchizedek was rather shadowy, Howard Kee and Franklin Young have observed how the Epistle to the Hebrews gave a new typological slant to his significance: "The thesis of Christ's priesthood is developed in relation to the mysterious Old Testament personage, Melchisedek. . . . By a method of interpretation common in the author's day, though it seems far-fetched today, he seeks to establish the superiority of Melchisedek over both Abraham and the Levitical priesthood descended from Abraham."[135]

Although Newman takes Heb. 7:3 as his epigraph, he fails altogether to develop the sacerdotal arguments more usually associated with Melchizedek. Instead—rather quirkishly—he focuses on the unlineaged priest-king as the type of all lonely people: "Thrice blest are they who feel their loneliness; / To whom nor voice of friend nor pleasant scene / Brings that on which the saddened heart can lean."[136] The beatitude formula is familiar from the Sermon on the Mount, except that here the blessing is tripled to signify the special holiness of the subjects. No longer will those that mourn simply be comforted as in Matt. 5:5; their isolation will help them escape entrammelment in earthly concerns. Here we have a hint of Newman's commitment to the celibate life, which, according to the *Apologia,* had been with him since boyhood: "another deep imagination . . . took possession of me,—there can be no mistake about the fact; viz. that it would be the will of God that I should lead a single life."[137] About this precocious vocation some critics have had much to say. Here, for example, are the plausible speculations of David Hilliard: "It seems inherently possible that young men who were secretly troubled by homosexual feelings that they could not publicly acknowledge may have been attracted by the prospect of devoting themselves to a life of celibacy, in the company of like-minded male friends, as a religiously sanctioned alternative to marriage."[138] Since Newman's celibacy might or might not be a function of an unacknowledged homosexuality, it is worth noting that he recurs here to another cryptohomosexual sonnet—Gray's on the death of his friend Richard West. There, in his bereavement, the poet is indeed repulsed by the fecundity and joy of nature—though grief drives him inward, whereas in Newman it provides an upward impulsion. Nonetheless, the parallels between the two utterances remain significant:

> Yet morning smiles the busy race to cheer,
> And new-born pleasure brings to happier men:
> The fields to all their wonted tribute bear;
> To warm their little loves the birds complain.
> I fruitless mourn to him that cannot hear,
> And weep the more because I weep in vain.[139]

For Newman, the "rich earth, garbed in its daintiest dress, / Of light and joy, doth but the more oppress" and for the same reason, viz., "nor voice of friend nor pleasant scene / Brings that on which the saddened heart can lean." That catachresis is symptomatic of unacknowledged confusion below the surface of the poem, where the physical embrace implied by "lean" clashes with the metonymic "heart" (rather as in "Guardian Angels" Newman projected "thoughtful mind's" *walking* with Christ"). Be that as it may, he chooses to connect the arguments of Heb. 7 with his own interest in celibacy. The sonnet resolves into a catalog of epithets and participial phrases that, by doing away with verbs, deletes the agents of change and movement, and mimics the rapt stasis of eternity:

> Fatherless, homeless, reft of age and place,
> Severed from earth, and careless of its wreck,
> Born through long woe His rare Melchizedek.

In this parthenogenesis of a different order, the celibate priest has been begotten of his sufferings, though an implicit pun on "borne" suggests the presence underneath of "everlasting arms."

"Siren Isles" needs to be taken along with "Messena," "Taurominium," and "Corcyra" as a suite of Mediterranean idylls all concerned with the tension between the classical past and the Christian present. Of course, the tension would be much stronger in an Oxford scholar steeped in Greek literature than it would be for an Evangelical tradesperson who, unbedeviled by such nostalgia, could more vigorously shake off the pagan past. "Siren Isles" broaches the problem and tries manfully to exorcise a sirenical distraction:

> Cease, Stranger, cease those piercing notes,
> The craft of Siren choirs;
> Hush the seductive voice, that floats
> Upon the languid wires.[140]

Sailing past the island of the sirens, Newman takes Odysseus as a pagan type of himself, attracted by a beauty that will deflect him from his course. This intense response can be attributed to Newman's musicality: he played the violin well and felt a passionate love for the music of Beethoven. Barry, indeed, has noticed the way in which this faculty has colored the whole of his creative process: "His sentences glide upon a musical scale; he flows along as a river, is not fixed on canvas."[141] But just as in Tom Stoppard's *Travesties* Lenin renounces the Beethoven he loves because of his bourgeois origins, so in "Siren Isles" Newman does violence to the feeling that music arouses in him. The tears that he was capable of shedding so freely—even to the extent of bathing a friend's hands with them—are imaged here as the solvent of clay, the undoing of the man. Self-expression cannot be squared with the militant propaganda of *Lyra Apostolica*. Yet even as he issues his stern directive, killing the thing he loves, Newman aligns himself with Odysseus, here called the "Man of many woes." (In *The Odyssey*, Athene cries "It is for Odysseus that my heart is wrung—the wise but unlucky Odysseus.")[142] To talk of the "Man of many woes," however, is inevitably to allude to the

"Man of Sorrow," the Suffering Servant of Isaiah. This imposes a goal of strenuous Christian striving upon a self that might otherwise be tempted to rest content in the knowledge that human nature has not changed over the centuries. In "Messena" (spelt "Messina" in the letter that carried the text to Jemima on 19 February 1833), Newman develops the same idea but in less censorious terms. The sonnet's octave once again acknowledges that tension between Christian allegiance and pagan sympathies: "Why, wedded to the Lord, still yearns my heart / Upon these scenes of ancient heathen fame?"[143] Bernard Anderson has pointed how Hosea, instead of "explaining the divine marriage by referring to the cycles of nature, . . . spoke of a historical marriage made in the wilderness between God and a people."[144] It is to just this sort of marriage that Newman refers in the opening line of his sonnet. The celibate priest is beset by adulterous yearnings for the ancient world. But far from plucking out his eye and cutting off his hand—which he comes close to doing in "Siren Isles"—Newman rationalizes his whoring after false gods not as mental impurity but as *homo humani nil a se alienum putans.* He semitizes this aphorism by referring to "Adam's race" in the sestet, which conceives classical history as dress rehearsal or dummy run for the greater drama of salvation.

It is odd that having been persuaded of the "unreal" Evangelical distinction between the saved and the reprobate, Newman should not have paused to assess contemporary ideas of the Fall. All he can do in "Taurominium" is to register a momentary incredulity that loveliness should persist through physical damnation; "Thou couldst but marvel to have found this blighted world so fair."[145] In "Corcyra" he does something even odder, trying reclaim the history of that violent city-state in terms of Christian individualism. He begins his sonnet with that sitting posture which has been associated with grief and recollection ever since Ps. 137:

> I sat beneath an olive's branches grey,
>   And gazed upon the site of a lost town
>   By sage and poet chosen for renown;
> Where dwelt a Race that on the sea held sway,
> And restless as its waters, forced a way
>   For civil strife a thousand states to drown.[146]

The warlike nature of the Corcyraeans had become legendary even before the time of Thucydides, who, in *The Peloponnesian War*, remarks that "the first naval battle on record is the one between the Corinthians and the Corcyraeans: this was about 260 years ago."[147] Newman, however, dispenses with the generalities to which historians have reduced past life by totalizing a mass of individuals "Whose spirits live in awful singleness, / Each in his self-formed sphere of light or gloom." It is difficult to see what "apostolic" purpose he hoped to serve by a poem as strange as this. Its speculations about the afterlife are, to say the least, unusual. Catholic orthodoxy forbade even the admission of virtuous pagans into heaven, but here Newman postulates a multitude of cellular afterlives, some beatific and some infernal. The implicit theme would seem to be this, that Christianity, a religion concerned with the salvation of individuals, not races, will necessarily impose a different perspective on the received commonplaces of historiography.

"Removal" is also an anagogical poem in which Newman addresses the Catholic practice of invocation, and—at this stage of his career, at least—decides against its legitimacy:

> Dear sainted Friends, I call not you
> To share this joy serene
> Which flows upon me from the view
> Of crag and steep ravine.[148]

Newman has here taken a rocky Mediterranean landscape to image the topography of Eden, defying such sentimental versions as the one that Keble would later offer in *Lyra Innocentium*:

> Round the margin breath'd and bloom'd
> Flowers from Eden: far below
> Gems from Heaven the sides illum'd:—
> But nor flower nor gems might show
> Half so fair as your soft charms,
> Who in your own Seraph's arms
> Here are wafted, in pure vest
> Rob'd, and wash'd, and seal'd, and bless'd.[149]

How bracingly harsh the texture of Newman's vision compared with these deliquescent charms and wafting sensations; how refreshingly different the nudity of his crags and steep ravines from a luxuriance of flowers and gems. He seems to have derived his idea of the "earthly paradise" from Dante, who similarly broke with convention: "this mountain rock / Was raised thus high to heaven, and lifted clear / Above all this, from where it's under lock.[150] In her note on this canto from *Purgatorio*, Dorothy Sayers has also remarked on "Dante's insistence on speaking always of 'the sacred *Forest*', 'the ancient *Forest*', and never employing the more usual and traditional image of a garden."[151] Newman's mountain cells likewise testify to the originality of *his* mind.

Since the saints are resting in sealed-off quiet, they cannot be importuned; nor can the busier race of angels, even though they mediate between heaven and earth: "Ye hear, and ye can sympathize— / Vain thought!" Invocation should accordingly be reserved for Christ alone, who, because he sustains his glorified body at the right hand of God, remains accessible to our human impetrations. The dynamic of the whole poem, with its strategic false starts and revocations, is strongly reminiscent of Herbert's formal changes of tack, which Helen Vendler has called "reinventions."[152] It is clear that Newman feels *some* attraction to the idea of invoking the saints, but, pulled in the opposite direction by his Evangelical heritage, he wrestles himself away from it. And indeed there is a lyric in *The Temple* that shows that Herbert was also beset by similar temptations, as Louis Martz has pointed out: "One of the finest tributes to the reluctance of conservative Anglicans to give up this devotion [to the Blessed Virgin Mary] is found, as we might expect, in George Herbert: in his remarkably ambiguous poem, 'To All Angels and Saints.'"[153] Newman dissolves a comparable attraction by reaffirming Christ's humanity, a fact that dispenses with the need for other human mediators.

"Rest" develops the imaginative conception of paradise that has been sketched in "Removal." Here those waiting for judgment once again sleep in mountain cells. While Barry has remarked that it treats "after Venerable Bede, of 'a meadow wherein the souls, not suffering, were detained, as yet unmeet for the Beatific Vision,'"[154] he fails to note that the traditional meadows of Fra Angelico and Giovanni di Paolo have given way to a bleaker topography (as in a Gethsemane painting by Bellini or Mantegna). As before, Newman advances this unusual conception as confidently as though it were a received dogmatic truth:

> They are at rest:
> We may not stir the heaven of their repose
> By rude invoking voice, or prayer addrest
> In waywardness to those

Who in the mountain grots of Eden lie,
And hear the fourfold river as it murmurs by.

They hear it sweep
In distance down the dark and savage vale;
But they at rocky bed, or current deep,
    Shall never more grow pale;
They hear, and meekly muse, as fain to know
How long untired, unspent, that giant stream shall flow.

And soothing sounds,
Blend with the neighbouring waters as they glide;
Posted along the haunted garden's bounds,
    Angel forms abide,
Echoing, as words of watch, o'er lawn and grove
The echoes of that hymn which Seraphs chant above.[155]

This strikes me as poetry of the highest order, comparable with such masterpieces as Tennyson's "Kraken":

Below the thunder of the upper deep;
Far, far beneath in the abysmal sea,
His ancient, dreamless, uninvaded sleep
The Kraken sleepeth: faintest sunlights flee
About his shadowy sides:[156]

The imaginative link between these two great poems might be called the Berkeleian principle—the poets' projection of consciousness upon unconscious or semiconscious beings, conferring reality on an environment barely grasped by the subjects. Another unifying factor is the sublimity of vagueness, of scumbled vision and half articulated forms, perceived as through a veil of sleep. Gray has perhaps supplied Newman with a hint or two in this regard, for in "The Descent of Odin. An Ode" the prophetess is equally reluctant to respond to the invocation of the god: "Who is he, with voice unblest, / That calls me from the bed of rest" and again "Unwilling I my lips unclose: / Leave me, leave me to repose."[157] Another echo of Gray is perhaps to be found in the vague sublimity of "angelic forms" (rather than specified angels), recalling on the one hand the "shaggy forms" in "The Progress of Poesy"[158] and the "angel forms" in the "Ode on the Death of a Favourite Cat."[159] There is also an interesting effort in this poem to reclaim the rocky landscape from the demonic associations it had acquired in countless Temptations of St. Anthony, and in such poems as "Kubla Khan":

> But oh! the deep romantic chasm which slanted
> Down the green hill athwart a cedarn cover!
> A savage place! as holy and enchanted
> As e'er beneath a waning moon was haunted
> By woman wailing for her demon lover.[160]

Newman does not *expunge* demonic color altogether—the vale, like Coleridge's chasm, still remains "dark and savage"—but simply ensures that the blessed feel no human fears at its prospect: "they . . . Shall never more grow pale." And yet this strange otherworldly peace is located within the real world, as witness the reference to the "fourfold river" (the Pison, Gihon, Tigris, and Euphrates), resuscitating (in 1833) an old medieval belief in the earthly paradise. This fantasticates an otherwise solemn meditation on the beatific state and adds a further element of mystery to a mysterious poem.

5

Newman's Contribution to
Lyra Apostolica: II

PRAYER" belongs to a group of poems that ponder the humbling function of sin. Our efforts at perfection will always be thwarted by ineradicable flaws that, like the errors for Allah in Persian carpets, serve to remind us of our human limitations. Newman clearly subscribed to the Mosaic authorship of the Pentateuch, the content of which he here presents as a pageant of priestly matter. The "shadows" in the second stanza could either signify that the cultus is a sacramental image of God's glory or that it *fore*shadows the activities of the Great High Priest so methodically spelled out by the author of Hebrews. Be that as it may, there can be no doubting that Newman has once gain found inspiration in Gray's "Bard," with its pageant of Tudor monarchs.[1] Into this rapt trance comes the "news flash" of infidelity at the foot of the mountain, a sort of knocking at the door that drags Moses back to the quotidian reality of sin and apostasy: "A sadder vision came, / Announcing all that guilty deed / Of idol rite."[2] But as it does, it turns the priestly office into something more than a sacrificial ministry. Moses, type of Christ, and finally of all priests after him, becomes an intercessor, tempering divine wrath with mercy. There is a bitter prophetic note in this poem. When Newman and Frederick Faber went their separate ways in Birmingham and London, the latter envisaged him in a study "with books up to the ceiling where [he] could be reading and people could come and see him" and where he could convert "intellectual infidels, lawyers and heretics rather than hearing the general confessions of dirty paddies,"[3] shocking witness to his prejudice against a disadvantaged congregation struggling, like Moses', "in the vale" below.

"Isaac" is also an undercutting exercise, since it claims that the patriarch's holiness was compromised by his mistakenly blessing Jacob. This is a harsh judgment indeed, since blame must rather be heaped on Jacob and his mother. We can therefore infer that Newman is articulating the new rigorism of the Tractarians, a counsel of perfection that turns a stern, censorious eye on things that ordinary people might find venial:

> Many the guileless years the Patriarch spent,
>   Blessed in the wife a father's foresight chose;
>   Many the prayers and gracious deeds which rose,
> Daily thank-offerings from his pilgrim tent.
> Yet these, though written in the heavens, are rent
>   From out truth's lower roll, which sternly shows
>   But one sad trespass of his history's close,
> Father's, son's, mother's, and its punishment.[4]

This heaping *(acervatio)*, followed by a carpet-tug, presents a parable about our vulnerability to sin, a precedent for which exists in Herbert:

> Blessings beforehand, tyes of gratefulnesse,
>   The sound of glorie ringing in our eares:
>   Without, our shame; within, our consciences;
> Angels and grace, eternall hopes and fears.
>   Yet all these fences and their whole aray
>   One cunning bosome-sinne blows quite away.[5]

Exactly the same rhythm of accumulation and sudden collapse informs "The Call of David," unusual in its being spoken by angels at David's coronation. Unlike Keble's, who crane into the abyss as they try to decipher the mystery of the Atonement, Newman's angels are virtually omniscient, whether by native talent or by instruction from the Deity the poem does not say. They simply gather round and, like the Norns, spin David's life-thread. Although they begin with a *prompemptikon* or Godspeed wish, they soon gloat over the accumulation of perils and failings :

> Go! and mid thy flocks awhile,
> At thy doom of greatness smile;
> Bold to bear God's heaviest load,
> Dimly guessing of the road,—
> Rocky road, and scarce ascended,

> Though thy foot be angel-tended;
> Double praise thou shalt attain,
> In royal court and battle plain;
> Then comes heart-ache, care, distress,
> Blighted hope, and loneliness;[6]

The source for this relentless hail of woes is easily found. Because the catalog is made all the more irremissive by the speed with which the couplets, missing the extra foot of heroic pentameter, snap shut on its victim, we can be fairly sure than Newman had Gray's "Fatal Sisters" in mind:

> Low the dauntless Earl is laid,
> Gored with many a gaping wound:
> Fate demands a nobler head;
> Soon a King shall bite the ground.[7]

But even as the sins are heaped up by the *acervatio*, they turn into *felices culpae*, partly canceled by the savior who will spring from the line of David. Hence the sudden indifference to posterity's verdict ("Dust unborn may bless or blame"), and its subordination to the more central work of redemption: "But we mould thee for the root, / Of man's promised healing fruit." This coda was an afterthought, for it is missing from the first draft that Newman sent his mother on 26 January 1833.[8]

"I saw thee once" takes its epigraph from Gal. 1:24—"They glorified God in me"—where individual imperfection is subsumed into, made perfect by, the Godhead it attempts to serve. An apocryphal document of the second century, *The Acts of Paul and Thecla*, describes the Apostle as "a man little of stature, thin-haired upon the head, crooked in the legs, of good state of body, with eyebrows joining, and a nose somewhat hooked, full of grace: for sometimes he appeared like a man and sometimes he had the face of an angel."[9] Commentators have remarked that it "is conceivable that this imaginative writing incorporates traditions about Paul that circulated in Iconium."[10] Since Newman came increasingly to relish saintly myths, we can be fairly certain that he drew on this source material when he wrote the lyric in hand, for, like St. Paul in *The Acts of Paul and Thecla*, his subject oscillates between ordinariness and divinity. There can be little doubt that the poem is about Keble, of whose face Georgina Battiscombe has remarked that it "might have belonged to an honest Gloucestershire farmer, but for the fine eyes."[11] To a mind conditioned by engravings of Renaissance St. Jeromes and St. Anthonys, such a pleasant, homely face would not at first glance have seemed the signifier of special piety—hence the ritualized "triple-take" of the poem as the conviction of Keble's sainthood dawns, accessed, no doubt, through those "beamy" eyes:

> I saw once more, and awe-struck gazed
>   On face, and form, and air;
> God's living glory round thee blazed—
>   A Saint—a Saint was there![12]

This uses an old narrative design in which deities disguise themselves to test the probity of mortals and then disclose themselves in all their glory. An early instance is the story of Philemon and Baucis in Ovid's *Metamorphoses*, where Jupiter and Mercury reward the couple by transforming their cottage into "a temple: marble columns took the place of its wooden supports, the thatch grew yellow, till the roof seemed to be made of gold."[13] Christian hagiography also adapted this sort of epiphany in the legends of St. Julian the Hospitaller ("One day they [St. Julian and his wife] succoured a man almost dead with cold, who before he disappeared in glory told Julian that Jesus Christ had accepted his penance")[14] and St. Christopher ("Reaching the other shore, Christopher inquired 'Who art thou, child, that placed me in such extreme peril? Had I carried the whole world on my shoulder, the burden had not been heavier.' 'Wonder not, Christopher,' the child replied. 'Thou hast not only borne the world, but Him who made the world on your shoulders. I am Jesus Christ the King'").[15] So much for Newman's transfiguration of ordinariness in a poem at once personal and—out of consideration, no doubt, of the subject's modesty—unspecific. Equally interesting is the way in which he renders the *process* of perception, as though the anagnorisis of a Greek drama had been boiled down from three acts to three stanzas. A mock-heroic precedent for an unfolding perception can be found in Gray's "Ode on the Death of a Favourite Cat," where variants of the prophetic *vidi* are placed at various stages of the poem to monitor the change of vision ("She saw and purred applause"; "Still had she gazed"; "The hapless nymph with wonder saw"),[16] just as each stanza of Newman's poem repeats but develops the act of viewing. And since revelation inevitably produces excitement and yearning, the expression reveals a comparable agitation—

the *epizeuxis,* for example. Who can doubt that Newman, passionate lover of Beethoven, knew the aria in *Fidelio* in which Florestan recognizes a succoring angel as his wife? There too we encounter what might be termed "cognitive" *epizeuxis:* "Ein Engel, Leonoren, Leonoren der Gattin, so gleich, der."[17] Further instances could be cited from Hopkins's "Carrion Comfort"—"I wretch lay wrestling with (my God!) my God,"[18] and from Keats's *Hyperion,* where Clymene hears someone twice saluting Apollo's godhead: "A voice came sweeter, sweeter than all tune, / And still it cried, 'Apollo, young Apollo!.'"[19] Whether Keble ever did luminesce as dramatically as Newman claims he did ("God's living glory round thee blazed") cannot now be determined, but it seems likely that Newman has blent personal experience with these various literary traditions.

"I dreamed that, with a passionate complaint" broaches a similar topic, except here a dream formula frames and distances the revelation of sainthood beneath a surface otherwise uncompelling or unattractive. On this occasion Newman rejects mythic elements as the products of a glamorizing fancy:

> Yet in the mood, he could with aptness speak,
> Or with stern force, or show of feelings keen,
> Marking deep craft, methought, or hidden pride:
> Then came a voice—"St. Paul is at thy side!"[20]

Whereas in "I saw thee once" Newman's presentation of Keble recalled the St. Paul of *The Acts of Paul and Thecla,* here he does the reverse, reconceiving the saint in distinctly Kebelian terms. I certainly do not recognize the St. Paul of the epistles in this Romney-like portrait of an English gentleman—are "courteous" and "grave" the epithets that spring to the minds of most readers? "Meek in mien" might likewise better describe the personae of St. John and St. James. More to the point, however, is the speaker's misconstruction of the face as "Marking deep craft," since this does indeed recall the famous Pauline *phronesis*—being all things to all people. But at this point Keble's broad farmer face goes out of focus, and Newman seems to glance at his own mirror. Archbishop Benson would later speak of "the terrible lines deeply ploughed all over his face, and the craft that sat upon his retreating forehead and sunken eyes."[21] Be that as it may, a voice confirms the apostolic credentials of a man whom the world might slight or even despise.

Keble was reluctant, as we know, to pass judgment on dubious elements in the Old Testament. Newman doubtless tried to follow his master in this as in other instances, but his more commodious and complex mind made it a difficult task. In spite of all his invective against heresy, he had the grace to admit that an auto-da-fé would have undone him, and he himself would soon know the pain of delation and persecution by the church which later received him. The epigraph of "Christ bade his followers" is accordingly ambivalent, being undercut rather than endorsed by the poem it prefaces: "Him that escapeth from the sword of Jehu shall Elisha slay". At first blush, this might seem to license violence in people otherwise committed to the service of God or misguided enough to think that God can be served through violence, a topic that Newman had already explored with Bowden in *St. Bartholomew's Eve.* However the very format of the poem, a tense sequence peculiar to what me might call historiographic moralizing, shows that a lesson has to be learned and a point taken. Stanza 1 adduces a historical event—St. Peter's violence in Gethsemane—and, naturally enough, is couched in the past tense. Stanza 2, on the other hand, is in the "gnomic" present, the tense which locates the perpetual recurrence of moral actions in and out of time, showing that we have moved from a specific to a general plane. The final strophe shifts from the indicative to the imperative mood, urging acceptance of the moral set forth in the second. But even though the poem conforms to this homiletic pattern of event, application and hortation, there is nothing pat or formulaic about it. The renovating energy flows from a contradiction between lines 1 and 2: "Christ bade His followers take the sword / And yet he chid the deed"[22]—which is Newman's way of separating figurative from literal interpretation. Militarism will cause few problems in the context of a psychomachia, but, taken out of that mental context, it will become a crass and anti-Christian thing. That is why Newman instantly displaces the actual sword of St. Peter with the notional sword of orthodoxy, legitimized and sanctified by St. Paul's military language in Eph. 6:13–17: "And take the helmet of salvation, and the sword of the Spirit, which is the word of God." Thus to spiritualize the sword of St. Peter is implicitly to condemn the sword of Elisha in the epigraph, an item finally unworthy of a prophet.

"Thou to wax fierce," like many other poems in *Lyra Apostolica* is the allomorphic twin of its predecessor, addressing the same topic from a slightly different angle:

> Thou to wax fierce
>   In the cause of the Lord,
> To threat and to pierce
>   With the heavenly sword;
> Anger and Zeal,
>   And the Joy of the brave,
> Who bade *thee* to feel,
>   Sin's slave.[23]

Newman probably intends the troubled, crinkly syntax of this stanza to show that the addressee has not been thinking clearly. "Sin's slave" is self-directed; but because of the syntactic torsion, it also tends to register as the answer to "Who bade thee to feel Anger and Zeal?" and momentarily suggests the figure of Satan. As St. Peter had confused physical violence with sustained aggression against sin, so the speaker in this poem rebukes himself for having luxuriated in a *saeva indignatio* that springs from self. The second stanza recasts the argument in terms of the old beam/mote formula, suggesting that the "apostolic" fervor ignited by the "national apostasy" has led the speaker to direct his attention outward at perceived enemies, losing sight of the insidious fifth column within.

Such self-arraignment is obviously salutory and just, but it has an attendant danger. Publicly to confess to sin demands heroism from the confessor, and bound up in that heroism is the temptation to admire one's own courage. So in "Thy words are good and freely given" Newman remarks that repeated confessions might simply be a form of self-display that trivializes the sacrament:

> Beware! such words may once be said,
>   Where shame and fear unite;
> But, spoken twice, they mark instead
>   A sin against the light.[24]

The same topic is rotated a few degrees and reexamined in "Deeds Not Words." Here words have all the rampancy of *natura naturans*, crying for the restraint and discipline of a gardener's tool:

> Prune thou thy words, the thoughts control
>   That o'er thee swell and throng;
> They will condense within thy soul,
>   And change to purpose strong.[25]

The verb "swell" provides an entrée into the image of condensation, since it applies as much to the vigor of sap as it does to the distillation of "swelling" gas—the gas of theory and profession—into nurturing liquid. Many anecdotes in Newman's biography point to his tearful tendencies. Responding to the stern task of *nosce teipsum*, he acknowledges the danger of such indulgence, for his chosen adjective "luxurious" comes from *luxus*, the Latin word for "excess":

> But he, who lets his feelings run,
>   In soft luxurious flow,
> Shrinks when hard service must be done,
>   And faints at every woe.

Newman here alludes obliquely to the definition of poetry as "the spontaneous overflow of powerful feelings,"[26] where feeling, marginalized by neoclassical theory, is given an aesthetic status of its own. Even in 1833, Newman seems to have sensed a potential danger in the Oxford Movement—confirmed by its development into Ritualism—viz., that of aestheticizing religious emotion. His final stanza, indeed, comes close to paraphrasing an utterance of an Evangelical predecessor, Reginald Heber. Compare

> Faith's meanest deed more favour bears,
>   Where hearts and wills are weighed,
> Than brightest transports, choicest prayers,
>   Which bloom their hour and fade

with the final strophe of the latter's hymn—"Brightest and best of the sons of the morning":

> Vainly we offer each ample oblation,
>   Vainly with gifts would his favour secure:
> Deeper by far is the heart's adoration,
>   Dearer to God are the prayers of the poor.[27]

But even while Newman censures the emotionalism that, encouraged by the Romantic cult of the *Gefühlsmensch*, has displaced proper religious feeling, he falls back on another key romantic doctrine, that of primitivism. The "meanest deed" of faith is first cousin to the "meanest flower that blows" in Wordsworth's *Intimations Ode*[28] and exalts simplicity and sincerity above elaborated grandeur.

Since the *via media* of Anglicanism centers on a none-too-stable compromise between the additions of Roman Catholicism and the subtractions of Protestantism, the dialectical oscillation of *Lyra Apostolica* is easily explained. Where "Deeds not Words" sounded a warning against aesthetic temptations that might otherwise deflect the life of faith, "How didst thou start" defends the sacerdotalism (and by implication the ceremoniousness) that had largely vanished from the Anglican Church after 1688. Newman takes St. John the Baptist as the type of priests who think their failings disqualify them from sacramental tasks—a *non sum dignus* theme going back at least as far as Herbert's "Aaron":[29] "How didst thou start, Thou Holy Baptist, bid / To pour repentance on the Sinless Brow!"[30] At the great sacramental climax of his ministry, the implication runs, St. John felt humility, not the pride of office that might otherwise have been expected of him. The idea is then applied and inverted in the second stanza, where the speaker sloughs traditional Protestant views of the priest and magnifies his office. It is interesting to note that scorn creeps in with the claim at the very moment it is made—the reference to "common eyes" calls to mind Horace's famous announcement at the start of his Roman odes—*Odi profanum vulgus et arceo.*[31] As soon as priests claim special privileges, they form a spiritual elite, and from that sense of difference there will spring traditional charges of priestcraft and Jesuitry, anticipated here as a "purpose deep."

Newman's "Sleep" will show the characteristic temper of the Tractarian sensibility if we set it against Keats's handling of the same topic. The romantic poet, filled with religious emotion that has no formal creed to channel it, is prone to a mythopoeia that deifies everything under the sun. This is how R. H. Barrow describes the religion of ancient Rome: "Every minute operation of nature and man . . . took place in the presence and by the energy of these vague powers, now becoming formless deities."[32] One such "formless deity" engendered by the romantic thirst for an immanent rather than a transcendent divinity is Keats's Sleep:

> O soft embalmer of the still midnight,
>   Shutting, with careful fingers and benign,
> Our gloom-pleas'd eyes, embower'd from the light,
>   Enshaded in forgetfulness divine:[33]

To pass from this to Newman's "Sleep" is to enter an entirely different world:

> Unwearied God! before whose face
> > The night is clear as day,
> Whilst we, poor worms, o'er life's brief race
> > Now creep, and now delay;
> We with death's foretaste alternate
> Our labour's dint and sorrow's weight,
> Save in that fever-troubled state
> > When pain and care hold sway.[34]

Keats's sonnet addresses an ad hoc deity, for whom, in a manner reminiscent of Collins's odes, it establishes an ad hoc cultus. The tone is blandishing, the format an intercessory prayer, the motive, exemption from suffering. Newman, by contrast is sternly orthodox, and the discomfort of human sleeplessness (which Keats evades by anesthetizing conscience) is here embraced as a penal consequence of sin. Indeed, as in conventional Catholic theology the sufferer is advised to unite his or her sufferings with the transcendent suffering of Christ, so in a strange but analogous way Newman here unites his sleeplessness with the sleeplessness of God, irradiating and divinizing what would otherwise appear to be a human disability. (In his first draft, Newman addressed the Deity as a "sleepless God"[35] but softened the anthropomorphism in his final version.) There is not a breath of romantic escapism in the poem; the speaker accepts the "disease" of insomnia because it extends the temporal scope of his awareness. This gives God the opportunity to impress upon the wakeful subject his lessons of humility and submission.

In "The Elements" we have a dress rehearsal for the argument of *The Tamworth Reading Room*, an essay in which Newman attacked the Benthamites' deification of knowledge. His epigraph, taken from Sophocles' *Antigone*, is a distich that E. F. Watling has rendered thus: "Wonders are many on the earth, and the greatest of these / Is man."[36] That sentiment, of course, is a variant of the Protagorean claim that humankind provides the measure of all things, a claim to which the nineteenth century increasingly gave its assent. Newman, needless to say, had little patience with what he perceived to be the hubris of such thinking—in the same chorus from *Antigone* Sophocles claims that "There is nothing beyond [humanity's] power,"[37] a doctrine espoused also by the proponents of Victorian meliorism. (We might therefore want to qualify the adjective "Aeschylean" that R. H. Hutton applied to lyric,[38] since the poem actually offers a *critique* of the Greek ethos of knowledge and comes close, as Stephen Thomas has observed in another context, to "identifying the *appetitus intellectivus* with deficiency of character, unreflective obscurantism with the fullness of orthodox truth.")[39] Newman starts with a passive verb so as to set an unspecified supernatural constraint upon the exercise of human will:

> Man is permitted much
> To scan and learn
> In Nature's frame;
> Till he can well-nigh tame
> Brute mischiefs,[40]

While human power might seem to have no limit, it is circumscribed by the permitting omnipotence of God. Newman stresses this by half-alluding to Rom. 8:28—"And we know that all things work together for good to them that love God"—a harmonization of which humankind is incapable.

The second stanza falls back on the apologetic position taken up in such texts as Job 26:7-8—we should submit to a God who can command the forces we cannot control ("He stretcheth out the north over the empty place, *and* hangeth the earth upon nothing"). However, the catalog of human *adynata* cannot be termed persuasive. Newton had indeed explained the restraint of "impious Ocean" a century before, and Henry Cavendish had used a "set scale" to explore, if not the "Air's weight," then certainly the earth's. Jenner had likewise made some advances in tracing the advent of the Plague. The trouble with theodicies that try to circumscribe the human sphere is that they are almost invariably overtaken by technology. (To be purely anecdotal, I knew an old woman who lost her faith when Neil Armstrong set foot on the moon; she had been taught that God had created humankind to stay on Earth.)

With Newman's reactionary middle term thus called into question, we cannot wholly assent to his conclusion in the third and final strophe. As a Roman Catholic apologist he would later argue that the Tractarians, by restricting their creed to the authority of the Fathers, had artificially "capped" the principle of doctrinal development, and yet he is just as ready to cap the technological advance of humankind in this poem, suggesting a cutoff point for the skills permitted by Providence: "man, when fully skilled, / Still gropes in twilight dim." In its resulting despondency, it will turn to God, and in that turning, repent of its quest for knowledge. No wonder

Kingsley and other Latitudinarians were appalled by such dissociations of religious and secular knowledge. In Herbert's "Pulley," God withheld rest from humanity to secure its allegiance; in Newman's Faustian adapation of the argument, God withholds information. And yet, whatever reservations the reader might have about the argument of "The Elements," there can be no denying the excitement of its lean, peristaltic stanza, which pushes the line of thought forward through a contraction of trimeter and dimeter lines.

Temptation is as old as religion itself, since most religions involve a negotiation between the better and worse selves. Even Medea in Ovid's *Metamorphoses* feels herself torn between reason and impulse: "I see which is the better course, and I approve it; but still I follow the worse."[41] While the Christian genre of the psychomachia formalizes these internal struggles as mental warfare, another less dramatic tradition—that of the *contentio*—turns the conflict into an internal debate:

> "Give any boon for peace!
> Why should our fair-eyed Mother e'er engage
> In the world's course and on a troubled stage,
> From which her very call is a release?
> No! in thy garden stand,[42]

The epigraph of this lyric, taken from Matt. 10:8, suggests that the gift of grace demands more than a posture of passive reception—it must be channeled into the world at large. Roman Catholicism had always made provision for the contemplative as well as the active life, but apart from Nicholas Ferrar's experiment at Little Gidding, the Anglican Church never sought to institutionalize the *via contemplativa*. The tenure of secular fellowships at the two universities was as far as Canterbury went in the direction of St. Benedict, which is why Newman changed "cloister's shade" to "learned shade."[43] So even while he comes down on the side of apostolic fervor and engagement with the world at large, he is sufficiently drawn to the alternative set forth so enticingly in the opening stanza. Indeed his retreat to Littlemore when he lay on his Anglican "deathbed" shows him opting for a solution different from the one offered here. The garden image seems almost certainly to have derived from Marvell's many celebrations of retirement, a retirement nonetheless condemned in *An Horatian Ode upon Cromwel's Return from Ireland* as being inappropriate to stirring times:

> The forward Youth that would appear
> Must now forsake his *Muses* dear,
>   Nor in the shadows sing
>   His numbers languishing.[44]

Marvell's epithet "languishing" here suggests that pastoral offers a feckless, inactive option. And in a similar way, Newman associates *his* garden with naïveté ("Thou guileless one") and unprogressive stasis ("in thy garden stand"), negative elements designed to qualify its attractiveness. He contrasts the human, "pious" hand in stanza 1 with the "rough hand" of God in stanza 2 to sanctify energy and commitment to the struggle and to remind us that conversion is a disruptive event that can effect no compromise with the world. As though remembering Marvell once again—this time the nuns' blandishing arguments in *Upon Appleton House*[45]—he furthermore implies that retirement is a selfish option. By ignoring the world to secure peace of mind, it betrays the apostolic mission. St. Paul, by this reasoning, would have been a sort of Levitical monk if he had not chosen to be an apostle!

"Time was, I shrank" is another conversion poem, placing a spiritual "before" and "after" in antithetic tension to each other. The "before" is the "garden"-self of effacement, the "after" the struggle for commitment. And, as in the preceding poem, the realignment involves moral definition, where the new self penetrates the shell of former virtues to reveal the vices they enclosed. In *Verses on Various Occasions*, Newman christened the poem "Sensitiveness," publicly confessing to a "vice" of which many found him guilty:

> But now I cast that finer sense
>   And sorer shame aside;
> Such dread of sin was indolence,
>   Such aim at heaven was pride.[46]

"Παυλου μιμητης" (The imitator of Paul) recurs to that saint as the pattern of apostolic perfection and advocates a sort of *imitatio Pauli* instead of that more traditional *imitatio Christi*. Here, to offset the militarism and recklessness of "Give any boon for peace," Newman counsels a Pauline *phronesis*—shrewd adaptability to circumstance. *Imitatio Pauli* will not necessarily produce heroic confrontations but rather a sense—by grace of God—of when it *is* right to pursue the cause. Here we have that reserve and prudence which, along with extraordinary lapses of judgment and confrontational tactics, characterized the leadership of the Oxford Movement:

> "Not so," He said:— "hush thee, and seek,
>   With thoughts in prayer and watchful eyes,
> My season sent for thee to speak,
>   And use them as they rise."[47]

And while "Παυλου μιμητης" contrasts the implicit heroism of the Apostle with the "unheroic" counsel of his nineteenth-century successors, "The Saint and the Hero" reverses the poles of the antithesis, if indeed St. Paul is the subject (as I suspect he is). In the "Keble" poem earlier in the collection ("I saw thee once, and naught discerned"),[48] the speaker recorded a gradual perception of holiness beneath an ordinary surface. Here, nuancing the topic in a slightly different way, he records a disappointing collision between the ideal and the humble reality it has mythicized. I find it difficult to construe the meaning of "far off" in the opening stanza: "O aged Saint! far off I heard / The praises of thy name."[49] Since Newman did not visit any holy men during his Mediterranean tour, and since Keble cannot have deserved the epithet "aged" in 1832-33, the saint in question is probably a biblical figure (St. Paul?), an object of abstract veneration in England but somehow made real by Newman's having partially retraced the course of his missionary journeys. Given the antithesis of worldly heroism and unflashy piety in the title of the lyric, the allusion to Caesar's *Veni, vidi, vici* has a special irony. Newman has omitted the third member of the design to show he recoils from a worldly desire to dominate:

> I came and saw; and, having seen,
>   Weak heart, I drew offence
> From thy prompt smile, thy simple mien,
>   Thy lowly diligence.

The recoil is not immediate, however. The speaker has first to swallow his disappointment at virtues so "unheroic" and Kebelian. Of course, it is possible that the saint is simply a generic saint and that the poem is simply a fable about spiritual education. Certainly the last stanza functions as an *epimythium*, its generality further indicated by the uppercase spellings:

> The Saint's is not the Hero's praise;—
> This have I found, and learn
> Nor to profane Heaven's humblest ways,
> Nor its least boon to spurn.

That, of course, is the very spirit of the Incarnation, which undercut the triumphalism of traditional messianic ideas.

"Jonah" takes us back to the tension between the contemplative and the active life, a tension that vibrates through most of the poems that surround it in *Lyra Apostolica.* The echoes of Marvell's "Garden" are even stronger than they were in "Give any boon for peace." Jonah, all but "stumbling on Melons,"[50] has all but fallen on grass:

> Deep in his meditative bower,
>   The tranquil seer reclined;
> Numbering the creepers of an hour,
>   The gourds which o'er him twined.[51]

Newman is obviously addressing those who deplored the party spirit and divisiveness that sprang from the Oxford Movement and pointing out that in times of crisis, there can be no striving for Horatian ideals of retirement and *aequa mens.* Whereas the Sabine farm had offered Horace refuge from urban corruption, Newman's austere Christian vision sees sin as an all-pervasive fact—*caelum non vitia mutant qui trans mare currunt.* There can be no doubt as to the answer he expects to the rhetorical questions at the end of "Jonah":

> What?—pride and sloth! man's worst of foes!
>   And can such guests invade
> Our choicest bliss, the green repose
>   Of the sweet garden shade?

Exactly the same solution is offered in "Jeremiah," where, without Keble's geographic exactness, Newman projects the prophet's lodging-place in the Wilderness—always a terrifying and inhospitable locus in Old Testament thought—as an attractive "bower of bliss":

> "O place me in some silent vale,
>   Where groves and flowers abound;
> Nor eyes that grudge, nor tongues that rail,
>   Vex the truth-haunted ground!"[52]

If a prophet should sin by thus neglecting his vocation, then a Tractarian would a fortiori prove himself even more blameworthy, for his task is even greater.

In *Lyra Apostolica* the energetic clarion poems like "Jonah" and "Jeremiah" are chastened and qualified by the lyrics that flank them. It is almost as if Keble were whispering in Newman's ear from time to time and drawing his attention back to the "trivial round, the common task." In "St. Paul at Melita," for example, the speaker moves from the saint's huge prophetic office to his humble fire-making:

> Secure in his prophetic strength,
>   The water-peril o'er,
> The many-gifted man at length
>   Stept on the promised shore.[53]

There is a hint here of trial by fire and water, and the immunity from human fears confirmed by such trials (in Mozart's *Zauberflöte*, for example). The promised shore also for a moment sounds like an arrival in Canaan and, typologically extended, an arrival in heaven. However, the anadiplosis between stanzas 1 and 2 connects transcendence and the everyday duties that (properly viewed) are its medium:

> He trod the shore; but not to rest,
>   Nor wait till Angels came;
> Lo! humblest pains the Saint attest,
>   The firebrands and the flame.

This humble task nonetheless has its own miraculous consequence when the viper in the faggots fails to kill St. Paul. From which Newman extracts the obvious moral that ripeness is all—"Christian! hence learn to do thy part, / And leave the rest to Heaven."

In "Give any boon for peace," in "Jonah," and in "Jeremiah," Newman had screwed his courage to the sticking point and accepted the fissions and factions that would result from his combative response to "Liberalism." "The time has been" shows that the peace that might have resulted from the Tractarians' withdrawing to a life of pietistic quiet would not be peace at all but rather the indifferentism of laissez-faire. Quiet, after all, as the Marquis in Schiller's *Don Carlos* reminds us, must not be confused with the quietus of death. The "Ruhe" that King Philip intends to bring to Flanders is "Die

Ruhe eines Kirchhofs"—the peace of a graveyard.[54] The poem begins by looking back:

> The time has been, it seemed a precept plain
>   Of the true faith, Christ's tokens to display;
> And in life's commerce still the thought retain,
>   That men have souls, and wait a judgment-day,
> Kings used their gifts as ministers of heaven,
> Nor stripped their zeal for God of means which God had given.[55]

This is Newman writing under the influence of Froude, yearning for the unity of (Western) Christendom before the Reformation. The nostalgia declares itself above all in the elegiac "The time has been" formula, one that often signals the wistful recollection of a vanished order, as witness this couplet from Goldsmith's *Deserted Village*: "A time there was, ere England's griefs began / When every rood of ground maintained its man."[56] The glorious "was" inevitably yields to a "now" of decadence and falling away: "But now the sounds of population fail, / No cheerful murmurs fluctuate in the gale."[57] In Newman, too:

> 'Tis altered now;—for Adam's eldest born
>   Has trained our practice in a selfish rule;
> Each stands alone, Christ's bonds asunder torn,

Some thirty years later Matthew Arnold would also employ the "was / now" polarity, when he mourned the dissolution of Christian unity in "Dover Beach":

> The sea of faith
> Was once, too, at the full, and round earth's shore
> Lay like the folds of a bright girdle furl'd;
> But now I only hear
> Its melancholy, long, withdrawing roar,[58]

But whereas for Arnold that faith remains irrecoverable—on more than one occasion he called Catholic orthodoxy a position "frankly impossible"—Newman's poem ends with a clarion summons, a gesture of defiant anachronism that seeks to displace the "now" with "was." It was precisely this flying in the face of received Victorian wisdom that earned the Tractarians the contempt of such progressive thinkers as Dickens and Carlyle:

> Brothers! spare reasoning;—men have settled long
>   That ye are out of date, and they are wise;
> Use their own weapons; let your words be strong,
>   Your cry be loud, till each scared boaster flies;
> Thus the Apostles tamed the pagan breast,
> They argued not, but preached; and conscience did the rest.

Whether this sweeping, anti-intellectual conclusion is entirely true to the details of the Book of Acts—what, for example, about St. Paul's sermon in Athens?—is scarcely to the point. Newman does violence to his own brilliant mind by suggesting that the only solution to infidelity was to shout it down. It is hard not to share Mark Pattison's irritation on this score:

> He was yet insular, like all his generation at Oxford, in idea not less than in knowledge. Dean Stanley's epigram is celebrated: "How different the fortunes of the Church of England, if Newman had been able to read German!" Pattison, who reports it, observes that "he assumed and adorned the narrow basis on which Laud had stood two hundred years before"; and he adds, not without bitterness, "All the grand development of human reason, from Aristotle down to Hegel, was a sealed book to him."[59]

This repellent smugness is of a piece with Newman's contemptuous reaction when he heard that Manning, as a member of the Metaphysical Society, had been present for Huxley's paper on the impossibility of the Resurrection. More interesting is the cadence of "The time has been," resolving not in noise but in conscience, and so anticipating the important place that Newman would later ascribe to this faculty in *The Grammar of Assent.*

A preacher who stresses godliness above comfort will almost certainly reshuffle other Gospel priorities in order to stiffen and sharpen his creed. The title of the next lyric, "Zeal before Love," belongs much more to the genocidal narrative of Joshua than it does to the Gospel of St. John. Conscious that the Tractarians' combativeness often seemed at odds with Christian demand for charity, Newman wrote apologetic poems to smother any stirrings of conscience. Sometimes, as in "Jonah" and "Jeremiah," the perceived conflict issued in a debate in which the opposing voices are given approximately equal weight; sometimes, as in "Zeal before Love," the opposition is drowned by strident declamation—Newman had, after all, urged his factional "Brothers" to the disruptive tactics that had characterized English elections before Reform: "let your words be strong, / Your cry be loud":

> And wouldst thou reach, rash scholar mine,
>   Love's high unruffled state?
> Awake! thy easy dreams resign:
>   First learn thee how to hate.[60]

Here Newman dismantles the Stoic ideal of ataraxia, of dispassionateness, as a mere construct of the study—a seeking to escape rather than to canalize human feelings. (Keble had always suggested that Catholics were more "poetic," gave fuller scope to feeling, than Liberals.) The "rash scholar" is therefore a compound familiar ghost, made up of Hoadley, Thomas Arnold, and other like-minded thinkers. There is a curious tension between "rash" and "unruffled," suggesting an unscholarly wildness beneath a professed calm. Of course the distressing line that ends stanza 1 has been set up as the "fall guy" for a *contre-rejet* at the start of the next, where the object of hatred is properly defined as sin. The trouble is that the Tractarians did not always distinguish between the sinner and the sin, as, inter alia, their vindictiveness towards Hampden attests. The lives of the Oxford Apostles contain many unedifying episodes—Newman's priggish letter to Whately after the suppression of the Irish bishoprics and Keble's refusing to shake the hand of an Arnoldian because he had "sacrificed at the altar of Jupiter." If you demonize your opposition—and the Tractarians leveled charges of heresy with very few qualms—it is easy to persuade yourself that your uncharity is a kind of holy wrath, the more so if you take your bearings from the likes of Elijah, who slaughtered the prophets of Baal, or Elisha, who set bears upon troublesome boys. So it is that in stanza 2 "Hatred of sin, and Zeal, and Fear" are all given primacy before Charity is allowed to emerge—the mere ghost of itself—as something ascetic and punitive, not warm and embracing. The same cold austerity informs "The Wrath to Come," where once again the Tractarians link hands with the Evangelicals against those Liberal theologians who suggested that the doctrine of eternal punishment blasphemed the charity of God. Newman informs us in the *Apologia*, "From this time [1816] I have held with a full inward assent and belief the doctrine of eternal punishment, as delivered by our Lord Himself."[61] Thus the fifteen-year-old Newman. Let us contrast this with the revelation that flashed upon the young Leigh Hunt: "I remember kneeling one day at the school-church during the Litany, when the thought fell upon me—'Suppose eternal punishment should be true.' An unusual sense of darkness and anxiety crossed me—but only for a moment. The next instant the extreme absurdity and impiety of the notion restored me to my ordinary feelings."[62] The Tractarians, of course, would have rejected the generous inclusiveness of Hunt's credo by pointing to its heterodoxy. Tampering with even one brick in the edifice of belief, they thought, would cause the entire structure to collapse. This tenacious fidelity was misplaced in an age of scientific advance, since many bricks in the structure were friable and soon began collapsing of their own accord. It was precisely Liberal theologians like F. D. Maurice (hounded out of a professorship for denying the doctrine of eternal punishment) who began redefining Christianity in terms more tenable in the nineteenth century, and more appropriate to it, than those offered by the fundamentalism of Evangelical and Tractarian alike. Saluting Maurice in a generous Horatian epistle, Tennyson drew attention to the social commitment of the Latitudinarians, a commitment that the Oxford Apostles could not begin to match (and had no interest in matching): "How best to help the slender store, / How mend the dwellings of the poor."[63] It was by their sense of social issues, not by Scholastic niceties of dogma, that the Latitudarians demonstrated the relevance of Christianity to the nineteenth century. The content of Newman's poem does not fare well by comparison, however grave and impressive the conduct of the verse. Personifying the Church as a tender mother is simply to sugar the pill of cruel dogma that Newman wants his readers to swallow.

"The Course of Truth" owes something to Keble, for it follows him in abstracting a moral type from a historical figure. Just as in "The Epiphany"[64] St. Mary and St. Joseph become Chastity and Reverence personified, so here Newman presents Christ as Truth (elaborating an equation made in the Gospel of John):

> When royal Truth, released from mortal throes,
> Burst his brief slumber, and triumphant rose,
>   Ill had the Holiest sued
>   A patron multitude,[65]

The substitution allows Newman to cut to the gist of his poem, for if Christ himself refrained from making a massive public disclosure of his resurrection, then it must follow that theological truth will not be universally held. The fact that the Tractarians constitute only a party within the body of the Anglican Church, far from compromising their claims, actually endorses them. Here, *in ovo*, is the argument of Isaac Williams's tract on reserve, of a sacred arcanum accessible only to those who are worthy of it.

"The Watchman" carries forward this concern with "remnant" theology, where the few who have earned redemption are confirmed as the missionaries of God, whose strength is made perfect in their weakness: "Weakness is aye Heaven's might."[66] Once again we recognize the austere sublimity of Newman's vision, for "Truth's grey height" (gray with mist, or gray with granite) recalls the rocky paradise of other poems. The watchman has his origin in Isaiah, but he has also been fashioned from 1 Cor. 16:13, Newman's epigraph. While it is one thing to counsel spiritual vigilance, it is another to institutionalize watchfulness and set up a sentry to monitor the course of evil. That course is traced through several Old Testament episodes where human failings would seem to have thwarted the purposes of God while actually advancing them. The refrain comes again and again, with an incremental adjustment here and another there, proving its sufficiency to all circumstances. Newman's model for this effect, as we have already seen, is the indomitable, resistant refrain of Ralegh's "Lie." Even when he does not explicitly state the idea of weakness, he implies it by force of a hidden equation. Thus Baal is undercut as a futile deity by occupying the first part of the sentence "When Baal would scan Heaven's might," because in all preceding instances of the refrain the nominative position was held by "weakness": "Weakness is aye Heaven's might"; "But weakness shall be Heaven's might"; "Our weakness shall be Heaven's might"; and so on.

So heroic a battle cry as "The Watchman" is all very well for a fight with grand satanic forces. However, the course of evil can often seem trivial and banal, and it is to this sort of ordinariness that Newman turns in "Vexations." His masochism declares itself in a romanticized vision of a martyr's suffering, but, rather as Keats had modified his death wish in the "Ode to a Nightingale" ("I have been half in love with easeful Death"),[67] so here Newman salvages part of his pain the better to savor it:

> The martyr's hope half wipes away the trace
>   Of flowing blood; the while life's humblest cares
> Smart more, because they hold in Holy Writ no place.[68]

Denied the benefit of that heroic kind of agony and consigned to trivial pricks and discomfitures, Newman then recalls the fall of the sparrow, realizing that all experience—even the least significant—belongs to the compass of Providence. Having divested himself of the Byronic mode of suffering, Newman begins "The Greek Fathers" by dismissing the poet who had recently hymned the isles of Greece. Using the jussive of contemptuous dismissal (as in Donne's "Good Morrow"—"Let sea-discoverers to new worlds have gone")[69] he cancels the pagan past to focus instead on Christian Greece:

> Let others sing thy heathen praise,
> Fallen Greece! the thought of holier times
> In my sad heart abides;[70]

Because neither the Evangelicals and the Liberals in the Anglican Church had much patience with patristics, the poem addresses a specifically Tractarian issue, viz., that of reinstating the Fathers as fathers. Newman gives them apostolic credentials by blending the legend of Danae with the narrative of Pentecost. The rest of the poem takes form as a patristic roll call, similar to those evocative lists of exotic names that we find in Elizabethan drama—in *Tamburlaine*,[71] for example.

"Athanasius" does homage to an illustrious Father, especially cherished by Newman for his opposition to Arianism. In order, however, to salvage the relevance of St. Athanasius and other Eastern saints, and take them from remote Alexandria into the life of contemporary England, Newman sets up parallels between Northern and Mediterranean saints. The lives of St. Cyprian and St. John Chrysostom, he claims, have been replicated in the life of St. Thomas of Canterbury: "Cyprian is ours, since the high-souled primate laid / Under the traitorous blade / His silvered head."[72] In the same way, Thomas More parallels the fearlessness of St. Ambrose (unless of course the champion who "crossed a king" "in dark times" refers once again to St. Thomas's feud with Henry II—St. Thomas More was canonized only in 1935). The series remains incomplete, however, and an analogue for St. Athanasius has still to be found. Newman almost certainly has Gray's ode "The Progress of Poesy" in mind here, where an apostolic succession of poets leads to the speaker, who flinchingly presents himself for the mantle. Newman likewise hints that he might turn out to be the true *fidei defensor*, crossing William IV and his parliament in comparably "dark times":

"Dim Future! shall we need / A prophet for Truth's creed?" The Tractarians had no doubt that they would. Not surprisingly, therefore, Newman focuses in his next poem on St. Gregory Nazianzus, a saint who, like himself, was retiring by temperament but who had had greatness thrust upon him. Just as in "The Elements" all human action was held subject to the permitting will of God, so here human choice has to be surrendered to the edicts of Providence: "So works the All-wise! our services dividing / Not as we ask."[73] Of interest here is the eccentric use of "divide," which Newman has taken over from 2 Tim. 15:2: "rightly dividing the word of truth." In that context, as here, "divide" virtually means "interpret." Our conception of our gifts may not be God's and the final form of our vocations will accordingly differ from our first ideas of service. Using St. Gregory in this way, as a sort of hagiological "type" for his own summons to lead a movement, Newman is able to reconcile himself to the task that lies before him. In the final stanza he recalls the saint's resignation after being bishop for a matter of weeks and his retirement to Arianzus. Again the subjection of human will to a divine dispensation registers in the disturbing metaphor of a fractured vessel, which implies that personalities are entirely extrinsic to the workings of Providence: "Heaven broke at last the consecrated tool / Whose work was done." On the heels of that harshness, however, there comes the fulfillment of St. Gregory's yearning for solitude— "According thee the lot thou lovest best,— / To muse upon times past, to serve, yet be at rest."

"When I would search the truths" also plays discordant interpretations against each other, only in this instance it is not a vertical clash between divine ordinance and human presumption but rather the lateral tension between the world and the Tractarian. The excited potentiality of the opening stanza recalls an exalted line from Gray's "Progress of Poesy" ("Thoughts that breathe and words that burn"):[74] "When I would search the truths that in me burn, / And mould them into rule and argument."[75] A crucial word here is "rule," which seems on the surface to imply the intellectual shaping and articulation of inchoate impulses, but which also carries the hint of monastic discipline—the austere stripping of worldly comforts. For Liberals such as Arnold and Whately, monasticism was so much irrecoverable baggage sloughed by Christianity in its march towards enlightenment; for Newman, committed to a celibate priesthood, it was a channel of grace that the Church of England needed urgently to restore to its corporate life. He finds, however, that even after dispensing with counsels of perfection, he is still shouted down. His comfort is set out in the second stanza, where after some self-searching, he rejects the arguments of his accusers and forges one of his peculiarly abstract types from the concrete documents of Scripture. We have already seen how in "The Course of Truth" Newman borrowed Keble's strategy of abstract displacement and rendered Christ as Truth personified. He does the same thing here and claims that truth can be claimed as truth only if it conforms to a pattern of general rejection and eventual triumph—conforms, in other words, with the gestalt of the Cross and the Resurrection. Truth is "without a home" because in Matt. 8:20 "The foxes have holes, and the birds of the air *have* nests; but the Son of Man hath not where to lay *his* head" and because the ideas and commitments of the Tractarians have as yet found no purchase within the established church.

Nervous perhaps of constituting a potential schism in that church, "Poor wanderers, ye are sore distrest" turns away from the disruptive relodging of Truth in Canterbury to address the issue of Dissent. Newman would later claim that whereas heresiarchs thirst for originality and difference, orthodox theologians repeat themselves *ad infinitum*: "St. Athanasius, St. Augustine, St. Leo are conspicuous for the repetition *in terminis* of their own theological statements."[76] The effect of such repetition registers here in the image of a track, the path of thronging orthodoxy. Similar reassurance springs from the idea of enclosure ("They fenced the rich bequest He made"), offering a fold and a home to the schismatic wanderers without. The complacency that often accompanies such "Safe in the arms of Jesus" thinking manifests itself again in "Patriarchal Faith." Nothing could more alienate the twentieth-century reader than the pre-Darwinian confidence of stanza 1. Newman intends a literal rather than a spiritual descent from Noah:

> We are not children of a guilty sire,
>> Since Noe stepped from out his wave-tossed home,
>> And a stern baptism flushed earth's faded bloom.[77]

Since, according to the speaker, the whole world was engulfed by the Deluge, we are de facto descended from the one person who survived it. Typological connections had long been made between the flood and the sacrament of baptism, but Newman reverses the prolepsis usually associated with typology to render the flood as a retrospective baptism, one that cleansed sin from the face of the earth.

It is hard not to sense a certain exultant schadenfreude in his account of the catastrophe, where, in contrast to his decision in "Corcyra" to separate individuals out of the "multitudinous stream," he conflates the "wicked" into a "faded bloom" and seems to feel no compassion at their fate. Writing more than a century later, Richard Wilbur, himself a fairly orthodox Episcopalian, manages to treat the story of Noah without that gloating, *extra Ecclesia nulla salus* confidence that perceives the other in terms of damnation. His poem "Still, Citizen Sparrow"[78] shows that some contemporary versions of the Christian faith have learned to broaden their horizons. But even as we resist the insular spirituality of this and other poems by Newman, we cannot help applauding the vigor of an imagination that can galvanize old tropes. The ark, a time-honored type of the Church, now traverses not the stormy sea of seventeenth-century woodcuts but a sheet of lava altogether more perilous to its wooden structure. And whereas in other eschatological writings, the arrival in paradise is conveyed either by swimming *(The Pilgrim's Progress)* or by toilsome ascent *(The Divine Comedy)*, in Newman the dissolution of the earth provides a mounting tide that bears up the ark to a gate otherwise inaccessible. If we were to enquire about the significance of the title—"Patriarchal Faith"—we would have to conclude that Newman is trying to recover the exclusionism of early Judaic thought before the great universal utterances of Deutero-Isaiah, and so to justify the sense of self-separation and purification that led the Tractarians to denounce thinkers and persecute theologians who differed from them.

Much the same pharisaic priggishness can be found in "Heathenism," where Newman sets up a facile distinction between the elect and the reprobate. He argues that since God was not deterred from persisting with the redemption of Israel even at times of apostasy, the superabundance of his grace can carry over into institutions otherwise unaffiliated with his "official" channels:

> If such o'erflowing grace
> From Aaron's vest e'en on the Sibyl ran,
> Why should we fear the Son now lacks His place,
> Where roams unchristened man?[79]

"Judaism" need not detain us, for, like Keble's poem on the topic, it mistakes human persecution for divine edict. The "isms" that follow are likewise designed to set the Tractarian version of the *via media* as an Aristotelian norm between the corrupt extreme of Romanism on the one hand ("Superstition") and Protestantism on the other ("Schism"). Newman never really came to terms with Eastern Orthodoxy—if he had, he might have been less persuaded by the Augustinian tag *(Securus judicat orbis terrarum)* so instrumental in his conversion to Rome. In "Schism," however, he speaks about *"Churches* of the South," presumably including the Eastern faith in his judgment. The plural nicely balances the "brethren of the North" at the start of "Schism." "Liberalism" recapitulates "Zeal before Love," but simply as a flat prohibition. We are told that "Liberals" "halve the Truth" by avoiding the sectarianism, persecution, and hatred that have always been the notes of "zeal," the unholy instrument by which the Tractarians sought to reinvigorate their church. Well might Whately and Arnold and Maurice have answered, with Hamlet, that if they *had* halved the Gospel, then they were living "the purer by the other half." Certainly the posture taken up by "Apostacy" shows Newman at his worst. His solution to the "Liberalism" associated with the French Revolution is simply to expunge France from the atlas. Stanza 1 lists various Christian events that figure in French history of the preceding centuries, and begins with a reactionary avowal that privileges the past above the present ("France! I will think of thee, as what thou wast").[80] That vocative is removed from the second stanza in order to dramatize Newman's petty vow of silence. Perhaps no poem provides more telling evidence of the skepticism that Isaac Williams attributed to him—it is surely a faith uncertain of itself that claims "It is not safe to place the mind and heart / On brink of evil." "Apostacy" makes feeble reading when it is set alongside Milton's resolve to immerse himself in the destructive element: "I cannot praise a fugitive and cloistered virtue, unexercised and unbreathed, that never sallies out and sees her adversary."[81] Few would assent to Newman's absurd judgment on the Revolution in France, but even if one tried by a supreme act of empathy to enter his feelings in this regard, one would still have wished him to engage the "enemy" instead of shunning it. He remarks in the *Apologia,* for example, that he could barely bring himself to look at the flag of France—"A French vessel was at Algiers; I would not even look at the tricolour"[82]—as though that ostrich gesture would somehow effect its abolition.

"Conversion" also points to conflict within Newman, one caused by the Oxford Movement's recommitment to biblical fundamentalism (which it called "fidelity") in defiance of the skeptical temper of the age. Seeing himself and his colleagues as heirs to the apostles, Newman records how, having heard some Continentals (Italians, presumably) discourse on religious topics, he longed to propound the "superior" truth of Anglicanism, and yet he lacked the linguistic skill to do so. Had he been an apostle at the time of Pentecost, however, he would have been endowed with the gift of tongues. This discrepancy between an unmiraculous present and the numinous records of Scripture had exercised other minds than Newman's. In "Decay," Herbert contrasts the time when God lodged with Lot and a present marked by his absence: "But now thou dost thy self immure and close / In some one corner of a feeble heart."[83] Herbert, like Donne, turned to Jacobean cosmology for an answer; Newman, for all his reactionary indifference to the advances of science, obviously could not put forward the same apology. Nor could he consider the answers proposed by the higher criticism in Germany and later espoused by *Essays and Reviews,* viz., that Scripture contained accretions of fabulous matter. All he *can* do in this little poem is muse on the disparity.

"There is one only Bond in the wide earth" takes the Hosean vision of covenant-breaking as spiritual adultery and blends it with the figure of a church wedded to Christ. It begins with an absolute proclamation, the ideal of monogamy, and then addresses the practical reality of life in a culture no longer uniformly Christian. The poem follows a familiar course from nostalgia for the past to denunciation of the present, and shows the intemperateness of a sensibility unable to handle compromise and toleration. Newman sounds a new note, however, in the final stanza, in which he begins to feel the isolation of the prophet's role, a Cassandra-like sense of dissociation. A curious anguish prompts the word "hot," suggesting all at once the speaker's discomfort, unchanneled indignation and unreality (by association with "hot air"): "to whom shall I not seem / Pained with hot thoughts, the preacher of a dream?"

"Weep, Mother mine," "The Beasts of Ephesus" and "How shall a child of God fulfil" continue to propound this almost pharisaical sense of separation from a world perceived to be unclean. The Christ who feasted with publicans and prostitutes is entirely forgotten in such counsels as these, all significantly looking back to Judaic norms of separation and self-enclosing sanctity:

> How shall a child of God fulfil
> His vow to cleanse his soul from ill,
> And raise on high his baptism-light,

> Like Aaron's seed in ritual white,
> And holy tempered Nazarite?[84]

The answer comes in the next stanza: "First let him shun the haunts of vice." It is hardly surprising, then, that, as Robert Pattison, has pointed out, the Oxford Movement was essentially elitist: "Newman was offended by the populism of Lammenais and squeamish about contact with anything vulgar. Under his leadership the Oxford Movement addressed itself more and more *ad clerum.*"[85] This bias *ad clerum,* however, was not simply a question of tactical mismanagement; it springs from a lack of social compassion. Poems such those under scrutiny urge the high-minded to avert their faces rather than gaze long and steadily at situations crying for humane action. Not surprisingly, a certain vindictiveness towards the world springs up in consequence of Newman's sense of alienation. While his ostensible regret centers on the wickedness of the wicked, his real regret (as in Psalm 94) is that they have not been consumed by God's anger ("LORD, how long shall the wicked, how long shall the wicked triumph. *How long* shall they utter *and* speak hard things? *and* all the workers of iniquity boast themselves?"): "How long, O Lord of grace, / Must languish Thy true race, / In forced friendship linked with Belial here."[86] How distressing Newman's exclusionary phrase "Thy true race" seems to twentieth-century ears, and his racial epithet "dog-breed," which recalls the language of Shylock and Gratiano while pretending learnedly to address the etymology of cynicism. And when we turn to the final stanza of "Weep, Mother mine" it is hard not to feel that the vehement italicization of "suffer" is of a piece with such codas as that of Ps. 137 ("Happy *shall he be,* that taketh and dasheth thy little ones against the stones"):

> When Wrath next walks his rounds, and in Heaven's ken
>   Thy charge and works appear . . .
>   Ah! thou must *suffer* then.[87]

William Barry suggests that this reassertion of illiberal elements in the Old Testament might have been a function of Froude's medievalism: "[A]s Froude 'delighted in the notion of an hierarchical system, of sacerdotal power, and of ecclesiastical liberty,' he would appear when professing openly his admiration for the Church of Rome and his hatred of the reformers, to be doing little more than copying out the Old Testament in black letter."[88] To restrict the scope of salvation, so nobly opened up by Deutero-Isaiah and so nobly defended by St. Paul against those Christian Judaizers who objected to his mission to the Gentiles, is, as Barry implies, to give a cryptoracist color to the already intolerant decision that *extra Ecclesia nulla salus [est]*—the redeemed are a privileged superrace, not to be contaminated by the "Helots" of the world.

Because "Autumn" deals in eschatological absolutes rather than prim adaptations of "remnant" theology, it seems an altogether more generous poem than those it follows. Newman seems to have recalled the opening lines of *Richard III* ("Now is the winter of our discontent / Made glorious summer by the sun of York")[89] and subverted their affirmation:

> Now is the Autumn of the Tree of Life;
>   Its leaves shed upon the unthankful earth,
> Which lets them whirl, a prey to the winds' strife,
>   Heartless to store them for the months of dearth
>   Men close the door, and dress the cheerful hearth,
> Self-trusting still; and in his comely gear
> Of precept and of rite, a household Baal rear.[90]

One imagines that Newman also had Shelley's "Ode to the West Wind" in mind, even though he undercuts all sense of cyclical renewal. Decay in Shelley is the prelude to renovation;[91] in Newman's dark vision, the decay subsists in life itself and compromises the very fact of renewal. The Dickensian Christmas and the English person's castle seem likewise to receive a glancing blow as idolatrous displacements of the proper calling of Advent—viz., the contemplation of the four last things. Newman sallies forth from the warmth and enclosure of an English home, bent on realizing his apostolic mission of austerity and renunciation, and, incidentally, recalling the figure of Keats's knight-at-arms in "La Belle Dame Sans Merci,"[92] whose disaffection also exiles him from the comfort of the hearth:

> But I will out amid the sleet, and view
>   Each shrivelling stalk and silent-falling leaf;
> Truth after truth, of choicest scent and hue,
>   Fades, and in fading stirs the Angels' grief,
>   Unanswered here;

The allegory is not the less powerful for being so vague and personal. Newman seems to have adapted the Nordic myth of Yggdrasil, the great world tree that "spread its limbs over every land."[93] The localized "tree of life" in Genesis, fused with this cosmic version, images a destruction that only Newman can perceive in his bleak prophetic isolation. For the complacent John and Joan Bulls at home, the tree of life is so much firewood for the hearth.

Since we have seen how Tractarians and Evangelicals often converged in condemning worldly pleasures, "When the first earth's rulers" will not surprise us by preaching a stern Sabbatarianism. The kind of arguments that *Little Dorrit* levels against such thinking would have cut no ice with zealots who failed to acknowledge the rights of people disadvantaged by the Industrial Revolution. For Dickens, a loveless Sabbath that banned all recreation blasphemed the goodness of God and regressed to the meaningless taboos and cruel prohibitions found in religions of fear:

> Everything was bolted and barred that could by possibility furnish relief to an overworked people. No pictures, no unfamiliar animals, no rare plants or flowers, no natural or artificial wonders of the ancient world—all *taboo* with that enlightened strictness, that the ugly South Sea gods in the British Museum might have supposed themselves at home again.[94]

Newman, by contrast (who would have remained indifferent even if he had been alerted to the plight of the working class) regards the violation of the Sabbath as further proof that Mammon has displaced Christ in the public life of Britain. He falls back, as the Tractarians habitually did, on a suppositious past in which the Sabbath was indeed honored, in order to highlight the "depravity" of the present:

> And e'en about the holiest day,
>   God's own in every time,
> They doubt and search, lest aught should stay,
>   The cataract of crime.[95]

How much wiser and prudent, by contrast, the charges against Sabbatarianism adduced in *Little Dorrit*, for there the "cataract of crime," far from being stayed, is exacerbated by the boredom and disaffection of people denied the humane distraction of a holiday.

Lyra Apostolica prides itself on its "unrepresentativeness," its John the Baptist cries in the Wilderness of a worldly and complacent establishment. Such unpopularity must, in Newman's view, serve to guarantee its "truth" in a world too dark to comprehend the light. That is why he writes so wistfully of pre-Constantinian Christianity in "Christ's Church was holiest in her youthful days."[96] After the dust had settled over the Irish bishoprics, some Tractarians came to believe that disestablishment would in fact secure the Anglican Church against the Erastianism that had so colored its history after the Tudor settlement. Here we find Newman trying the idea upon his tongue and striving to like its flavor. Even as he bravely lists the advantages of such an eventuality, we feel a certain tremulous distress in such phrases as "that hand of force" and "The curse of breaking down." Instead of offering the more usual apostolic counsel of action and vigorous address, Newman here urges a martyrlike quiescence on his readers. Hence that most curious poem which follows "Christ's Church was holiest." Prefaced by a Greek epigram that we can roughly paraphrase as "Let sleeping dogs lie," it takes the distressing narrative of Uzzah and Obed-edom in 2 Sam. 6, and without turning a hair at the primitive conception of *numen* the anecdote underwrites, suggests that each figure provides a typological index to ways of responding to the "crisis" of 1833. One might officiously meddle with the ark as Uzzah had done, and be struck down for one's (entirely blameless) pains, or one might simply lodge it in one's home in the manner of Obed-edom, and let it transfuse one's life with a holy contagion:

> Read, who the Church would cleanse, and mark
> How stern the warning runs:
> There are two ways to aid her ark,
> As patrons and as sons.[97]

The definitive, oracular tone of this stanza demonstrates the poet's commitment to the "truth" of what he relays, as unflinching in his acceptance of the scriptural letter as his mentor in *The Christian Year.*

"Prosperity" is Newman's homage to Herbert's "Vertue," and much the better for once again reaching towards general human truths instead of taking up intemperate positions and raining *odium theologicum* on all who beg to differ. In "Vertue" the idea of transience is imaged by the abbreviated dimeter in stanza after stanza:

> Sweet day, so cool, so calm, so bright,
> The bridal of the earth and skie:

> The dew shall weep thy fall to night;
> For thou must die.[98]

Since that metrical abbreviation has a solemn, lapidary force, we can see its influence on Newman's poem:

> When mirth is full and free,
> Some sudden gloom shall be;
> When haughty power mounts high,
> The watcher's axe is nigh;
> All growth hath bound: when greatest found,
> It hastes to die.[99]

Gnomic certainty is generated by the trimeter couplets, for proverbs sometimes take trimetric form ("A stitch in time saves nine"); and the effect is heightened when the internal rhyme of the penultimate line effectively breaks the tetrameter into a run-on dimeter couplet. What might otherwise have offered relief from the insistence of the rhyme scheme has thus the very opposite effect, and the stanza brakes on yet another dimeter affirming the transience of life. In Herbert's poem the pattern of transitoriness is broken by the adversative structure of the final stanza ("Onely a sweet and vertuous soul"), and in Newman's also, Truth is exempted from the onward momentum of decay and resists it as a snag might a hectic current: "All gives below, save Truth, but grow / Towards an end." In the light of this metric adventurousness, I find it strange that Charles Harrold should find a "lack of force or color, of 'hidden music' or passionate expression"[100] in the poem.

The title of "Faith Against Sight" points to one of Newman's typical preferences, his exaltation of dogmatic principles above the relativity of sense experience. Even though the Christian conception of history is of a linear forward march toward an eschatological resolution, he falls back here on the notion of *anacyclosis* (familiar from Polybius), and relates this principle of recurrence (through his epigraph from St. Luke's Gospel) to the recapitulations of typology, on the one hand, and the recurrent and therefore circular impulse to sin, on the other. (It is worth recording that Newman has in fact misquoted the Evangelist in his epigraph; his substitution of "Lot" for "Noe" in Luke 17:26 probably springs from his sense that Lot provides a further type of vigilance. No better index could be found of Newman's

confident sense of biblical lore—a legacy of his Evangelical youth—
than this small lapse of memory):

> The world has cycles in its course, when all
>   That once has been, is acted o'er again:
> Not by some fated law, which need appal
>   Our faith, or binds our deeds as with a chain;
> But by men's separate sins, which blended still
>   The same bad round fulfil.[101]

Herbert showed the same sense of circular futility when in "Sinnes
round" he used anadiplosis to forge an inexorable sequence from
the first to the last line, lines identical with each other ("Sorrie I am,
my God, sorrie I am").[102] For even while Christian history is drawing toward its apocalyptic climax, its underlying tenets declare themselves again and again in variant but essentially similar forms. That
is why in the second stanza, Newman sets up New Testament types
for the present circumstances of the Church. In trying to revive the
dogmatic principle in the nineteenth century, Newman obviously
fell foul of the Benthamites. These he accordingly figures as Gallio,
a Roman deputy from Acts 18:15 who also rejected theological terms
and formularies: "But if it be a question of words and names and *of
your law, look ye to it; for I will be no judge of such matters.*" No
judge because such matters are insusceptible of judgment. Pattison
has pointed out that for Newman, nineteenth-century Liberalism
had reincarnated the thought of Arius. He was appalled, for example,
by Thomas Arnold's readiness to include non-Trinitarians within
the Church: "Not only did Arnold extend the hand of fellowship to
the Church's Arian foes, but he adopted the central tenet of their
heresy—that belief is after all only a form of words, and words are
incapable of expressing divine truths."[103] In the light of this,
Newman's "true hearts" refer not only to faithfulness (as to a cause)
but also to doctrinal fidelity. To be marginalized by the dominant
thought of the time is accordingly to be certain of the truth that that
thought, according to the Tractarians, is incapable of accepting.

Because the Anglican establishment seemed hand in glove with
the liberal forces that had contributed to England's economic ad-
vancement, the equation of that country with Tyre in "England" is
meant ironically—Tyre, after all, was the center of Baalism, and it
was from Tyre that Jezebel came to marry Ahab. Newman, like all
his fellow Tractarians, sets his face against any material prosperity

that is unsupported by the Athanasian Creed. One recalls that hor-
rifying passage, restated without remorse in the *Apologia*:

> The Catholic Church holds it better for the sun and moon to drop
> from heaven, for the earth to fail, and for all the many millions on it
> to die of starvation in the extremest agony, as far as temporal afflic-
> tion goes, than that one soul, I will not say, should be lost, but should
> commit one single venial sin, should tell one wilful untruth, or should
> steal one poor farthing without excuse.[104]

Such intemperateness is enough to drive most people into the arms
of Bentham. Whereas St. Peter wields the sacred keys of heaven and
hell, Newman's England is a *claviger* manqué: "Wielding Trade's
master-keys, at thy proud will / To lock or loose its waters, England!"

The image of Tyre also has tangential bearing on the lyric that
follows ("Say, who is he in deserts seen"), for Newman has lifted his
epigraph from Ps. 45, which envisages the Israel's marriage to the
messianic king:

> 13 And the daughter of Tyre shall be there with a gift: like as the
> rich also among the people shall make their supplication before thee.

To move from such pageantry into Newman's poem is to enter the
world of the Desert Fathers. Nothing could be more remote from an
epithalamion than the first stanza:

> Say, who is he in deserts seen,
>   Or at the twilight hour;
> Of garb austere and dauntless mien,
> Measured in speech, in purpose keen,
> Calm as in heaven he had been,
>   Yet blithe when perils lower?[105]

Newman enhances the sublimity of this vision with a biblical formula—the antiphonic question and answer that serve dramatically
to disclose the identity of a figure, as for example in Matt. 21: 10–11:

> 10 And when he was come into Jerusalem, all the city was moved,
> saying, Who is this?
> 11 And the multitude said, This is Jesus the prophet of Nazareth
> of Galilee.

Newman's antiphonic answer comes in stanza 2, where the bridal panoply of Ps. 45 gives way to the desert exile of the New Eve in Rev. 12:14:

> My holy Mother made reply,
>   "Dear Child, it is my priest.
> The world has cast me forth, and I
> Dwell with wild earth and gusty sky;
> He bears to men my mandates high,
>   And works my sage behest.["]

Although the speaker flinches at the deprivation of the exiled church, he will nonetheless come to in time to share it.

The epigraph of "The Afflicted Church" urges a lion to endure the unendurable, but that heroic vigor is at once subverted by the opening lines: "Bide thou thy time! / Watch with meek eyes the race of pride and crime."[106] This is Newman trying once again to temper and control the impatience he feels at the slow pace of reform—one of several instances in *Lyra Apostolica* where the individual is counseled to surrender the initiative to providence. The effect on this occasion is slightly repulsive, since those "meek eyes" conceal an inward self-possession, smilingly smug. It is the tone of Uriah Heep, in fact—the tone that so infuriated Kingsley. In *What, Then, Does Dr. Newman Mean?* he indignantly quotes a sermon that celebrates "the humble monk, and the holy nun" with "calm faces, and sweet plaintive voices, and spare frames, and gentle manners, and hearts weaned from the world, and wills subdued; and for their meekness meet with insult."[107] It is hard not to feel that a "humble monk" comes close to being an "'umble" one in a definition so concerned with superficialities of voice timbre and physical build. The cunning watchfulness counseled to the meek eyes in "The Afflicted Church" springs from much the same source.

We ought, perhaps, in fairness to the poet, remember that he is trying to some extent to recuperate the idea of passivity as a posture that can in some instances prove as useful as resolute action. Newman's impulse was to take up cudgels, and yet, finding himself blocked by circumstance and policy, he had to relearn the virtue of patience in lyric after lyric. The pattern of his journey home from the Mediterranean is a parable for the course of his subsequent career:

I was aching to get home; yet for want of a vessel I was kept at Palermo for three weeks. I began to visit the Churches, and they calmed my impatience, though I did not attend any services. I knew nothing of the Presence of the Blessed Sacrament there. At last I got off in an orange boat, bound for Marseilles. . . . At length I got to Marseilles, and set off for England. The fatigue of travelling was too much for me, and I was laid up for several days at Lyons. At last I got off again, and did not stop night and day, (except a compulsory delay at Paris,) till I reached England, and my mother's house.[108]

The pattern here is of eager impulses crossed and tempered by the ordinations of Providence. Newman's desires center not only on seeing his mother in the flesh but also the ecclesiastical mother whom he perceives to be beleaguered by the Reform movement. Writing of *Lyra Apostolica*, Charles Dessain has remarked:

The bulk of Newman's poetry was written between November 1832, just as he was about to leave England, and his return, the following summer. It shows how full he was of the evils threatening the Church, and the harsh necessity of reforming it. His tone is very different from that of the gentle verse of Keble in the *Christian Year*. Newman is forceful and fierce and tormented, but with an underlying security—God's providence will enable him to fulfil His tasks, in spite of his weakness.[109]

That underlying security did not, however, engender much peace of mind, or the poet would have felt less need to repeat and repeat the lesson of patience. Indeed, in "The Church in Prayer" he has even to remind himself—a curious memento from an ordained clergyman—that prayer is not a futile exercise. He has even so far forgotten his Bible that he places the house of Simon the tanner alongside the Dead Sea instead of at Joppa, eager as always to image landscapes so craggy and inhospitable that they cannot inspire tranquil thoughts:

> Why loiterest within Simon's walls,
>   Hard by the barren sea,
> Thou Saint! when many a sinner calls
>   To preach and set him free?
>
> Can this be he, who erst confessed
>   For Christ affection keen,

> Now truant in untimely rest,
> The mood of an Essene.[110]

The "mood of an Essene" refers, on the one hand, to the strict dietary rules connected with that sect and, on the other, to their strategy of withdrawal. The poem moves on to show that St. Peter's vision abrogated the dietary rules that Judaizing Christians (of which he had been one) set against St. Paul's more liberal response to the Law. It also shows how the apparent "inactivity" of prayer ultimately broadened the Church's scope. Even so, the use of "loiter" in the first stanza is symptomatic of the discomposure Newman feels at doing so little.

This discomposure recurs in "The Church in Bondage" where it likewise embodies a forced suspension of missionary work in a spineless, recreational verb:

> Say did impatience first impel
> The heaven-sent bond to break?
> Or couldst thou bear its hind'rance well,
> Loitering for Jesu's sake?[111]

This particular line of thought finds a resolution of sorts in "The Prospects of the Church" where, surveying Old Testament types of active engagement (Moses and David), the speaker concludes that Christ alone, by virtue of his godhead, was able to cry *consummatum est*—all others have had to be content with adumbrations and approximations. In "When I have fears that I might cease to be,"[112] Keats resolved the clash between imminent death and surging creativity by putting it *sub specie aeternitatis*; Newman here takes a leaf from the book of that stoic unbeliever by contemplating his own death in a ripeness-is-all frame of mind:

> Christ will unloose His Church; yea, even now
> Begins the work, and thou
> Shalt spend in it thy strength; but, ere He save,
> Thy lot shall be the grave.[113]

Of course, the Church in question is the Anglican Church, for Newman is still in the grip of his Evangelical conviction that, as Dessain has phrased it, "the Roman Church was bound up with the cause of Antichrist."[114]

"Rome" draws on the standard nineteenth-century belief that the book of Daniel, far from being a Maccabean document, was actually written at the time of the Exile, and that the four empires of the prophecy were the Babylonian, Persian, Greek and Roman:

> Far sadder musing on the traveller falls
>   At sight of thee, O Rome!
> Than when he views the rough sea-beaten walls
>   Of Greece, thought's early home;
> For thou wast of the hateful Four, whose doom
>   Burdens the Prophet's scroll;
> But Greece was clean, till in her history's gloom
>   Her name and sword a Macedonian stole.[115]

The logic of this escapes me, since Greece cannot be dissociated from the history of the Alexandrian conquest. One might just as well say that Rome ought not properly to included because in its Republican phase it had never persecuted Palestine. (Still, logic seldom obtains in fundamentalist readings of prophetic books.) The confusion extends into the second stanza, for Newman feels uncertain how to separate the Rome of primitive Christianity from its "anti-Christian" evolution and registers that confusion in a formula lifted, perhaps, from Wordsworth's lines "To a Cuckoo" ("O Cuckoo! shall I call thee Bird, / Or but a wandering Voice"):[116]

> And next a mingled throng besets the breast
>   Of bitter thoughts and sweet;
> How shall I name thee, Light of the Wide West,
>   Or heinous error-seat?

The effect is of a baffled suspension of alternate jigsaw pieces, neither of which seems quite appropriate to the space the assembler has to fill.

Newman's confused sensations over the Roman Catholic Church manifest themselves also in the contradictions and shifts of "The Cruel Church," which invokes Isa. 49:15—"Can a woman forget her sucking child, that she not have compassion on the son of her womb? yea, they may forget, yet will I not forget thee"—to demonstrate that Rome lacks this divine note of fidelity. He refers to Pope Pius V's excommunication of England in such a way as to stress the latter's truth and integrity. If that were so, one might have more logically deduced that the censure of Rome was a matter of indifference, not a cause for prostration and debility:

> . . . beneath thy censure's smart
> Long days we writhed, who would not be beguiled;
> While thy keen breath, like blast of winter wild,
> Froze, till it crumbled, each sublimer part
> Of rite or work, devotion's flower and prime.
> Thus have we lain, thy charge, a dreary time,
> Christ's little ones, torn from faith's ancient home,
> To dogs a prey. And now thou sendest foes
> Bred from thy womb, lost Church! to mock the throes
> Of thy free child, thou cruel-natured Rome![117]

As a moral statement, this is all over the place, and points to a crux in Anglo-Catholicism that virtually defies resolution. If the child is free, how are we to account for its death throes? And if Rome is "lost" and "cruel-natured," why should that child pay the slightest regard to her mockery? "The Good Samaritan" places Rome as a typological Samaria in relation to Anglican Judah, a comparison that carries a charge of schism. Here, however, she is not the neglectful mother of Isa. 49 but a source of relief and restoration. Newman is clearly alluding to his visits to Sicilian churches while waiting for a vessel to take him back to England:

> I almost fainted from the long delay,
> That tangles me within this languid bay,
> When comes a foe, my wounds with oil and wine to tend.[118]

Because the poem ends where it does, it hints that the speaker might be on the point of revising his traditional prejudices. The word "foe" clashes with the nurturement and attentiveness celebrated later in the poem.

Rome is also implicitly present in "When I am sad, I say," a "stock-taking" lyric that ponders the whole cycle of reform and corruption. Loathe Milton though he might, Newman cannot help recalling the sonnet on his blindness. If, he seems to say, he were to succeed in recatholicizing Anglicanism, would it not open the door to the unapostolic developments exemplified by Rome, and so require a new effort of purification. The historiographic model behind such thinking is once again the pagan one of *anacyclosis:*

> Alas! what good will come,
>   Though we our prayer obtain,
> To bring old times triumphant home,
>   And Heaven's lost sword regain?
>
> Would not our history run
>   In the same weary round,
> And service, in meek faith begun,
>   One time in forms be bound?[119]

Newman concludes his poem by breaking the mould of human historiography and placing the enterprise *sub specie aeternitatis.* "Moses Seeing the Land" offers an altogether more sober assessment of the Oxford Movement's prospect for success—indeed, it is curiously downbeat, even resentful. The poem might on the surface of things have invited comparison with Gray's "Bard," but in that poem a vision of future restitution is grandly articulated:

> "A voice as of the cherub-choir
> "Gales from blooming Eden bear;
> "And distant warblings lessen on my ear,
> "That lost in long futurity expire["][120]

and leads to a triumphal acceptance of death. Moses experiences nothing of same repleteness and confidence. In this instance, he ventriloquizes the poet's fears that Tractarianism might founder:

> Ah! now they melt . . . they are but shades . . .
>   I die!—yet is no rest,
> O Lord! in store, since Canaan fades
>   But seen, and not possest![121]

Whereas for Gray's bard the vision is an ontological earnest of future triumph, for Moses it seems a mere mirage.

In "Israel," however, Newman gives himself a good shaking and tries once again to sound the note of resolute struggle that Tennyson was also sounding in 1833, though "Ulysses" would be published only nine years later. His starting point is the grief that Jacob felt at the apparent death of Joseph and the slightly willful way in which he remained inconsolable: "And all his sons and all his daughters rose up to comfort him: but he refused to be comforted." Disappointment and grief ought not to issue in this sort of injured withdrawal, he claims. Even so, Newman's retreat to Littlemore would later give the lie to the self-chastening vigor of this poem:

> O specious sin, and Satan's subtle snare,
> That urges sore each gentlest, meekest heart,
> When its kind thoughts are crushed and its wounds smart,
> World-sick to turn within and image there
> Some idol dream to lull the throbbing care![122]

Defiant resistance presents itself as an alternative—upward- surging aspiration. By enjambing the final lines, Newman beautifully registers this dogged, ineluctable moving up through impediments: "when man from self is called / Up through this thwarting outward world to Heaven."

Insofar as "Do not their souls" bases itself on the doctrine of purgatory, it recalls other poems in *Lyra Apostolica* that moot an intermediate state for souls. In a curious but imaginative extrapolation from his own experience and also from the parable of Dives and Lazarus, Newman suggests that the those in limbo are no less obliged to practice patience than those who remain on earth. Such contentious doctrines as that of purgatory itself could be clarified by a single angelic visit, but Providence has ordained the continuous trial of Christians, one in which hope and fear contend for the soul and in which the outcome (in a way foreign to Evangelical modes of thinking) can never be predicted:

> Dearest! he longs to speak, as I to know,
> And yet we both refrain:
> It were not good; a little doubt below,
> And all will soon be plain.[123]

It is hard not to break down the superlative of that invocation into "dear rest"—the resolution and finality of paradise.

Such yearning for rest, as with the earlier invocations of patience and submission, in no way moderates the ardor of Newman's poetry, and the final impression left by his contribution to *Lyra Apostolica* is of energetic commitment to a cause. G. B. Tennyson remarks that because of "the sense of urgency that informs the volume, the *Lyra* has overall much tauter verse and much more vigorous diction than *The Christian Year*, as suits its more polemic intent."[124] That polemic intent, however, is part of a trade-off. Anglo-Catholicism has long since made its peace with Newman's bête noir, the "Liberal" theologian. Indeed its distinctive color today--something that prevents it from merging into the Romanism with which it is popularly identified—lies in that very marriage of the "poetic" tradition of Catholicism (its ritual) with a theology more humanistic and socially responsible than that promulgated by John Paul II. It is precisely those parts of *Lyra Apostolica* that fulminate against the Liberal ideas accommodated by modern Anglo-Catholicism that, in the words of Stephen Prickett, supply a "reminder of how emotionally alien much of the Oxford Movement would be to corresponding sensibilities today."[125]

Epilogue

IT will have become apparent by now that renunciation and *contemptus mundi* are central tenets of Tractarian poetry. The presence of an unresolved regionalism in *The Christian Year*, and the overlay of decorative diction acquired from poets of the eighteenth century, to some extent obscure and soften the austerity and even the toughness of Keble's vision. Newman, who initially perceived himself as a sort of popularizer and disseminator of Kebelism, took this vision (as so much else in Keble) much further than his master was willing to take it. Uncomplicated by any sort of earthly allegiance, sealed into the aureole of a beatific solipsism in which only God and himself had any self-evident reality, Newman's poetry realized the bleakness of his vision in verse that is comparably bleak. Gone in his contributions to *Lyra Apostolica* are the diction of Sensibility and the comfortable Gloucestershire landscapes it mediated in so much of *The Christian Year*—in its place is a lean, Housmanesque expression far in advance of its time and a spiritual topography of rocky cells and chasms. Given the color of his sensibility, it should not surprise us that when Newman defected to Rome, he gravitated toward what—for want of a better term—we might call the "Gallican" pole of English Catholicism. The reticence and self-effacement that were part and parcel of the Tractarian view recoiled from the baroque glare, the triumphalism, of the Ultramontane party. We can see this if we contrast Newman's poetry with that of Frederick Faber, his Oratorian rival, a leader in the opposing camp. In Faber there is none of that bleak, uncompromising Stoic discipline that tempered Newman's utterance as rigorously as his literal discipline scourged his body. Instead we have a kind of transposed voluptuousness as foreign to Newman as Crashaw's Continental Catholicism was to

Herbert. It is true that in *The Temple*, Herbert repeatedly baptized
the apparatus of Petrarchism, transposing God and mistress, but he
was quite incapable of the sort of displaced eroticism that we find,
say, in Crashaw's "Hymn to St. Teresa":

> Love touch't her HEART, and lo it beates
> High, and burnes with such brave heates;
> Such thirsts to dy, as dares drink up.
> A thousand cold deaths in one cup.
> Good reason. For she breathes All fire.
> Her weake brest heaves with strong desire
> Of what she may with fruitles wishes
> Seek for amongst her MOTHER's kisses.[1]

And here is Faber on "The Grandeurs of Mary":

> O Mary, what ravishing pageants I see,
> What wonders and works centre round thee in heaven,
> What creations of grace fall like light from thy hands,
> What creator-like powers to thy prudence are given.
>
> What vast jurisdiction, what numberless realms,
> What profusion of dread and unlimited power,[2]

If this is Faber's version of *hyperdulia*, the sense faints as it attempts
to picture his flights of *latria*!

An anecdote will further illustrate the temperamental divide
between the Tractarian austerity that Newman carried with him into
Rome (and which earned him the reproach of crypto-Protestantism)
and the Ultramontane exuberance of Faber. Whereas during his last
days as an Anglican Newman wistfully pondered St. Macarius's diet
of palm leaf, Frederick Faber seems to have conceived the devotional apparatus of Catholicism as so much decor:

> Meanwhile Faber's happiness was completed by getting into a
> back room again, away from the traffic. 'The sun never shines there
> and fresh air is at a discount,' he said, 'but a bright yellow and red
> paper creates an artificial sunshine, and F. Antony has bought me a
> *glowing* rug and a *gleaming* chintz curtain, and Burns has given me a
> brilliantly painted S. Joseph and there is a water closet in my room; in
> fact my room was ye lobby to ye refreshment room water closet. It
> will make a nice confessional.[3]

That "brilliantly painted S. Joseph" seems to present itself as a metonym for an entirely different spiritual temper. Not surprisingly, Faber's poetry and devotional prose reveal something of the same "brilliance" (or garishness, if the real truth be told of the devotional images that populate Victorian churches, whether Roman or Ritualist). At Littlemore, little *glowed* and *gleamed* in heated italics, and the presence throughout *Lyra Apostolica* of discomfiting rocky landscapes ("Truth's grey height" in "The Watchman") furnish images of a spirituality altogether more austere and disciplined than the brightly colored, cozy imagination of Frederick Faber.

The poets of the Oxford Movement were fighting a lost cause; their intransigent rejection of the Liberal thought that has shaped our century has placed them at the margin of history. Fortunately, however, the value of poetry (at least in the eyes of a qualified formalist like myself) has never been fully commensurate with its intellectual relevance. Indeed in terms of Matthew Arnold's romantic prejudices the very marginality of poems affirming baptismal regeneration and the "heresy" of "halving" the Gospel will supply an additional poetic condiment:

> It is exactly what is expressed by the German word "Aberglaube," *extra-belief*, belief beyond what is certain and verifiable. Our word "superstition" had by its derivation this same meaning, but it has come to be used in a merely bad sense, and to mean a childish and craven religiosity. With the German word it is not so; therefore Goethe can say with propriety and truth: "*Aberglaube* is the poetry of life,— *der Aberglaube ist die Poesie des Lebens.*" It is so. *Extra-belief*, that which we hope, augur, imagine, is the poetry of life, and has the rights of poetry.[4]

If Arnold is right, then the spiritual antiquarianism associated with the Oxford Movement becomes a poetic asset, an imaginative escape from the rational constraints and limitations of a Benthamite worldview. At the same time, however, we need to recall that, whatever the dilettantish, picturesque color of contemporary Anglo-Catholicism, the Tractarians were in deadly earnest about their efforts. There is nothing very decorative about the fasts that, according to *Tract 18*, ought to be reinstated in the Church. Indeed, most modern sensibilities, conditioned by some famous lines by Blake ("And Priests in black gowns were walking their rounds / And binding with briars my joys & desires"),[5] would probably flinch at Pusey's language of bondage: "Their silence [the silence of church authorities] on this subject is rather to be ascribed to the supposed hopelessness of attempting to bind our modern manners to Ancient Discipline, than to any disparagement of the institutions themselves."[6] Even so, anyone approaching the poems of *The Christian Year* and *Lyra Apostolica* in the right frame of mind, able to suppress his or her irritation at postures and positions no longer tenable, will find, as I hope I have shown, a great deal to admire—qualities of form and even qualities of content.

Notes

Preface and Acknowledgments

1. Raymond Chapman, *Faith and Revolt* (London: Weidenfeld and Nicolson, 1970).
2. G. B. Tennyson, *Victorian Devotional Poetry: The Tractarian Mode* (Cambridge: Harvard University Press, 1981).
3. Gregory Goodwin, "Keble and Newman: Tractarian Aesthetics and the Romantic Tradition," *Victorian Studies* 30 (1987): 474–94.
4. Stephen Prickett, *Romanticism and Religion* (Cambridge: Cambridge University Press, 1976).
5. John Henry Newman (Cardinal Newman), *The Poems of John Henry Newman, Afterwards Cardinal* (London: John Lane, n.d.), 329.
6. William Cowper, *Poetical Works*, edited by H. S. Milford, revised by Norma Russell (London: Oxford University Press, 1967), 289.
7. John Henry Newman (Cardinal Newman), preface to John Keble, *Occasional Papers and Reviews of John Keble* (London and Oxford: James Parker, 1877), xii.
8. Ibid., 80–81.
9. George Herbert, *The Works of George Herbert*, edited by F. E. Hutchinson (Oxford: Clarendon Press, 1941), 57.
10. Ibid., 146.
11. R. W. Church, *The Oxford Movement* (London: Macmillan, 1904), 69–70.
12. Geoffrey Tillotson, "Newman's Essay on Poetry," in *John Henry Newman: Centenary Essays* (London: Burns, Oates and Washbourne, 1945), 184.

Chapter 1. The Nature of Tractarian Poetry

1. Geoffrey Faber, *The Oxford Apostles* (London: Faber and Faber, 1933), 91.
2. Georgina Battiscombe, *John Keble* (London: Constable, 1963), 106.
3. Samuel Taylor Coleridge, *Poetical Works*, edited by Ernest Hartley Coleridge (London: Oxford University Press, 1912), 364.
4. G. B. Tennyson, *Victorian Devotional Poetry* (Cambridge: Harvard University Press, 1981), 93.

5. Ibid., 104–5.

6. Patrick Scott, "Rewriting the Book of Nature: Tennyson, Keble and *The Christian Year*," *Victorians Institute Journal* 17 (1989): 141.

7. Raymond Chapman, *Faith and Revolt* (London: Weidenfeld and Nicolson, 1970), 62–63.

8. John Henry Newman, *Apologia Pro Vita Sua*, edited by David DeLaura (New York: W. W. Norton, 1968), 27–28.

9. Battiscombe, *John Keble* (above, note 2), 110–11.

10. Ibid., 84.

11. Faber, *Oxford Apostles* (above, note 1), 342.

12. Ibid., 342.

13. Ibid., 343.

14. Edmund Sheridan Purcell, *Life of Cardinal Manning*, 2 vols. (London: Macmillan, 1895), 1:68.

15. J. C. Shairp, "Keble and 'The Christian Year'," *North British Review* 45 (1866): 233.

16. Alexander Whyte, *Newman* (London: Oliphant, Anderson and Ferrer, 1901), 76.

17. William Cowper, *Poetical Works*, edited by H. S. Milford, revised by Norma Russell (London: Oxford University Press, 1967), 444.

18. [John Keble], *The Christian Year* (London: Oxford University Press, n.d.), 38.

19. Cowper, *Poetical Works* (above, note 17), 216–17.

20. Keble, *Christian Year* (above, note 18), 51.

21. *Poetry of the Landscape and the Night*, edited by Charles Peake (London: Edward Arnold, 1967), 91.

22. Keble, *Christian Year* (above, note 18), 119–20.

23. Ibid., 36.

24. Cowper, *Poetical Works* (above, note 17), 463.

25. John Henry Newman, *Loss and Gain* (London: Burns, Oates, 1867), 290–91.

26. John Henry Newman (Cardinal Newman), *The Poems of John Henry Newman, Afterwards Cardinal* (London: John Lane, n.d.), 5–6.

27. Julie Billiart, *Thoughts of Blessed Julie Billiart* (London: Burns, Oates and Washbourne, 1934), 16.

28. Newman, *Loss and Gain* (above, note 25), 349

29. Chapman, *Faith and Revolt* (above, note 7), 122.

30. Quoted in Walter Lock, *John Keble* (London: Methuen, 1893), 75.

31. [John Henry Newman], "Thoughts on the Ministerial Commission," *Tracts for the Times*, 6 vols. (London: J. G. and F. Rivington, 1838–42), I, 1.

32. Mario Praz, *The Romantic Agony*, translated by Angus Davidson (1933; rpt. London: Oxford University Press, 1970), 156–57.

33. Tobin Siebers, "The Werther Effect: The Esthetics of Suicide," *Mosaic* 26 (1993): 17.

34. John Keble, *Lyra Innocentium* (London: Parker, n.d.), 97–98.

35. Hurrell Froude, *The Remains of Hurrell Froude*, 4 vols. (London: J. G. and F. Rivington, 1838–39), I, 42.

36. Charles Dickens, *Little Dorrit*, edited by John Holloway (Harmondsworth: Penguin, 1967), 74.

37. Froude, *Remains* (above, note 35), I, 49.

38. Faber, *Oxford Apostles* (above, note 1), 399–400.

39. Keble, *Lyra Innocentium* (above, note 34), 35.

40. W. J. A. M. Beek, *John Keble's Literary and Religious Contribution to the Oxford Movement* (Nijmegen: Centrale Drukkerij, 1959), 70.

41. Quoted in Lock, *John Keble* (above, note 30), 216.

42. Chapman (above, note 7), 123.

43. Faber (above, note 1), 442.

44. Quoted in Alfred Lord Tennyson, *Poems*, edited by Christopher Ricks (London: Longman, 1969), 542.

45. Newman, *Loss and Gain* (above, note 25), 104.

46. Cowper, *Poetical Works* (above, note 17), 196–97.

47. Donald Attwater, *The Penguin Dictionary of Saints* (Harmondsworth: Penguin, 1965), 140.

48. Stephen Prickett, *Romanticism and Religion* (Cambridge: Cambridge University Press, 1976), 105.

49. Cowper, *Poetical Works* (above, note 17), 198.

50. Ibid., 199.

Chapter 2. *The Christian Year* Surveyed: I

1. Stephen Prickett, *Romanticism and Religion* (Cambridge: Cambridge University Press, 1976), 104.

2. Robert Pattison, *The Great Dissent* (New York: Oxford University Press, 1991), 44.

3. John Keble, "Life of Sir Walter Scott," in *Occasional Papers and Reviews by John Keble M. A.* (London and Oxford: James Parker, 1877), 18.

4. Roger Lonsdale, ed., *The Poems of Gray, Collins and Goldsmith* (London: Longman, 1969), 175.

5. Thomas Gray, *Correspondence of Thomas Gray*, edited by Paget Toynbee and Leonard Whibley, 3 vols. (London: Oxford University Press, 1935), 1:192.

6. Quoted in Georgina Battiscombe, *John Keble* (London: Constable, 1963), 105.

7. Walter Lock, *John Keble* (London: Methuen, 1893), 53–54.

8. [John Keble], *The Christian Year* (London: Oxford University Press, n.d.), 1.

9. Samuel Taylor Coleridge, *The Poetical Works of Samuel Taylor Coleridge*, edited by Ernest Hartley Coleridge (London: Oxford University Press, 1912), 364.

10. *A Book of Common Prayer* (London: Oxford University Press, 1954), 8–9.

11. John Keble, *Miscellaneous Poems* (Oxford and London: James Parker, 1869), 124.

12. Coleridge, *Poetical Works* (above, note 9), 378.

13. Ibid., 378–79.

14. Keble, *Occasional Papers* (above, note 3), 88.

15. W. A. J. M. Beek, *John Keble's Literary and Religious Contribution to the Oxford Movement* (Nijmegen: Central Drukkerij, 1959), 22.

16. Lonsdale, *Poems of Gray, Collins and Goldsmith* (above, note 4), 48–49.

17. John Keble, *Lyra Innocentium* (London: Parker, n.d.), 60.

18. Brian W. Martin, *John Keble* (London: Croom Helm, 1976), 73.

19. Ibid., 150.

20. R. W. Church, *The Oxford Movement* (London: Macmillan, 1904), 25.

21. Josef Haydn, *Correspondence and London Notebook*, edited by H. C. Robbins Landon (London: Barrie and Rockliff, 1959), 141.

22. John N. Burke, *The Life and Works of Beethoven* (New York: Random House, 1943), 47.

23. Mary Moorman, *William Wordsworth*, 2 vols. (Oxford: Clarendon Press, 1957–65), 2:480n.

24. William Wordsworth, *Poetical Works*, edited by Thomas Hutchinson, revised by Ernest de Selincourt (Oxford: Oxford University Press, 1969), 743.

25. Ibid., 736.

26. George Saintsbury, "Lesser Poets of the Middle and Later Nineteenth Century," in *The Cambridge History of Literature*, edited by A. W. Ward and A. R. Waller (Cambridge: Cambridge University Press, 1916), 13:170.

27. *Breviarum Romanum*, Pars Hiemalis, 4 vols. (Turin: Sumptibus et Typis Mame, 1949), 4:19.

28. Wordsworth, *Poetical Works* (above, note 24), 165.

29. George Herbert, *Poetical Works*, edited by F. E. Hutchinson (Oxford: Clarendon Press, 1941), 56.

30. Ibid., 185.

31. Ibid., 160.

32. Keble, *Christian Year* (above, note 8), 3.

33. John K. Hale, "'Hail! Gladdening Light': A Note on John Keble's Verse Translations," *Victorian Poetry* 24 (1986): 93.

34. Keble, *Miscellaneous Poems* (above, note 11), 23–27.

35. *Hymns Ancient and Modern Revised* (London: William Clowes, n.d.), 30.

36. Libretto for Verdi's *Requiem* (London: HMV AN 133–34, 1964).

37. John Milton, *Complete Poems and Major Prose*, edited by Merritt Y. Hughes (New York: Odyssey, 1957), 469.

38. Keble, *Christian Year* (above, note 8), 5–6.

39. John Keats, *Poetical Works*, edited by H. W. Garrod (London: Oxford University Press, 1970), 206.

40. John Henry Newman, *Meditations and Devotions* (London: Longman, Green, 1953), 1.

41. Keble, *Christian Year* (above, note 8), 9.

42. Percy Bysshe Shelley, *Selected Poems*, edited by Timothy Webb (London: Dent, 1977), 159.

43. Ibid., 160.

44. John Carey, *The Violent Effigy* (1973; rpt., London: Faber, 1977), 140.

45. St. Ignatius, *Spiritual Exercises*, translated by W. H. Longridge (London: A. R. Mowbray, 1919), 85.

46. Elbert N. S. Thompson, "*The Temple* and *The Christian Year*," *PMLA* 54 (1939): 1023.

47. Keble, *Christian Year* (above, note 8), 11.

48. Lonsdale, *Poems of Gray, Collins and Goldsmith* (above, note 4), 633.

49. Herbert, *Poetical Works* (above, note 29), 67.

50. Thompson, "*The Temple*" (above, note 46), 1023.

51. Keble, *Occasional Papers* (above, note 3), 56.

52. Ibid.

53. Quoted in Martin, *John Keble* (above, note 18), 67.

54. Keble, *Christian Year* (above, note 8), 13–14.

55. Alfred Lord Tennyson, *Poems*, edited by Christopher Ricks (London: Longman, 1969), 1459.

56. Lonsdale, *Poems of Gray, Collins and Goldsmith* (above, note 4), 200.

57. *Hymns Ancient and Modern Revised* (above, note 35), 226.

58. Herbert, *Poetical Works* (above, note 29), 57.

59. T. S. Eliot, *The Complete Poems and Plays* (London: Faber and Faber, 1969), 261.

60. Charles Wheatly, *A Rational Illustration of the Book of Common Prayer of the Church of England* (London: J. Knapton, R. Wilkin, A. Bettesworth, J. Osburn and T. Longman, 1728), 216.

61. Keble, *Christian Year* (above, note 8), 16.

62. Keble, *Lyra Innocentium* (above, note 17), 1.

63. Quoted in Martin, *John Keble* (above, note 18), 45.

64. Thompson, *"The Temple"* (above, note 46), 1020.

65. John Henry Newman, *Essays Critical and Historical* (London: Basil Montagu Pickering, 1873), 2:453.

66. Maria Grazia Ciardi Dupré, *Raphael* (London: Bloomsbury Books, 1985), plate 27.

67. Keble, *Christian Year* (above, note 8), 19.

68. Donald Attwater, *The Penguin Dictionary of Saints* (Harmondsworth: Penguin, 1965), 189.

69. Keble, *The Christian Year* (above, note 8), 21.

70. John Marsh, *The Gospel of St John* (Harmondsworth: Penguin, 1968), 674.

71. Keble, *Christian Year* (above, note 8), 22.

72. Lonsdale, *The Poems of Gray, Collins and Goldsmith* (above, note 4), 58.

73. Ibid., 135–36.

74. Ibid., 139.

75. Keble, *Lyra Innocentium* (above, note 17), 11.

76. Wordsworth, *Poetical Works* (above, note 24), 462.

77. Keble, *Christian Year* (above, note 8), 24.

78. Lonsdale, *Poems of Gray, Collins and Goldsmith* (above, note 4), 173.

79. Attwater, *Penguin Saints* (above, note 68), 345.

80. Herbert, *Poetical Works* (above, note 29), 59.

81. Attwater, *Penguin Saints* (above, note 68), 284.

82. William Shakespeare, *Antony and Cleopatra*, edited by M. R. Ridley (London: Methuen, 1954), 214.

83. Keble, *Christian Year* (above, note 8), 27.

84. Quoted in William Shakespeare, *The Winter's Tale*, edited by H. P. Pafford (London: Methuen, 1963), 103n.

85. W. S. Gilbert, *The Savoy Operas* (London: Macmillan, 1962), 4.

86. *Hymns Ancient and Modern Revised* (above, note 35), 461.

87. Keble, *Christian Year* (above, note 8), 30.

88. *Requiem* (above, note 36).

89. Keble, *Lyra Innocentium* (above, note 17), 3.

90. Keble, *Christian Year* (above, note 8), 32.

91. St. Ignatius, *Spiritual Exercises* (above, note 45), 92.
92. Wordsworth, *Poetical Works* (above, note 24), 145.
93. Keble, *Christian Year* (above, note 8), 34.
94. Ibid., 3.
95. Lonsdale, *Poems of Gray, Collins and Goldsmith* (above, note 4), 140.
96. Wordsworth, *Poetical Works* (above, note 24), 462.
97. Church, *Oxford Movement* (above, note 20), 339.
98. Ibid., 343.
99. Ibid., 71.
100. Quoted in Lock, *John Keble* (above, note 7), 60.
101. Wordsworth, *Poetical Works* (above, note 24), 104.
102. Keble, *Occasional Papers* (above, note 3), 43.
103. Lonsdale, *Poems of Gray, Collins and Goldsmith* (above, note 4), 186.
104. Ibid., 92.
105. Ibid., 50.
106. Ibid., 63.
107. Herbert, *Poetical Works* (above, note 29), 165.
108. Keble, *Christian Year* (above, note 8), 36.
109. Lonsdale, *Poems of Gray, Collins and Goldsmith* (above, note 4), 192–93.
110. Ibid., 174.
111. Ibid., 199.
112. Keble, *Christian Year* (above, note 8), 39.
113. Wordsworth, *Poetical Works* (above, note 24), 149.
114. Coleridge, *Poetical Works* (above, note 9), 149.
115. *Hymns Ancient and Modern Revised* (above, note 35), 89.
116. Keble, *Christian Year* (above, note 8), 43.
117. Helen Vendler, *The Poetry of George Herbert* (Cambridge: Harvard University Press, 1975).
118. Keble, *Christian Year* (above, note 8), 44.
119. Ibid., 50.
120. *Hymns Ancient and Modern Revised* (above, note 35), 225.
121. Keble, *Christian Year* (above, note 8), 52.
122. Lock, *John Keble* (above, note 7), 64.
123. Joseph Butler, *The Analogy of Religion Natural and Revealed* (London: John and Paul Knapton, 1736), vi.
124. Keble, *Christian Year* (above, note 8), 53.
125. Herbert, *Poetical Works* (above, note 29), 87–88.
126. Ibid., 59.
127. Keble, *Christian Year* (above, note 8), 56.
128. Shelley, *Selected Poems* (above, note 42), 157.
129. Keble, *Christian Year* (above, note 8), 59.
130. Walter Scott, *The Heart of Midlothian* (London: Caxton, n.d.), 459.
131. Quoted in Martin, *John Keble* (above, note 18), 110.
132. Beek, *John Keble's Contribution* (above, note 15), 37.
133. Thomas Paine, *The Complete Writings,* ed. Philip S. Foner, 2 vols. (New York: Citadel, 1945), 1:523.
134. Keble, *Lyra Innocentium* (above, note 17), 68.
135. Lock, *John Keble* (above, note 7), 101.

136. Lonsdale, *Poems of Gray, Collins and Goldsmith* (above, note 4), 59.

137. Keble, *Christian Year* (above, note 8), 67.

138. Martin, *John Keble* (above, note 18), 128.

139. Keble, *Christian Year* (above, note 8), 64.

140. *Hymns Ancient and Modern Revised* (above, note 35), 131.

141. Keble, *Christian Year* (above, note 8), 67.

142. Ibid., 70.

143. Keble, *Occasional Papers* (above, note 3), xiii.

144. Lock, *John Keble* (above, note 7), 229.

145. Keble, *The Christian Year* (above, note 8), 69.

146. Ben Jonson, *Poems*, edited by George Burke Johnston (London: Routledge and Kegan Paul, 1954), 115–16.

147. Keble, *Christian Year* (above, note 8), 72.

148. Martin, *John Keble* (above, note 18), 101.

149. Lonsdale, *Poems of Gray, Collins and Goldsmith* (above, note 4), 192.

150. Keble, *Christian Year* (above, note 8), 79.

151. Battiscombe, *John Keble* (above, note 6), 80.

152. A. M. Hayes, "Counterpoint in Herbert," *Studies in Philology* 35 (1938): 43–60.

153. Keble, *Christian Year* (above, note 8), 81.

154. Milton, *Complete Poems* (above, note 37), 72.

155. Ibid., 73.

156. Keble, *Christian Year* (above, note 8), 85.

157. Battiscombe, *John Keble* (above, note 6), 106.

158. Keble, *Christian Year* (above, note 8), 88.

159. Geoffrey Faber, *Oxford Apostles* (London: Faber, 1933), 134–35.

160. Keble, *Christian Year* (above, note 8), 90.

161. Herbert, *Poetical Works* (above, note 29), 186.

162. Keble, *Christian Year* (above, note 8), 92.

163. Herbert, *Poetical Works* (above, note 29), 41.

164. Ibid., 75.

165. Keble, *Christian Year* (above, note 8), 94.

166. Ibid., 96–97.

167. Ibid., 99.

168. Joseph A. Seiss, *Holy Types; or The Gospel in Leviticus* (Houston, Tex.: St. Thomas Press, 1972).

169. Keble, *Christian Year* (above, note 8), 101.

170. Lonsdale, *Poems of Gray, Collins and Goldsmith* (above, note 4), 186.

171. Alexander Pope, *Poems*, edited by John Butt (1963; London: Methuen, 1968), 155.

172. Keble, *Christian Year* (above, note 8), 104.

173. William Shakespeare, *The Tempest*, edited by Frank Kermode (1954; rpt. London: Methuen, 1962), 84.

174. Keble, *Christian Year* (above, note 106).

175. Herbert, *Poetical Works* (above, note 29), 114.

176. Battiscombe, *John Keble* (above, note 6), 80.

177. Keble, *Christian Year* (above, note 8), 109.

178. Ibid., 113.

179. *Hymns Ancient and Modern Revised* (above, note 35), 226.

180. Keble, *Christian Year* (above, note 8), 115.

181. Thompson, *"The Tempest"* (above, note 46), 1025.

182. Battiscombe, *John Keble* (above, note 6), 110.

183. Keble, *Christian Year* (above, note 8), 117.

184. R. T. Davies, ed., *Medieval English Lyrics* (London: Faber, 1963), 155.

185. Keble, *Christian Year* (above, note 8), 119.

186. Lonsdale, *Poems of Gray, Collins and Goldsmith* (above, note 4), 122.

187. Keble, *Christian Year* (above, note 8), 122.

188. Herbert, *Poetical Works* (above, note 29), 185.

189. Ibid., 167.

190. Keble, *Christian Year* (above, note 8), 125 and 127.

191. Quoted in Martin, *John Keble* (above, note 18), 175.

192. Keble, *Christian Year* (above, note 8), 125.

193. Franz Schubert, *Sixty Songs* (London: Boosy, n.d.), 138–39.

194. Keats, *Poetical Works* (above, note 39), 46.

195. Herbert, *Poetical Works* (above, note 29), 128.

196. Keble, *Christian Year* (above, note 8), 196.

197. Quoted in Edmund Sheridan Purcell, *Life of Cardinal Manning*, 2 vols. (London: Macmillan, 1895), 1:194.

198. Keble, *Christian Year* (above, note 8), 130.

199. Lonsdale, *Poems of Gray, Collins and Goldsmith* (above, note 4), 71.

200. Keble, *Christian Year* (above, note 8), 132.

201. Horace, *Satires, Epistles and Ars Poetica*, translated by H. Rushton Fairclough (London: William Heinemann, 1970), 324.

Chapter 3. *The Christian Year* Surveyed: II

1. [John Keble], *The Christian Year* (London: Oxford University Press, n.d.), 134.

2. Charles Peake, ed., *The Poetry of the Landscape and the Night* (London: Edward Arnold, 1967), 40.

3. Roger Lonsdale, ed., *Poems of Gray, Collins and Goldsmith* (London: Longman, 1969), 466.

4. Franz Schubert, *Sixty Songs* (London: Boosey, n.d.), 210–11.

5. Keble, *Christian Year* (above, note 1), 21.

6. Ibid., 76.

7. Ibid., 137.

8. Ibid., 140.

9. George Herbert, *The Works of George Herbert*, edited by F. E. Hutchinson (Oxford: Clarendon Press, 1941), 166.

10. Ibid., 74.

11. *Hymns Ancient and Modern Revised* (London: William Clowes, n.d.), 66.

12. Ibid., 135.

13. Keble, *Christian Year* (above, note 1), 142.

14. Ibid., 146.

15. Ibid., 147.

16. Quoted in Geoffrey Faber, *The Oxford Apostles* (London: Faber and Faber, 1933), 189.

17. Keble, *Christian Year* (above, note 1), 150.

18. Ibid., 16

19. John Keats, *Poetical Works*, edited by H. W. Garrod (London: Oxford University Press, 1970), 206.

20. Keble, *Christian Year* (above, note 1), 151.

21. Lonsdale, *Poems of Gray, Collins and Goldsmith* (above, note 3), 465.

22. Ibid., 71.

23. Walter Lock, *John Keble* (London: Methuen, 1893), 19–20.

24. Keble, *Christian Year* (above, note 1), 153.

25. Herbert, *Poetical Works* (above, note 9), 160.

26. Keble, *Christian Year* (above, note 1), 157.

27. Lonsdale, *Poems of Gray, Collins and Goldsmith* (above, note 3), 59.

28. J. T. Coleridge, *A Memoir of the Rev. John Keble* (Oxford and London: James Parker, 1869), 171.

29. B. W. Martin, *John Keble* (London: Croom Helm, 1976), 133.

30. Keble, *Christian Year* (above, note 1), 159.

31. Keats, *Poetical Works* (above, note 19), 220.

32. William Wordsworth, *Poetical Works*, edited by Thomas Hutchinson, revised by Ernest de Selincourt (London: Oxford University Press, 1969), 87.

33. Keble, *Christian Year* (above, note 1), 160–61.

34. Ibid., 162.

35. Quoted in A. O. J. Cockshut, *Anglican Attitudes* (London: Collins, 1959), 26.

36. *Hymns Ancient and Modern Revised* (above, note 11), 461.

37. Keble, *Christian Year* (above, note 1), 165.

38. Herbert, *Poetical Works* (above, note 9), 67.

39. Keble, *Christian Year* (above, note 1), 167.

40. Herbert, *Poetical Works* (above, note 9), 128.

41. Andrew Marvell, *The Poems and Letters of Andrew Marvell*, edited by H. M. Margoliouth, revised by Pierre Legouis with the collaboration of E. E. Duncan-Jones, 2 vols. (Oxford: Clarendon Press, 1971), 1:17.

42. Keble (above, note 1), 174.

43. *The Poems of Gray, Collins and Goldsmith* (above, note 3), 162.

44. Wordsworth (above, note 32) 448.

45. William Shakespeare, *Love's Labour's Lost*, edited by R.W. David (London: Methuen, 1951), 185–86.

46. Keble (above, note 1), 176.

47. Ibid., 178.

48. Wordsworth (above, note 32), 460.

49. *The Poems of Gray, Collins and Goldsmith* (above, note 3), 176.

50. Faber (above, note 16), 89.

51. George Saintsbury, "Lesser Poets of the Middle and Late Nineteenth Centuries," *The Cambridge History of Literature*, edited by A. W. Ward and A. R. Waller (Cambridge: Cambridge University Press, 1916), 13:170.

52. Keble (above, note 1), 179.

53. Johann Wolfgang Goethe, *Sämtliche Werke*, 45 vols. (Berlin: Im Propnläen Verlag, n.d.), 4: 194–95.

54. Geoffrey Tillotson, *Augustan Poetic Diction* (London: Athlone Press, 1964), 30.

55. Matthew Arnold, *The Poems of Matthew Arnold* (London: Oxford University Press, 1909), 401.

56. *The Poems of Gray, Collins and Goldsmith* (above, note 3), 57.

57. Percy Bysshe Shelley, *Selected Poems*, edited by Timothy Webb (London: Dent, 1977), 76.

58. Lonsdale, *Poems of Gray, Collins and Goldsmith* (above, note 3), 121–22.

59. John Donne, *Devotions upon Emergent Occasions* (Ann Arbor: University of Michigan Press, 1959), 108.

60. Arnold, *Poems* (above, note 55), 135.

61. Ibid.

62. Keble, *Christian Year* (above, note 1), 182.

63. Wordsworth, *Poetical Works* (above, note 32), 164–65.

64. Lonsdale, *Poems of Gray, Collins and Goldsmith* (above, note 3), 177.

65. Alexander Pope, *The Poems of Alexander Pope*, edited by John Butt (London: Methuen, 1963), 515.

66. Keble, *Christian Year* (above, note 1), 183.

67. Alfred Tennyson, *The Poems of Tennyson*, edited by Christopher Ricks (London: Longman, 1969), 907.

68. Ibid., 907.

69. Wordsworth, *Poetical Works* (above, note 32), 62.

70. Keble, *Christian Year* (above, note 1), 185.

71. Ibid., 187.

72. Wordsworth, *Poetical Works* (above, note 32), 206.

73. John Keble, *Lyra Innocentium* (London: Parker and Co., n.d.), 49.

74. John Keble, "On the Mysticism Attributed to the Fathers of the Early Church," *Tracts for the Times*, 6 vols. (J. G. and F. Rivington, 1838–42), 6:105.

75. Keble, *Christian Year* (above, note 1), 190.

76. Keats, *Poetical Works* (above, note 19), 196.

77. Keble, *Christian Year* (above, note 1), 51.

78. Ibid., 192–93.

79. Aristotle, *Poetics*, translated by S. H. Butcher (New York: Hill and Wang, 1961), 68.

80. Keble, *Christian Year* (above, note 1), 195.

81. Charles Dickens, *Little Dorrit*, edited by John Holloway (Harmondsworth: Penguin, 1967), 485.

82. Keble, *Christian Year* (above, note 1), 198–99.

83. W. Peacock, ed., *English Verse*, 5 vols. (London: Oxford University Press, 1929), 2:14.

84. Keble, *The Christian Year* (above, note 1), 201.

85. Herbert, *Poetical Works* (above, note 9), 174.

86. Keble, *Christian Year* (above, note 1), 203.

87. Keats, *Poetical Works* (above, note 19), 211.

88. Lonsdale, *Poems of Gray, Collins and Goldsmith* (above, note 3), 463.

89. *Breviarium Romanum*, 4 vols. (Turin: Sumptibus at Typis Mame, 1949), 4: 10.

90. R. T. Davies, ed., *Medieval English Lyrics* (London: Faber, 1963), 53.

91. Keble, *Christian Year* (above, note 1), 205.

92. Ibid., 206–7.

93. Herbert, *Poetical Works* (above, note 9), 153.

94. Marvell, *Poems and Letters* (above, note 41), 1:14–15.

95. Keble, *Christian Year* (above, note 1), 208–9.

96. Donne, *Complete English Poems* (above, note 59), 82.

97. Lonsdale, *Poems of Gray, Collins and Goldsmith* (above, note 3), 59.

98. Ibid., 134.

99. Keble, *Christian Year* (above, note 1), 212–13.

100. Lonsdale, *Poems of Gray, Collins and Goldsmith* (above, note 3), 167–68.

101. Keble, *Christian Year* (above, note 1), 214.

102. Samuel Taylor Coleridge, *The Poems of Samuel Taylor Coleridge*, edited by Ernest Hartley Coleridge (London: Oxford University Press, 1912), 240

103. W. H. Auden, *Collected Shorter Poems* (London: Faber, 1966), 107.

104. Keble, *Christian Year* (above, note 1), 217.

105. Lonsdale, *Poems of Gray, Collins and Goldsmith* (above, note 3), 173.

106. Ibid., 131.

107. Keble, *Christian Year* (above, note 1), 219.

108. William Shakespeare, *King Lear*, edited by Kenneth Muir (1952; rpt. London: Methuen, 1972), 202.

109. Shelley, *Selected Poems* (above, note 57), 79.

110. Keble, *Christian Year* (above, note 1), 222.

111. Wordsworth, *Poetical Works* (above, note 32), 214.

112. Herbert, *Poetical Works* (above, note 9), 59.

113. Keble, *Christian Year* (above, note 1), 226.

114. Ibid., 229–30.

115. Ibid., 231–32.

116. Lonsdale, *Poems of Gray, Collins and Goldsmith* (above, note 3), 50.

117. Keble, *Lyra Innocentium* (above, note 73), xii.

118. Donne, *Complete English Poems* (above, note 59), 163.

119. Keble, *Christian Year* (above, note 1), 234.

120. Ibid., 238.

121. Lock, *John Keble* (above, note 23), 166–67.

122. Georgina Battiscombe, *John Keble* (London: Constable, 1963), 111.

123. Keble, *Lyra Innocentium* (above, note 73), 1.

124. Ibid., 37.

125. Herbert, *Poetical Works* (above, note 9), 75.

126. Lonsdale, *Poems of Gray, Collins and Goldsmith* (above, note 3), 172.

127. Wordsworth, *Poetical Works* (above, note 32), 460.

128. Keble, *Christian Year* (above, note 1), 242.

129. Marvell, *Poems and Letters* (above, note 41), 1:73.

130. Keble, *Christian Year* (above, note 1), 243.

131. Martin, *John Keble* (above, note 29), 166.

132. Keble, *Christian Year* (above, note 1), 242–43.

133. Ibid., 246.

134. Lonsdale, *Poems of Gray, Collins and Goldsmith* (above, note 3), 678.

135. Ibid., 67.

136. Keble, *Christian Year* (above, note 1), 246.

137. John Milton, *The Complete Poems and Major Prose*, edited by Merritt Y. Hughes (New York, Odyssey, 1957), 72.

138. Lonsdale, *Poems of Gray, Collins and Goldsmith* (above, note 3), 268.

139. Keble, *Lyra Innocentium* (above, note 73), 48.

140. Wordsworth, *Poetical Works* (above, note 32), 599.

141. Ibid., 600.

142. Ibid., 601.

143. Keble, *Lyra Innocentium* (above, note 73),

144. Keble, *Christian Year* (above, note 1), 249.

145. William Shakespeare, *The Sonnets*, edited by John Dover Wilson (Cambridge: Cambridge University Press, 1966), 39.

146. Herbert, *Poetical Works* (above, note 9), 56.

147. Shakespeare, *Sonnets* (above, note 145), 67.

148. Wordsworth, *Poetical Works* (above, note 32), 206.

149. Keats, *Poetical Works* (above, note 19), 3.

150. Keble, *Christian Year* (above, note 1), 250.

151. Herbert, *Poetical Works* (above, note 9), 59.

152. Keble, *Lyra Innocentium* (above, note 73), 139.

153. Ibid., 175.

154. Keble, *Christian Year* (above, note 1), 252.

155. Ibid., 254.

156. Lonsdale, *Poems of Gray, Collins and Goldsmith* (above, note 3), 127.

157. William Shakespeare, *The Tempest*, edited by Frank Kermode (1954; rpt. London: Methuen, 1962), 35–36.

158. Herbert, *Poetical Works* (above, note 9), 109.

159. Keble, *Christian Year* (above, note 1), 257.

160. Charlotte Brontë, *Villette* (London: Collins, 1953), 649.

161. Marvell, *Poems and Letters* (above, note 41), 91.

162. H. G. Wells, *An Outline of History* (1920; rpt. London: Cassell, 1932), 806.

163. Keble, *Christian Year* (above, note 1), 259.

164. Ibid., 261.

165. Nicholas Jose, *Ideas of the Restoration in English Literature: 1660–71* (London: Macmillan, 1984), 47.

166. Keble, *Christian Year* (above, note 1), 263.

Chapter 4. Newman's Contribution to *Lyra Apostolica:* I

1. Walter Lock, *John Keble* (London: Methuen, 1893), 54.

2. Ian Ker, *John Henry Newman* (London: Oxford University Press, 1990), 54.

3. Cf. chapter 1, pp. 20–21.

4. Alexander Whyte, *Newman* (London: Oliphant, Anderson & Ferrier, 1901), 72.

5. Ibid.

6. Maisie Ward, *Young Mr. Newman* (London: Sheed & Ward, 1948), 48.

7. William Barry, *Newman* (London: Hodder and Stoughton, 1905), 101.

8. Meriol Trevor, *Newman: The Pillar of the Cloud* (London: Macmillan, 1962), 112–13.

9. J. M. Cameron, *John Henry Newman* (London: Longman, Green, 1956), 35.

10. Trevor, *Newman* (above, note 8), 562.

11. John Keats, *Poetical Works*, edited by H. W. Garrod (London: Oxford University Press, 1970), 209.

12. John Henry Newman (Cardinal Newman), *The Poems of John Henry Newman, Afterwards Cardinal* (London: John Lane, n.d.), 131.

13. William Blake, *A Selection of Poems and Letters*, edited by J. Bronowski (Harmondsworth: Penguin, 1958), 52.

14. George Herbert, *Works*, edited by F. E. Hutchinson (Oxford: Clarendon Press, 1941), 66.

15. William Shakespeare, *A Midsummer Night's Dream*, edited by Harold F. Brooks (London: Methuen, 1979), 99.

16. Newman, *Poems* (above, note 12), 132.

17. John Henry Newman, *The Letters and Diaries of John Henry Newman*, edited by Ian Ker and Thomas Gornall (Oxford: Clarendon Press, 1979), 3:134.

18. Roger Lonsdale, ed., *The Poems of Gray, Collins and Goldsmith* (London: Longman, 1969), 126.

19. Ibid., 175.

20. Andrew Marvell, *The Poems and Letters of Andrew Marvell*, edited by H. M. Margoliouth, revised by Pierre Legouis with the collaboration of E. E. Duncan-Jones, 2 vols. (Oxford: Clarendon Press, 1971), 1:51.

21. John Keble, *The Christian Year* (London: Oxford University Press, n.d.), 204.

22. Trevor, *Newman* (above, note 8), 112.

23. Lonsdale, *Poems of Gray, Collins and Goldsmith* (above, note 18), 641.

24. Johann Wolfgang Goethe, *Poems of Goethe*, translated by Edgar Alfred Bowring (London: George Bell, 1885), 183.

25. William Shakespeare, *Macbeth*, edited by Kenneth Muir (1953; rpt. London: Methuen, 1976), 56.

26. John Henry Newman, *The Dream of Gerontius* (London: Heath Cranton, n.d.), 63.

27. Lonsdale, *Poems of Gray, Collins and Goldsmith* (above, note 18), 67.

28. Newman, *Poems* (above, note 12), 134.

29. Newman, *Letters* (above, note 17), 3:150.

30. Alexander Pope, *The Complete Poems of Alexander Pope*, edited by John Butt (London: Methuen, 1963), 594.

31. Lonsdale, *Poems of Gray, Collins and Goldsmith* (above, note 18), 53.

32. Newman, *Poems* (above, note 12), 135.

33. John Henry Newman, *Loss and Gain* (London: Burns, Oates, 1876), 426.

34. Percy Bysshe Shelley, *Selected Poems*, edited by Timothy Webb (London: J. M. Dent, 1977), 153.

35. Newman, *Poems* (above, note 12), 136.

36. Ibid., 137.

37. Trevor, *Newman* (above, note 8), 113.

38. Herbert, *Poetical Works* (above, note 14), 114.

39. Newman, *Poems* (above, note 12), 138.

40. Herbert, *Poetical Works* (above, note 14), 42.

41. Marvell, *Poems and Letters* (above, note 20) 14–15.

42. Newman, *Poems* (above, note 12), 139.

43. John Milton, *The Complete Poems and Major Prose*, edited by Merritt Y. Hughes (New York: Odyssey, 1957), 168.

44. John Henry Newman, *Meditations and Devotions* (London: Longman, Green, 1953), 305.

45. Herbert, *Poetical Works* (above, note 14), 153.

46. Lock, *John Keble* (above, note 1), 210.

47. John Henry Newman, *Apologia Pro Vita Sua*, edited by David J. DeLaura (New York: W. W. Norton, 1968), 16.

48. Newman, *Loss and Gain* (above, note 33), 6.

49. Ibid., 19.

50. Newman, *Poems* (above, note 12), 140.

51. Gerard Manley Hopkins, *Poems and Prose*, edited by W. H. Gardner (Harmondsworth: Penguin, 1953), 27.

52. William Shakespeare, *The Sonnets*, edited by John Dover Wilson (Cambridge: Cambridge University Press, 1966), 19.

53. Alfred Tennyson, *The Poems of Tennyson*, edited by Christopher Ricks (London: Longman, 1969), 1458.

54. Newman, *Poems* (above, note 12), 141.

55. Keats, *Poetical Works* (above, note 11), 38.

56. Lock, *John Keble* (above, note 1), 213–14.

57. Newman, *Poems* (above, note 12), 142.

58. *Hymns Ancient and Modern Revised* (London: William Clowes, n.d.), 261.

59. Newman, *Poems* (above, note 12), 143.

60. Edmund Wilson, *Patriotic Gore* (London: André Deutsch, 1962), 40–41.

61. Herbert, *Poetical Works* (above, note 14), 41.

62. John Keble, *Occasional Papers and Reviews* (London and Oxford: James Parker, 1877), 94.

63. Newman, *Poems* (above, note 12), 144.

64. *Hymns Ancient and Modern Revised* (above, note 58), 132.

65. Newman, *Poems* (above, note 12), 145.

66. Newman, *Letters* (above, note 17), 197.

67. Keats, *Poetical Works* (above, note 11), 38.

68. Newman, *Poems* (above, note 12), 146.

69. William Shakespeare, *Twelfth Night*, edited by J. M. Lothian and T. W. Craik (London: Methuen, 1975), 46.

70. Newman, *Poems* (above, note 12), 147.

71. Newman, *Letters* (above, note 17), 161.

72. Newman, *Poems* (above, note 12), 148.

73. Pope, *Complete Poems* (above, note 30), 593.

74. *Hymns Ancient and Modern Revised* (above, 58), 461.

75. Newman, *Poems* (above, note 12), 149.

76. Ibid., 150.

77. Ker, *John Henry Newman* (above, note 2), 79.

78. Trevor, *Newman* (above, note 8), 138.

79. John Donne, *The Complete English Poems*, edited by A. J. Smith (Harmondsworth: Penguin, 1971), 72.

80. Newman, *Poems* (above, note 12), 151.

81. *Hymns Ancient and Modern Revised* (above, note 58), 131.

82. Horace, *The Odes and Epodes*, translated by C. E. Bennett (London: William Heinemann, 1968), 282.

83. Keble, *Christian Year* (above, note 21), 8.

84. Milton, *Complete Poems* (above, note 43), 254.

85. Lonsdale, *Poems of Gray, Collins and Goldsmith* (above, note 18), 67.

86. Newman, *Poems* (above, note 12), 152.

87. John Bunyan, *The Pilgrim's Progress*, introduced by G. B. Harrison (London: J. M. Dent, 1954), 296.

88. Blake, *Selection* (above, note 13), 162.

89. Alexander W. Allison, Herbert Barrows, Caesar R. Blake, Arthur J. Carr, Arthur M. Eastman and Hubert M. English Jr., eds., *The Norton Anthology of Poetry* (1970; rpt., New York: W. W. Norton, 1983), 107.

90. Herbert, *Poetical Works* (above, note 14), 110.

91. Ibid., 176.

92. Shelley, *Selected Poems* (above, note 34), 160.

93. Newman, *Poems* (above, note 12), 153.

94. Blake, *Selection* (above, note 13), 162.

95. Herbert, *Poetical Works* (above, note 14), 100.

96. Ibid., 41.

97. Newman, *Poems* (above, note 12), 153.

98. Dante, *The Divine Comedy*, translated by Dorothy Sayers and Barbara Reynolds, 3 vols. (Harmondsworth: Penguin, 1949–62), 3:75.

99. Keble, *Christian Year* (above, note 21), 184.

100. Newman, *Poems* (above, note 12), 155.

101. Herbert, *Poetical Works* (above, note 14), 46.

102. Newman, *Apologia* (above, note 47), 14.

103. Newman, *Poems* (above, note 12), 156.

104. Ibid., 157.

105. Shakespeare, *Sonnets* (above, note 52), 17.

106. Newman, *Poems* (above, note 12), 158.

107. Shakespeare, *Macbeth* (above, note 25), 100

108. Virginia Woolf, *To the Lighthouse* (Harmondsworth: Penguin, 1964), 87.

109. *Hymns Ancient and Modern Revised* (above, note 58), 544.

110. Newman, *Poems* (above, note 12), 159.

111. Edmund Sheridan Purcell, *Life of Cardinal Manning*, 2 vols. (London: Macmillan, 1895), 2:31.

112. Newman, *Poems* (above, note 12), 160.

113. Lonsdale, *Poems of Gray, Collins and Goldsmith* (above, note 18), 120.

114. Ibid., 132.

115. C. B. Caird, *The Gospel of St Luke* (Harmondsworth: Penguin, 1963), 224.

116. Newman, *Poems* (above, note 12), 161.

117. Ibid., 162.

118. *Hymns Ancient and Modern Revised* (above, note 58), 418.

119. Ibid., 261.

120. Newman, *Poems* (above, note 12), 163.

121. Newman, *Letters* (above, note 17), 145.

122. Tennyson, *Poems* (above, note 53), 534.

123. Newman, *Poems* (above, note 12), 164.

124. Ward, *Young Mr. Newman* (above, note 6), 77.

125. W. D. Snodgrass, Richard Wilbur, and Aidan C. Matthews, "Writers and Wrongs: W. D. Snodgrass, Richard Wilbur and Aidan C. Matthews in Conversation," *Crane Bag* 7 (1983): 125.

126. Newman, *Poems* (above, note 12), 165.

127. Shakespeare, *Twelfth Night* (above, note 69), 58.

128. Donne, *Complete English Poems* (above, note 79), 60.

129. Louis Untermeyer, ed., *The Albatross Book of Verse* (London: Collins, 1933), 579.

130. Newman, *Poems* (above, note 12), 166.

131. Plato, *The Republic*, translated by Desmond Lee (Harmondsworth: Penguin, 1974), 317–18.

132. William Wordsworth, *Poetical Works*, edited by Thomas Hutchinson, revised by Ernest de Selincourt (London: Oxford University Press, 1969), 164.

133. Ibid., 164.

134. Keats, *Poetical Works* (above, note 11), 242.

135. Howard Kee and Franklin Young, *The Living World of the New Testament* (London: Darton, Longman and Todd, 1960), 424.

136. Newman, *Poems* (above, note 12), 167.

137. Newman, *Apologia* (above, note 47), 19.

138. David Hilliard, "UnEnglish and Unmanly: Anglo-Catholicism and Homosexuality," *Victorian Studies* 25 (1982): 185.

139. Lonsdale, *Poems of Gray, Collins and Goldsmith* (above, note 18), 68.

140. Newman, *Poems* (above, note 12), 168.

141. Barry, *Newman* (above, note 7), 60.

142. Homer, *The Odyssey*, translated by E. V. Rieu (Harmondsworth: Penguin, 1946), 26.

143. Newman, *Poems* (above, note 12), 169.

144. Bernard W. Anderson, *The Living World of the Old Testament* (1957; rpt., London: Longman, 1967), 247.

145. Newman, *Poems* (above, note 12), 170.

146. Ibid., 171.

147. Thucydides, *The Peloponnesian War*, translated by Rex Warner (Harmondsworth: Penguin, 1954), 20.

148. Newman, *Poems* (above, note 12), 172.

149. John Keble, *Lyra Innocentium* (Oxford: James Parker, n.d.), 4.

150. Dante, *Divine Comedy* (above, note 98), 2:291–92.

151. Ibid., 293.

152. Helen Vendler, *The Poetry of George Herbert* (Cambridge: Harvard University Press, 1975).

153. Louis L. Martz, *The Poetry of Devotion* (1954; rpt., New Haven: Yale University Press, 1962), 97.

154. Barry, *Newman* (above, note 7), 209.

155. Newman, *Poems* (above, note 12), 173.

156. Tennyson, *Poems* (above, note 53), 246.

157. Lonsdale, *Poems of Gray, Collins and Goldsmith* (above, note 18), 225.

158. Ibid., 169.

159. Ibid., 82.

160. Samuel Taylor Coleridge, *Complete Poems*, edited by Ernest Hartley Coleridge (London: Oxford University Press, 1912), 297.

Chapter 5. Newman's Contribution to *Lyra Apostolica:* II

1. Roger Lonsdale, ed., *The Poems of Gray, Collins and Goldsmith* (London: Longman, 1969), 196–97.

2. John Henry Newman (Cardinal Newman), *The Poems of John Henry Newman, Afterwards Cardinal* (London: John Lane, n.d.), 174.

3. Quoted in Meriol Trevor, *Newman: The Pillar of the Cloud* (London: Macmillan, 1962), 476.

4. Newman, *Poems* (above, note 2), 175.

5. George Herbert, *The Works of George Herbert*, edited by F. E. Hutchinson (Oxford: Clarendon Press, 1941), 45–46.

6. Newman, *Poems* (above, note 2), 176.

7. Lonsdale, *Poems of Gray, Collins and Goldsmith* (above, note 1), 219.

8. John Henry Newman, *The Letters and Diaries of John Henry Newman*, edited by Ian Ker and Thomas Gornall (Oxford: Clarendon Press, 1979), 3:208.

9. Howard Clark Kee and Franklin W. Young, *The Living World of the New Testament* (1957; rpt., London: Darton, Longman and Todd, 1960), 227.

10. Ibid.

11. Georgina Battiscombe, *John Keble* (London: Constable, 1963), 49.

12. Newman, *Poems* (above, note 2), 178.

13. Ovid, *Metamorphoses*, translated by Mary Innes (Harmondsworth: Penguin, 1955), 214.

14. Donald Attwater, *The Penguin Dictionary of Saints* (Harmondsworth: Penguin, 1965), 207.

15. Gertrude Grace Sill, *A Handbook of Symbols in Christian Art* (New York: Macmillan, 1975), 182.

16. Lonsdale, *Poems of Gray, Collins and Goldsmith* (above, note 1), 82–83.

17. Joseph von Sonnleithner, Libretto for *Fidelio* (London: Decca MET 272–72, 1964).

18. Gerard Manley Hopkins, *Poems and Prose of Gerard Manley Hopkins*, edited by W. H. Gardner (1953; rpt., Harmondsworth: Penguin, 1963), 61.

19. John Keats, *Poetical Works*, edited by H. W. Garrod (London: Oxford University Press, 1970), 237.

20. Newman, *Poems* (above, note 2), 179.

21. Quoted in Trevor, *Newman* (above, note 3), 431–32.

22. Newman, *Poems* (above, note 2), 180.

23. Ibid., 181.

24. Ibid., 182.

25. Ibid., 183.

26. William Wordsworth, *Poetical Works*, edited by Thomas Hutchinson and Ernest de Selincourt (London: Oxford University Press, 1963), 740.

27. *Hymns Ancient and Modern Revised* (London: William Clowes, n.d.), 89.

28. Wordsworth, *Poetical Works* (above, note 26), 462.

29. Herbert, *Poetical Works* (above, note 5), 174.

30. Newman, *Poems* (above, note 2) 184.

31. Horace, *Odes and Epodes*, translated by C. E. Bennett (London: William Heinemann, 1968), 168.

32. R. H. Barrow, *The Romans* (Harmondsworth: Penguin, 1949), 15.

33. Keats, *Poetical Works* (above, note 19), 368.

34. Newman, *Poems* (above, note 2), 185.

35. Newman, *Letters* (above, note 8), 174.

36. Sophocles, *The Theban Plays*, translated by E. F. Watling (Harmondsworth: Penguin, 1947), 135.

37. Ibid., 136.

38. R. H. Hutton, *Cardinal Newman* (London: Methuen, 1891), 11.

39. Stephen Thomas, *Newman and Heresy* (Cambridge: Cambridge University Press, 1991), 45.

40. Newman, *Poems* (above, note 2), 186.

41. Ovid, *Metamorphoses* (above, note 13), 168.

42. Newman, *Poems* (above, note 2), 188.

43. Newman, *Letters* (above, note 8), 318.

44. Andrew Marvell, *The Poems and Letters of Andrew Marvell*, edited by H. M. Margoliouth, revised by Pierre Legouis and Elsie Duncan-Jones, 2 vols. (Oxford: Clarendon Press, 1971), 1:91.

45. Ibid., 65.

46. Newman, *Poems* (above, note 2), 189.

47. Ibid., 190.

48. Ibid., 178.

49. Ibid., 191.

50. Marvell, *Poems and Letters* (above, note 44), I, 52.

51. Newman, *Poems* (above, note 2), 192.

52. Ibid., 193.

53. Ibid., 194.

54. Friedrich Schiller, *Schillers Sämmtliche Werke*, 12 vols. (Stuttgart und Tübingen: J. C. Gotta'sscher, 1847), 3:298.

55. Newman, *Poems* (above, note 2), 195.

56. Lonsdale, *Poems of Gray, Collins and Goldsmith* (above, note 1), 678.

57. Ibid., 681.

58. Matthew Arnold, *The Poems of Matthew Arnold* (London: Oxford University Press, 1909), 402.

59. William Barry, *Newman* (London: Hodder and Stoughton, 1905), 38.

60. Newman, *Poems* (above, note 2), 197.

61. John Henry Newman, *Apologia Pro Vita Sua*, edited by David J. DeLaura (New York: W. W. Norton, 1968), 18.

62. Leigh Hunt, *The Autobiography of Leigh Hunt* (London: Smith, Elder, 1867), 33.

63. Alfred Tennyson, *The Poems of Tennyson*, edited by Christopher Ricks (London: Longman, 1969), 1024.

64. John Keble, *The Christian Year* (London: Oxford University Press, n.d.), 33.

65. Newman, *Poems* (above, note 2), 199.

66. Ibid., 201.

67. Keats, *Poetical Work* (above, note 19), 208.

68. Newman, *Poems* (above, note 2), 203.

69. John Donne, *The Complete English Poems*, edited by A. J. Smith (Harmondsworth: Penguin, 1971), 60.

70. Newman, *Poems* (above, note 2), 204.

71. Christopher Marlowe, *The Complete Plays*, edited by G. B. Steane (Harmondsworth: Penguin, 1969), 197.

72. Newman, *Poems* (above, note 2), 205.

73. Ibid., 207.

74. Lonsdale, *Poems of Gray, Collins and Goldsmith* (above, note 1), 175.

75. Newman, *Poems* (above, note 2), 209.

76. John Henry Newman, *An Essay on the Development of Christian Doctrine* (London: Longman, Green, 1906), 366.

77. Newman, *Poems* (above, note 2), 211.

78. Richard Wilbur, *New and Collected Poems* (London: Faber and Faber, 1989), 318.

79. Newman, *Poems* (above, note 2), 212.

80. Ibid., 218.

81. John Milton, *The Complete Poems and Major Prose*, edited by Merritt Y. Hughes (New York: Odyssey, 1957), 728.

82. Newman, *Apologia* (above, note 61), 39.

83. Herbert, *Poetical Works* (above, note 5), 99.

84. Newman, *Poems* (above, note 2), 223.

85. Robert Pattison, *The Great Dissent* (New York: Oxford University Press, 1991), 18.

86. Newman, *Poems* (above, note 2), 222.

87. Ibid., 221.

88. Barry, *Newman* (above, note 59), 34.

89. William Shakespeare, *King Richard III*, edited by Antony Hammond (London: Methuen, 1981), 125.

90. Newman, *Poems* (above, note 2), 224.

91. Percy Bysshe Shelley, *Selected Poems*, edited by Timothy Webb (London: J. M. Dent, 1977), 76.

92. Keats, *Poetical Works* (above, note 19), 350.

93. H. R. Ellis Davidson, *Gods and Myths of Northern Europe* (Harmondsworth: Penguin, 1964), 191.

94. Charles Dickens, *Little Dorrit*, edited by John Holloway (Harmondsworth: Penguin, 1967), 66.

95. Newman, *Poems* (above, note 2), 225.

96. Ibid., 226.

97. Ibid., 227.

98. Herbert, *Poetical Works* (above, note 5), 87.

99. Newman, *Poems* (above, note 2), 228.

100. Charles Frederick Harrold, *Newman* (London: Longman, Green, 1945), 273.

101. Newman, *Poems* (above, note 2), 221.

102. Herbert, *Poetical Works* (above, note 5), 122.

103. Pattison, *Great Dissent* (above, note 85), 142.

104. Newman, *Apologia* (above, note 61), 190.

105. Newman, *Poems* (above, note 2), 231.

106. Ibid., 232.

107. Quoted in Newman, *Apologia* (above, note 61), 313.

108. Ibid., 40.

109. Charles Stephen Dessain, *John Henry Newman* (Stanford, Calif.: Stanford University Press, 1966), 34.

110. Newman, *Poems* (above, note 2), 234.

111. Ibid., 235.

112. Keats, *Poetical Works* (above, 19), 366.

113. Newman, *Poems* (above, note 2), 236.

114. Dessain, *John Henry Newman* (above, note 109), xi.

115. Newman, *Poems* (above, note 2), 237.

116. Wordsworth, *Poetical Works* (above, note 26), 145.

117. Newman, *Poems* (above, note 2), 238.

118. Ibid., 239.

119. Ibid., 240.

120. Lonsdale, *Poems of Gray, Collins and Goldsmith* (above, note 1), 199.

121. Newman, *Poems* (above, note 2), 241.

122. Ibid., 242.

123. Ibid., 244.

124. G. B. Tennyson, *Victorian Devotional Poetry* (Cambridge: Harvard University Press, 1981), 129.

125. Stephen Prickett, *Romanticism and Religion* (Cambridge: Cambridge University Press, 1976), 112.

Epilogue

1. Richard Crashaw, *The Complete Poetry of Richard Crashaw*, edited by George Walton Williams (New York: New York University Press, 1972), 54–55.

2. Frederick William Faber, *Hymns* (London: Thomas Richardson, 1871), 147–48.

3. Meriol Trevor, *Newman: The Pillar of the Cloud* (London: Macmillan, 1962), 489.

4. Matthew Arnold, *Literature and Dogma* (London: Smith, Elder, 1891), 58.

5. William Blake, *A Selection of Poems and Letters*, edited by J. Bronowski (Harmondsworth: Penguin, 1958), 51.

6. Edward Bouverie Pusey, "Thoughts on the Benefits of the System of Fasting," in *Tracts for the Times*, 6 vols. (London: J. G. and F. Rivington, 1838–42), 1:26.

Bibliography

Primary Sources

[Keble, John.] *The Christian Year*. London: Oxford University Press, n.d.

———. *Lyra Innocentium: Thoughts in Verse on Christian Children, Their Ways, and Their Privileges*. London: Parker & Co., n.d.

———. *Miscellaneous Poems*. Oxford and London: James Parker and Co., 1869.

Newman, John Henry. *Apologia Pro Vita Sua: An Authoritative Text, Basic Texts of the Newman-Kingsley Controversy, Origin and Reception of the Apologia, Essays in Criticism*. Edited by David J. DeLaura. New York: W. W. Norton, 1968.

———*The Dream of Gerontius (1865) by John Henry Afterwards (1879) Cardinal Newman With Some Words on the Poem and its Writer by W. F. P. Stockley*. London: Heath Cranton Limited, n.d.

———. *An Essay in Aid of a Grammar of Assent*. London: Longman, Green, 1907.

———. *An Essay on the Development of Christian Doctrine*. London: Longman, Green, and Co., 1906.

———. *Essays Historical and Critical*. 2 vols. London: Longman, Green, 1901 (vol. 1) and London: Basil Montagu Pickering, 1873 (vol. 2).

———. *The Letters and Diaries of John Henry Newman*. Edited by Ian Ker, Gerard Tracey, Charles Stephen Dessain, and Thomas Gornall, S.J. 31 vols. Oxford: Clarendon Press, 1977–84.

———. *Loss and Gain: The Story of a Convert*. London: Burns, Oates, 1876.

———. *Meditations and Devotions*. London: Longman, Green, 1953.

———. *The Poems of John Henry Newman, Afterwards Cardinal*. Introduced by Frederic Chapman. London: John Lane, n.d.

Secondary Sources

Alexander W. Allison, Herbert Barrows, Caesar R. Blake, Arthur J. Carr, Arthur M. Eastman, Hubert M. English, Jr., eds. *The Norton Anthology of Poetry*. 1970. Reprinted and revised, New York: W. W. Norton, 1983.

Allsopp, Michael E., and Ronald R. Burke, eds. *John Henry Newman: Theology and Reform*. New York and London: Garland, 1992.

Anderson, Bernard W. *The Living World of the Old Testament*. 1957. Reprint, London: Longman, 1967.

Apostolos-Capadona, Diane. "Oxford and the Pre-Raphaelites from the Perspective of Nature and Symbol." *The Journal of Pre-Raphaelite and Aesthetic Studies* 20 (1981): 90–110.

Aristotle. *Aristotle's Poetics*. Translated by S. H. Butcher. Introduced by Francis Fergusson. New York: Hill and Wang, 1961.

Arnold, Matthew. *Literature and Dogma: An Essay Towards a Better Understanding of the Bible*. London: Smith, Elder, 1891.

———. *The Poems of Matthew Arnold: 1840–1867*. Introduced by Arthur Quiller-Couch. London: Oxford University Press, 1909.

Attwater, Donald. *The Penguin Dictionary of Saints*. Harmondsworth: Penguin, 1965.

Auden, W. H. *Collected Shorter Poems: 1927–1957*. London: Faber, 1966.

Barrow, R. H. *The Romans*. Harmondsworth: Penguin, 1949.

Barry, William. *Newman*. London: Hodder and Stoughton, 1905.

Battiscombe, Georgina. *John Keble: A Study in Limitations*. London: Constable, 1963.

Beek, Willem Joseph Antoine Marie. *John Keble's Literary and Religious Contribution to the Oxford Movement: Academisch Proefschrift van de Graad van Doctor in Letteren Wijsbegeerte aan de R. K. Universiteit te Nijmegen, op Gezag van de Rector Magnificus Mr L. G. A. Schlichting, Hoogleraar in de Faculteit der Rechtsgeleerdheid, volgens besluit van de Senaat in he Openbaar te Verdediging op Vrijdag 18 Dec. 1959, des Namiddags te 2 Uur*. Nijmegen: Centrale Drukkerij N. V., 1959.

Bentley, D. M. R. "The Pre-Raphaelites and the Oxford Movement." *Dalhousie Review* 57 (1977): 525–39.

Billiart, Julie. *Thoughts of Blessed Julie Billiart Selected and Arranged for Every Day in the Year by a Sister of Notre Dame (of Namur)*. London: Burns Oates & Washbourne, 1934.

Blake, William. *A Selection of Poems and Letters*. Edited by J. Bronowski. Harmondsworth: Penguin, 1958.

Blehl, Vincent Ferrer. "Early Criticism of the *Apologia*." In *Apologia Pro Vita Sua*, by John Henry Newman. Edited by David J. DeLaura. New York: W. W. Norton, 1968.

———. "John Henry Newman: Some Texts and Commentaries." *Thought* 52 (1977): 95–102.

———. "The Patristic Humanism of John Henry Newman." *Thought* 50 (1975): 266–74.

A Book of Common Prayer. London: Oxford University Press, 1954.

A Book of Common Prayer, and Administration of the Sacraments and Other Rites and Ceremonies of the Church, According to the Use of the Church of England: Together with the Psalter or Psalms of David, Pointed as They Are to Be Sung or Said in Churches. Cambridge: John Baskerville, 1760.

Brendon, Piers. "Newman, Keble and Froude's *Remains*." *English Historical Review* 87 (1972): 697–716.

Breviarium Romanum Ex Decreto Sacrosancti Concilii Tridentini Restitutum S. Pii V Pontificis Maximi Jussu Editum Aliorumque Pontificum Cura Recognitum Pii Papae X Auctoritate Reformatum Cum Nova Psalterii Translatione Pii Papae XII Jussu Edita Editio Vigesima Sexta Juxta Typicam. 4 Parts. Turonibus: Sumptibus et Typis Mame Sanctae Sedis Apostolicae et Sacrae Rituum Congregationis Typographorum, 1949.

Bright, Michael H. "English Literary Romanticism and the Oxford Movement." *Journal of the History of Ideas* 40 (1979): 385–404.

Brontë, Charlotte. *Villette.* Introduced by Phyllis Bentley. London: Collins, 1953.

Bunyan, John. *The Pilgrim's Progress.* Introduced by G. B. Harrison. London: J. M. Dent, 1954.

Burk, John N. *The Life and Works of Beethoven.* New York: Random House, 1943.

Butler, Joseph. *The Analogy of Religion Natural and Revealed, to the Constitutional Course of Nature. To Which Are Added Two Brief Dissertations: I. Of Personal Identity II. Of the Nature of Virtue.* London: John and Paul Knapton, 1736.

Butts, Denis. "Newman's Influence on Matthew Arnold's Theory of Poetry." *Notes and Queries* 203 (1958): 255–56.

Caird, C. B. *The Gospel According to St. Luke.* Harmondsworth: Penguin, 1963.

Calkins, Arthur Burton. "John Henry Newman on Conscience and the Magisterium." *Downside Review* 87 (1969): 358–69.

Cameron, J. M. *John Henry Newman.* London: Longman, Green, 1956.

Capps, Donald. "A Biographical Footnote to Cardinal Newman's 'Lead, Kindly Light.'" *Church History* 41 (1972): 480–86.

———. "John Henry Newman: A Study of Vocational Identity." *Journal for the Scientific Study of Religion* 9 (1970): 33–35.

Carey, John. *The Violent Effigy: A Study of Dickens's Imagination.* 1973. Reprint, London: Faber, 1979.

Chapman, Raymond. *Faith and Revolt: Studies in the Literary Influence of the Oxford Movement.* London: Weidenfeld and Nicolson, 1970.

Church, R. W. *The Oxford Movement: Twelve Years 1833–1845.* London: Macmillan, 1904.

Cockshut, A. O. J. *Anglican Attitudes: A Study of Victorian Religious Controversies.* London: Collins, 1959.

Colby, Robert A. "The Poetical Structure of Newman's *Apologia pro Vita Sua*." In *Apologia Pro Vita Sua*, by John Henry Newman. Edited by David J. DeLaura. New York: W. W. Norton, 1968.

———. "The Structure of Newman's *Apologia pro Vita Sua* in Relation to His Theory of Assent." In *Apologia Pro Vita Sua*, by John Henry Newman. Edited by David J. DeLaura. New York: W. W. Norton, 1968.

Coleridge, J. T. *A Memoir of the Rev. John Keble, M. A..* London and Oxford: James Parker, 1869.

Coleridge, Samuel Taylor. *The Poetical Works of Samuel Taylor Coleridge.* Edited by Ernest Hartley Coleridge. London: Oxford University Press, 1912.

Converse, Florence. *The House of Prayer.* 1908. Reprint, London: Dent, 1935.

Corbett, Edward P. J. "Some Rhetorical Lessons from John Henry Newman." *College Composition and Communication* 31 (1980): 402–12.

Cowper, William. *Poetical Works*. Edited by H. S. Milford and Norma Russell. London: Oxford University Press, 1967.

Crashaw, Richard. *The Complete Poetry of Richard Crashaw*. Edited by George Walton Williams. New York: New York University Press, 1972.

d'Amico, Diane. "Christina Rossetti's *Christian Year*: Comfort for the 'Weary Heart'." *Victorian Newsletter* 72 (1987): 36–42.

Dante. *The Divine Comedy*. Translated by Dorothy L. Sayers and Barbara Reynolds. 3 vols. Harmondsworth: Penguin, 1949–62.

Dark, Sidney. *Newman*. London: Duckworth, 1934.

Davies, R. T., ed. *Medieval English Lyrics: A Critical Anthology*. London: Faber, 1963.

Deen, Leonard W. "The Rhetoric of Newman's *Apologia*." In *Apologia Pro Vita Sua*, by John Henry Newman. Edited by David J. DeLaura. New York: W. W. Norton, 1968.

DeLaura, David. "Matthew Arnold and John Henry Newman: The 'Oxford Sentiment' and Religion of the Future." *Texas Studies in Literature and Language* 6 (1965): 571–702.

———. "Newman's *Apologia* as Prophecy" in Newman, John Henry. *Apologia Pro Vita Sua*. Edited by David J. DeLaura. New York: W. W. Norton, 1968.

Dessain, Charles Stephen. "Cardinal Newman's Theology and Philosophy." *Victorian Poetry* 12 (1974): 268–69.

———. *John Henry Newman*. Stanford, Calif.: Stanford University Press, 1966.

Dickens, Charles. *Little Dorrit*. Edited by John Holloway. Harmondsworth: Penguin, 1967.

Dilworth-Harrison, T. *Every Man's Story of the Oxford Movement*. London: A. R. Mowbray, 1932.

Donne, John. *The Complete English Poems*. Edited by A. J. Smith. Harmondsworth: Penguin, 1971.

———. *Devotions upon Emergent Occasions Together with Death's Duel*. Ann Arbor: University of Michigan Press, 1959.

Dupré, Maria Grazia Ciardi. *Raphael*. London: Bloomsbury Books, 1985.

Eliot, T. S. *The Complete Poems and Plays*. London: Faber and Faber, 1969.

Ellis Davidson, H. R. *Gods and Myths of Northern Europe*. Harmondsworth: Penguin, 1964.

Engel, Elliot. "Heir of the Oxford Movement: Charlotte Mary Yonge's *The Heir of Redclyffe*." *Etudes Anglaises* 33 (1980): 132–41.

The English Hymnal with Tunes. London: Oxford University Press and A. R. Mowbray & Co., 1933.

Evans, Gillian R. "'An Organon More Delicate, Versatile and Elastic': John Henry Newman and Whately's *Logic*." *Downside Review* 97 (1979): 175–91.

Faber, Frederick William. *Hymns*. London: Thomas Richardson, 1871.

———. *Poems*. London: Thomas Richardson, 1857.

———. *The Rosary, and Other Poems*. London: James Toovey, 1845.

————. *The Styrian Lake, and Other Poems*. London: J. G. F. Rivington, 1842.

Faber, Geoffrey. *Oxford Apostles: A Character Study of the Oxford Movement*. London: Faber and Faber, 1933.

Flood, J. M. *Cardinal Newman and Oxford*. London: Ivor Nicholson and Watson, 1933.

Froude, Hurrell. *Remains of the Late Reverend Hurrell Froude, Fellow of Oriel College*. 4 vols. London: J. G. and F. Rivington, 1838–39.

Fulweiler, Howard W. "The Oxford Movement." *Victorian Poetry* 12 (1974): 271–73.

————. "Tractarians and Philistines: *The Tracts for the Times* Versus Victorian Middle-Class Values." *Historical Magazine of the Protestant Episcopal Church* 31 (1962): 36–53.

Gates, Lewis E. "Newman as Prose-Writer." In *Apologia Pro Vita Sua*, by John Henry Newman. Edited by David J. DeLaura. New York: W. W. Norton, 1968.

Gilbert, W. S. *The Savoy Operas, Being the Complete Text of the Gilbert and Sullivan Operas as Originally Produced in the Years 1875–1896*. London: Macmillan, 1962.

Goethe, Johann Wolfgang. *Poems of Goethe: Translated in the Original Metres*. Translated by Edgar Alfred Bowring. London: George Bell, 1885.

————. *Sämtliche Werke*. 45 vols. Berlin: Propnläen-Verlag, n.d.

Goodwin, Gregory. "Keble and Newman: Tractarian Aesthetics and the Romantic Tradition." *Victorian Studies* 30 (1987): 475–94.

Gray, Thomas. *Correspondence of Thomas Gray*. Edited by Paget Toynbee and Leonard Whibley. London: Oxford University Press, 1935.

Griffin, John. "Cardinal Newman as Historian of the Oxford Movement." *Faith and Reason* 11 (1985): 130–35.

————. "Dr. Pusey and the Oxford Movement." *Historical Magazine of the Protestant Episcopal Church* 42 (1973): 137–53.

————. "John Keble: A Report from the Devil's Advocate." *Historical Magazine of the Protestant Episcopal Church in America* 48 (1979): 219–37.

————. "John Keble and *The Quarterly Review*." *Review of English Studies* 29 (1978): 452–56.

————. "John Keble: Radical." *Anglican Theological Review* 43 (1971): 167–73.

————. "The Meaning of *National Apostasy*: A Note on Newman's *Apologia*." *Faith and Reason* 2 (1975): 19–33.

————. "The Social Implications of the Oxford Movement." *Historical Magazine of the Protestant Episcopal Church* 44 (1975): 155–65.

————. "Tractarians and Metaphysicals: The Failure of Influence." *John Donne Journal* 4 (1985): 291–301.

Hale, John K. "'Hail! Gladdening Light': A Note on John Keble's Verse Translations." *Victorian Poetry* 24 (1986): 92–95.

Harrold, Charles Frederick. *John Henry Newman: An Expository and Critical Study of His Mind, Thought and Art*. London: Longman, Green, 1945.

Haydn, Josef. *Collected Correspondence and London Notebook*. Edited by H. C. Robbins Landon. London: Barrie and Rockliff, 1959.

Hayes, A. M. "Counterpoint in Herbert." *Studies in Philology* 35 (1938): 43–60.

Herbert, George. *The Poetical Works of George Herbert*. Edited by F. E. Hutchinson. Oxford: Clarendon Press, 1941.

Hilliard, David. "UnEnglish and Unmanly: Anglo-Catholicism and Homosexuality." *Victorian Studies* 25 (1982): 181–210.

Homer. *The Odyssey*. Translated by E. V. Rieu. Harmondsworth: Penguin, 1946.

Hopkins, Gerard Manley. *Poems and Prose of Gerard Manley Hopkins*. Selected with an Introduction and Notes by W. H. Gardner. Harmondsworth: Penguin, 1953.

Horace. *The Odes and Epodes*. Translated by C. E. Bennett. London: William Heinemann, 1968.

———. *Satires, Epistles and Ars Poetica*. Translated by H. R. Fairclough. London: William Heinemann, 1970.

Houghton, Esther Rhoads. "*The British Critic* and the Oxford Movement." *Studies in Bibliography* 16 (1963): 119–37.

Houghton, Walter E. "The Issue Between Kingsley and Newman." In *Apologia Pro Vita Sua*, by John Henry Newman. Edited by David J. DeLaura. New York: W. W. Norton, 1968.

———. "Style and the Dramatic Re-creation of the Past." In *Apologia Pro Vita Sua*, by John Henry Newman. Edited by David J. DeLaura. New York: W. W. Norton, 1968.

Hunt, Leigh. *The Autobiography of Leigh Hunt*. London: Smith, Elder, 1867.

Hutton, R. P. *Cardinal Newman*. London: Methuen, 1891.

Hymns Ancient and Modern Revised. London: William Clowes and Sons, n.d.

Ignatius of Loyola, Saint. *The Spiritual Exercises*. Translated by W. H. Longridge. London: A. R. Mowbray, 1919.

Jay, Elisabeth, ed. *The Evangelical and Oxford Movements*. Cambridge: Cambridge University Press, 1983.

Jones, O. W. *Isaac Williams and His Circle*. London: S.P.C.K., 1971.

Jonson, Ben. *Poems*. Edited by George Burke Johnston. London: Routledge and Kegan Paul, 1954.

Jose, Nicholas. *Ideas of the Restoration in English Literature, 1660–71*. London: Macmillan, 1984.

Keats, John. *Poetical Works*. Edited by H. W. Garrod. London: Oxford University Press, 1970.

Keble, John. *Occasional Papers and Reviews by John Keble, M. A.*. Oxford and London: James Parker, 1877.

Kee, Howard Clark, and Franklin W. Young. *The Living World of the New Testament*. London: Darton, Longman and Todd, 1960.

Ker, Ian. *John Henry Newman: A Biography*. Oxford: Oxford University Press, 1990.

Kollar, Dom René. "The Oxford Movement and the Heritage of Benedictine Monasticism." *Downside Review* 101 (1983): 281–90.

Kulishek, Patricia Jo. "John Henry Newman at Alton." *Notes and Queries* (1989): 188–90.

Landow, George P. "Thomas Seddon's 'Moriah' and His *Jerusalem and the Valley of Jehosophat*." *The Journal of Pre-Raphaelite and Aesthetic Studies* 1 (1987): 59–65.

Lock, Walter. *John Keble: A Biography*. London: Methuen, 1893.

Lonsdale, Roger, ed. *The Poems of Gray, Collins and Goldsmith*. London: Longman, 1969.

Love, Nicholas. *Mirror of the Blessed Life of Jesus Christ*. Edited by Michael G. Sargent. New York: Garland, 1992.

Marlowe, Christopher. *The Complete Plays*. Edited by G. B. Steane. Harmondsworth: Penguin, 1969.

Marsh, John. *The Gospel of St John*. Harmondsworth: Penguin, 1968.

Martin, Brian W. *John Keble: Priest, Professor and Poet*. London: Croom Helm, 1976.

———. "Wordsworth, Faber and Keble: Commentary on a Triangular Relationship." *Review of English Studies* 26 (1975): 436–47.

Martz, Louis L. *The Poetry of Meditation: A Study in English Religious Literature of the Seventeenth Century*. 1954. Reprint, New Haven: Yale University Press, 1962.

Marvell, Andrew. *The Poems and Letters of Andrew Marvell*. Edited by H. M. Margoliouth. Revised by Pierre Legouis with the collaboration of E. E. Duncan-Jones. 2 vols. Oxford: Clarendon Press, 1971.

McElrath, Damian. "Richard Simpson and John Henry Newman: *The Rambler*, Laymen and Theology." *Catholic Historical Review* 52 (1966): 509–33.

McGreevy, Michael A. "John Keble on the Anglican Church and the Church Catholic." *Heythrop Journal* 5 (1964): 27–35.

———. "John Keble's Way to Christian Unity." *One in Christ* 1 (1965): 53–61.

Mendel, Sydney. "Metaphor and Rhetoric in Newman's *Apologia*." *Essays in Criticism* 23 (1973): 357–71.

Moorman, Mary. *William Wordsworth: A Biography*. 2 vols. Oxford: Clarendon Press, 1957–65.

Milton, John. *The Complete Poems and Major Prose*. Edited by Merritt Y. Hughes. New York: Odyssey Press, 1957.

Noonkester, Myron C. "An Unpublished Letter of J. H. Newman." *Notes and Queries* 36 (1989): 188.

Osborne, John W. "John Henry Newman and the Idea of a University." *Journal of the Rutgers University Libraries* 42 (1980): 40–46.

Ovid. *The Metamorphoses of Ovid*. Translated by Mary M. Innes. Harmondsworth: Penguin, 1955

Paine, Thomas. *The Complete Writings with a Biographical Essay, and Notes and Introductions Presenting the Historical Background of Paine's Writings*. Edited and Collected by Philip S. Foner. 2 vols. New York: Citadel Press, 1945.

Pattison, Robert. *The Great Dissent: John Henry Newman and the Liberal Heresy*. New York: Oxford University Press, 1991.

———. "John Henry Newman and the Arian Heresy." *Mosaic* 11 (1978): 139–53.

Peacock, W., ed. *English Verse*. 5 vols. London: Oxford University Press, 1929.

Peake, Charles, ed. *Poetry of the Landscape and the Night: Two Eighteenth-Century Traditions*. London: Edward Arnold, 1967.

Pearsall, Ronald. "The Oxford Movement in Retrospect." *Quarterly Review* 204 (1966): 75–83.

Pfaff, Richard W. "The Library of the Fathers: The Tractarians as Patristic Translators." *Studies in Philology* 70 (1973): 329–44.

Plato. *The Republic*. Translated by Desmond Lee. 1955. Reprinted and revised,
Harmondsworth: Penguin, 1974.

Pope, Alexander. *The Poems of Alexander Pope*. Edited by John Butt. 1963. Reprint,
London: Methuen, 1968.

Poston, Lawrence. "'Worlds Not Realised': Wordsworthian Poetry in the 1830s."
Texas Studies in Literature and Language 28 (1986): 51–80.

Praz, Mario. *The Romantic Agony*. Translated by Angus Davidson. 1933. Reprint,
London: Oxford University Press, 1970.

Prickett, Stephen. *Romanticism and Religion: The Tradition of Coleridge and Wordsworth
in the Victorian Church*. Cambridge: Cambridge University Press, 1976.

Purcell, Edmund Sheridan. *Life of Cardinal Manning, Archbishop of Westminster*. 2
vols. London: Macmillan, 1895.

Rees, Daniel. "Martin Murphy's *Blanco White*." *Downside Review* 107 (1989): 229–
236.

"Sacred Poetry." *The British Critic* 21 (1837): 167–85.

Saintsbury, George. "Lesser Poets of the Middle and Late Nineteenth Century." In
The Cambridge History of English Literature, edited by A. W. Ward and A. R. Waller,
13:147–224. Cambridge: Cambridge University Press, 1916.

Schiller, Friedrich. *Schillers Sämmtliche Werke*. 12 vols. Stuttgart und Tübingen: J. C.
Gotta'sscher, 1847.

Schubert, Franz. *Sixty Songs with German and English Words, the Latter by Maria X.
Hayes*. London: Boosey, n.d.

Scott, Patrick. "Rewriting the Book of Nature: Tennyson, Keble, and *The Christian
Year*." *Victorians Institute Journal*: 141–55.

Scott, Walter. *The Heart of Mid-lothian*. London: Caxton Publishing Company, n.d.

Seiss, Joseph A. *Holy Types; or, The Gospel in Leviticus. A Series of Lectures on the
Hebrew Ritual*. Houston, Tex.: St. Thomas Press, 1972.

Selby, Robin C. *The Principle of Reserve in the Writings of John Henry Cardinal Newman*.
London: Oxford University Press, 1975.

Shairp, J. C. "Keble and 'The Christian Year'." *North British Review* 45 (1866): 229–
64.

Shakespeare, William. *Antony and Cleopatra*. Edited by M. R. Ridley. London:
Methuen, 1954.

———. *King Lear*. Edited by Kenneth Muir. 1952. Reprint, London: Methuen, 1972.

———. *King Richard III*. Edited by Antony Hammond. London and New York:
Methuen, 1981.

———. *Love's Labour's Lost*. Edited by R. W. David. London and New York: Methuen,
1951.

———. *Macbeth*. Edited by Kenneth Muir. 1953. Reprint, London: Methuen, 1972.

———. *A Midsummer Night's Dream*. Edited by Harold F. Brooks. London and New
York: Methuen, 1979.

———. *The Sonnets.* Edited by John Dover Wilson. Cambridge: Cambridge University Press, 1966.

———. *The Tempest.* Edited by Frank Kermode. 1954. Rpt. London: Methuen, 1961.

———. *Twelfth Night.* Edited by J. M. Lothian and T. W. Craik. London: Methuen, 1975.

———. *The Winter's Tale.* Edited by J. H. P. Pafford. London: Methuen, 1963.

Shelley, Percy Bysshe. *Selected Poems.* Edited by Timothy Webb. London: J. M. Dent and Sons, 1977.

Siebers, Tobin. "The Werther Effect: The Esthetics of Suicide." *Mosaic* 26 (1993): 15–34.

Sill, Gertrude Grace. *A Handbook of Symbols in Christian Art.* New York: Macmillan, 1975.

Smith, Jean, and Rosemary Smith. "Newman and Sicily." *Downside Review* 107 (1989): 155–82.

Snodgrass, W. D., Richard Wilbur and Aidan C. Matthews. "Writers and Wrongs: W. D. Snodgrass, Richard Wilbur and Aidan C. Matthews in Conversation." *Crane Bag* 7 (1983): 122–26.

Sophocles. *The Theban Plays.* Translated by E. F. Watling. Harmondsworth: Penguin, 1947.

Svalgic, Martin J. "Newman: Man and Humanist." *Victorian Poetry* 12 (1974): 269–71.

———. "The Structure of Newman's *Apologia*." In *Apologia Pro Vita Sua,* by John Henry Newman. Edited by David J. DeLaura. New York: W. W. Norton, 1968.

———. "Why Newman Wrote the *Apologia*." In *Apologia Pro Vita Sua,* by John Henry Newman. Edited by David J. DeLaura. New York: W. W. Norton, 1968.

Tennant, R. C. "The Anglican Response to Locke's Theory of Personal Identity." *Journal of the History of Ideas* 43 (1982): 73–90.

Tennyson, Alfred. *Poems.* Edited by Christopher Ricks. London: Longman, 1969.

Tennyson, G. B. *Victorian Devotional Poetry: The Tractarian Mode.* Cambridge: Harvard University Press, 1981.

Thirlwall, John C. "John Henry Newman: His Poetry and Conversion." *Dublin Review* 242 (1968): 75–88.

Thomas, Stephen. *Newman and Heresy: The Anglican Years.* Cambridge: Cambridge University Press, 1991.

Thompson, Elbert N. S. "*The Temple* and *The Christian Year*." *PMLA* 54 (1939): 1018–25.

Thucydides. *The Peloponnesian War.* Translated by Rex Warner. Harmondsworth: Penguin, 1954.

Tillman, Mary Katherine. "The Tension Between Intellectual and Moral Education in the Thought of John Henry Newman." *Thought* 60 (1985): 322–44.

Tillotson, Geoffrey. *Augustan Poetic Diction.* London: Athlone Press, 1964.

———. "Newman's Essay on Poetry." In *John Henry Newman: Centenary Essays.* London: Burns, Oates and Washbourne, 1945.

Tolhurst, James. "The Idea of the Church as a Community in the Anglican Sermons of John Henry Newman." *Downside Review* 101 (1983): 140–64.

Tracts for the Times by Members of the University of Oxford. London: J. G. and F. Rivington, 1838–42.

Trevor, Meriol. *Newman: Light in Winter*. London: Macmillan, 1962.

———. *Newman: The Pillar of the Cloud*. London: Macmillan, 1962.

Untermeyer, Louis, ed.*The Albatross Book of English Verse: English and American Poetry from the Thirteenth Century to the Present Day*. London: Collins, 1933.

Vendler, Helen. *The Poetry of George Herbert*. Cambridge: Harvard University Press, 1975.

Verdi, Giuseppe. *Requiem*: Libretto. London: HMV AN 133–34, 1964.

Vitanza, Dianna. "*The Cloister and the Hearth*: A Popular Response to the Oxford Movement." *Religion and Literature* 18 (1986): 71–88.

Von Sonnleithner, Joseph. Libretto for Beethoven's *Fidelio*. London: Decca MET 272-3, 1964.

Waddell, James. "Keble and the Reader's Imagination." *Christianity and Literature* 13 (1985): 39–56.

Wakeman, Henry Offley. *An Introduction to the History of the Church of England from the Earliest Times to the Present Day*. London: Rivingtons, 1898.

Walmsley, Geoffrey. "Newman's *Dream of Gerontius*." *Downside Review* 91 (1973): 167–85

Ward, Maisie. *Young Mr. Newman*. London: Sheed and Ward, 1948.

Wells, H. G. *The Outline of History, Being a Plain History of Mankind*. 1920. Reprinted and revised, London: Cassell and Company, 1932.

Wheatly, Charles. *A Rational Illustration of the Book of Common Prayer of the Church of England*. London: J. and J. Knapton, R. Knaplock, R. Wilkin, A. Bettesworth, J. Osborn, and T. Longman, 1728.

Whyte, Alexander. *Newman: An Appreciation in Two Lectures: With the Choicest Passages of His Writings Selected and Arranged by Alexander Whyte. The Appendix Contains Six of His Eminence's Letters Not Hitherto Published*. London: Oliphant Anderson & Ferrier, 1901.

Wilbur, Richard. *New and Collected Poems*. London and Boston: Faber, 1989.

Williams, Isaac. *The Cathedral; or, The Catholic and Apostolic Church in England*. Oxford: John Henry Parker, 1848.

Wilson, Edmund. *Patriotic Gore: Studies in the Literature of the American Civil War*. London: André Deutsch, 1962.

Woolf, Virginia. *To the Lighthouse*. Harmondsworth: Penguin, 1964.

Wordsworth, William. *Poetical Works*. Edited by Thomas Hutchinson. Revised by Ernest de Selincourt. Oxford and New York: Oxford University Press, 1969.

Index